*Détente and the
Democratic Movement
in the USSR*

Détente and the Democratic Movement in the USSR

Frederick C. Barghoorn

THE FREE PRESS
A Division of Macmillan Publishing Co., Inc.
NEW YORK

Collier Macmillan Publishers
LONDON

The Free Press
A Division of Macmillan Publishing Co., Inc.
866 Third Avenue, New York, N.Y. 10022

Collier Macmillan Canada, Ltd.

Library of Congress Catalog Card Number: 76-4425

Printed in the United States of America

printing number

1 2 3 4 5 6 7 8 9 10

Library of Congress Cataloging in Publication Data

Barghoorn, Frederick Charles
    Détente and the democratic movement in the USSR.

    Includes bibliographical references and index.
    1. Russia--Foreign relations--1953-1975. 2. Russia--
Foreign relations--1975-   3. Russia--Politics and
government--1953-   4. Dissenters--Russia. I. Ti-
tle.
DK274.B28   327.47   76-4425
ISBN 0-02-901850-1

To the participants in the Soviet Democratic Movement, whose struggle for freedom in the USSR has instructed and inspired the world.

Contents

Preface

THE UNDERLYING THESIS of this book is that the current "détente" between the United States and the Soviet Union is and will remain seriously flawed and limited as long as the Soviet rulers maintain an oppressive internal regime. Of course I hope that even under the difficult conditions imposed on statesmen by the anarchic structure of international politics (compounded by ideological conflicts), worthwhile achievements can continue in such mutually beneficial fields as scientific, technical, and cultural exchanges, trade, and above all, armaments control.

Realism requires, however, that we keep in mind the proposition, surely difficult to disprove, that a political regime that deprives its own citizens of elementary civil rights and freedoms cannot, in its foreign policy, promote humane and democratic values. On the contrary, as the noted Soviet physicist and civil rights advocate Andrei Sakharov has pointed out, such a regime is a danger to the people it rules and to the whole world. Only if we fully understand the links pointed out by Sakharov and the other leaders of the Soviet Democratic Movement between Soviet dictatorship and Soviet foreign policy can we cope with the very difficult problems faced by the West, especially the United States, in "coexisting" with the Kremlin without compromise of principle or weakening of national security.

This book owes its inception to two of my long term research interests, namely, Soviet foreign policy, and dissent in the USSR. Specifically, it originated as an unclassified study commissioned by the Office of External Research, of the Department of State. This study of course, reflects my own personal opinions, which do not necessarily reflect or coincide with those of the Department of State or its personnel. I would like to thank all those who helped me in the inception, conduct, and completion of the research and writing of this book, including especially Abraham A. Brumberg and other helpful persons in the Department of State, Charles E. Smith, Assistant Vice

ix

President, Macmillan Publishing Co., Patricia Jarvis of the Free Press, Robert Cohen, Thomas A. Remington, and David E. Powell. I am grateful to Yale University and the Yale Department of Political Science, and in particular to Professor Joseph LaPalombara, its chairman, for granting me leave during the second semester of the academic year 1974–75, which enabled me to devote full time to writing; and to Joseph Warner, of the Yale University Office of Grants and Contracts, for administrative assistance. Finally, I am grateful to Mesdames Karen Gaunt and Anne Dennehy for expert typing and other indispensable clerical assistance, and especially for coping with my virtually indecipherable handwriting; and to my wife, Nina, who married me in spite of the project.

1.

Conflict between the Regime and the Dissenters

BASIC TO THE ARGUMENT SET FORTH IN THIS BOOK is the assumption that the foreign policy of any international actor is in large part shaped by its internal political regime and political culture. If this is true, then it is obvious that Soviet foreign policy cannot be understood without a deep understanding of its domestic context. That context includes, in particular, Russian and Soviet traditions of vigilance and suspicion regarding the outside world, perhaps reflected in a political system designed to ensure tight control over participation in and expression of opinions about political affairs, especially in the field of foreign policy.

All of this would perhaps be too trivial to mention if it had not so often been forgotten, with resultant misunderstanding and frustration especially on the American side. The seasoned professionals who conduct or advise on foreign affairs in the USSR assume that they are engaged in a deadly serious business—requiring, if disaster is to be avoided, great discipline and patience. They are thus prepared for the worst. All but a few Americans who are interested in foreign affairs seem predisposed to assume that, given good will, the conflicting interests of nations may be brought into harmony; and when this hope is proved false, they tend to be perplexed or angry, *especially* at their own leaders. Thus, wide sections of American public opinion, including elite opinion, assumed in the now half-forgotten days of the American–British–Soviet "coalition" against

1

Nazi Germany and its allies that Moscow shared their hope that the war would be followed by a long period of fruitful and intimate cooperation among the nations that had banded together to eliminate the Fascist threat. We are all more or less familiar with the unhappy consequences both of these illusions and of their dissipation.

Doubtless in large part because of the skepticism engendered by years of frustration in post–World War II dealings with the Soviet Union, and—to mention a matter of great relevance to this book—partly because of their knowledge of the warnings sounded by Soviet dissenters regarding the possible dangers of false "détente" and of the penalty paid by many dissenters for having uttered such warnings, Americans have responded less euphorically to the current "détente" than to the hopes associated with the wartime "coalition." However, it seems clear that in the United States and in the West generally there are strong and widespread tendencies toward excessive optimism about the possible benefits of "détente." Above all, we can easily forget that "détente"—or, as it is called in Soviet parlance, "relaxation of international tensions" (in Russian, "razryadka napryazhennosti")—is subordinate, in the Kremlin's strategy, to the concept of "peaceful coexistence of states with different social systems." This amounts in turn to legitimizing the Kremlin's continued pursuit of power by all means short of large-scale military operations. This is indicated by Soviet texts which invariably warn their Soviet and foreign Communist readers that "peaceful coexistence" is by no means so peaceful as to allow for any relaxation of the political struggle between Soviet-style "socialism" and "imperialism," a code word for the United States and its allies.

Now the foregoing should not be interpreted as meaning that I am an unqualified opponent of "détente." Far from it. I am aware that given the anarchic pattern of relations among states in what the Soviets before the era of "détente" called the "international arena," and given, above all, the malign magic of contemporary weapons technology, a measure of regularization and accommodation among states possessing significant nuclear capabilities is imperative. I would add that motives of rational calculation and—dare I mention it—idealism argue for expanding "East-West" transactions in trade, science and health, the arts, sports, and other fields. But it should be remembered that there are numerous and difficult problems involved in all kinds of transactions between political systems with cultures and institutions as different as are those of the United States and the Soviet Union. Unless we are well informed and businesslike, the mood of cordiality and the imagery of community of purpose that can be generated by "exchanges of persons" and joint activities with the Soviets can easily distract our attention from the single-minded pursuit of power that dominates the Soviet rulers' attitude toward all aspects of foreign policy. Of course, individual Soviet participants involved in such exchange activities do not always fully share the instrumental approach of their government toward all transactions with the non-Soviet world. But it is very clear that the officials in charge of planning and administering Moscow's cultural strategy expect Soviet participants, as a matter of civic duty and also in return for the rare privilege of being trusted to travel or otherwise meet with foreigners, to fulfill their information-gathering and propaganda missions in such a fashion as to promote the Soviet national interest. Furthermore, both abroad and at home, participants are expected to refrain from indiscreet disclosure of information or opinion and from embarrassing conduct, on pain of exclusion from further participation or more severe sanctions.

Rejecting the Kremlin's machiavellianism, some Soviet dissenters began, as "détente" got under way, to offer cautionary advice regarding the potential dangers to the West of playing the "détente" game according to rules laid down by Moscow. It seems to me that there is much merit in the dissenters' analyses and warnings. Indeed, I believe that in their writings one finds some of the best available thinking about "détente." I would add that underlying the "democratic" dissenters' critique of Soviet domestic and foreign policy there seems to be a pattern of thought bearing a remarkable resemblance to the beliefs making up the conceptual structure basic to what Robert A. Dahl calls "polyarchy." Certainly the thinking of Soviet "democratizers" is a thousand times more akin to the Western democratic ethos than is the official Soviet creed of Marxism-Leninism, a kinship that doubtless helps explain the Kremlin's animosity toward the Soviet democrats, about which I shall subsequently have a good deal to say.

I contend in this book that acquaintance with the thinking of leading members of the "Democratic Movement" in the post-Khrushchev USSR, in the context of official attitudes and policies, can deepen our understanding of Soviet policies. I shall also argue that the limited and expediential character of the official Soviet conception of "détente" is clearly indicated by the unresponsive, contemptuous, and punitive stance of the Soviet leadership toward dissenters who have expressed opinions and offered proposals fully compatible with Western democratic standards. Soviet "democrats" have, for example, advocated the rule of law, freedom of conscience and information, and freedom to leave and return to their country.* (There is reason to believe, incidentally, that the unwillingness of the authorities to grant this last freedom—implying, as it does, a striking lack of trust on the part of Soviet rulers toward Soviet citizens—is deeply resented by many patriotic Soviet citizens.) Some dissenters have criticized what they term the "messianic" component in the official approach toward foreign affairs. Implicitly, and to some extent explicitly, Soviet "democratizers" are, in effect, demanding that the Soviet Union join with other nations in creating the conditions necessary for the kind of "safe" "détente" advocated by numerous British, American, and Western European foreign affairs opinion leaders—one which, I believe, presupposes a far greater measure of overlap than now exists between Soviet and Western political cultures. The relatively open-minded outlook of some advocates of what we might term the Soviet democratic approach to "détente"—some Soviet dissidents, for example, have discriminatingly called attention to what they regard as positive aspects of "capitalist" systems, while sharply criticizing others—is attractive to adherents of polyarchy. But those who hold such views are obviously regarded as subversive by the Soviet Communist Party leadership and the KGB.† It would not be fanciful to characterize the activists of the Democratic Movement—or at least some of them, such as Andrei Sakharov, the exiled physicist Valeri Chalidze; or the mathematician Igor Shafarevich—as the best friends of genuine, rather than formalistic if not disingenuous "détente." Moreover, I would assert that if a leadership committed to democratic norms and values were ever to come to power in the USSR, prospects for a stable and lasting peace—and even for making a start on the task of constructing something more closely resembling an international political community than the present fiercely competitive, semi-anarchic structure of world politics—would be immeasurably enhanced. At present this much-to-be-desired outcome seems as unlikely as it ever has. Indeed, current trends in East–West relations and in world affairs generally seem to render it more and more remote. Yet we should not forget that under the leadership of Nikita

* We use the term "Soviet Democratic Movement" in this book to refer to those who articulate these and other civil liberties demands.
† Formally, Committee for the State Security; in actuality, the secret police.

Khrushchev an attempt was made in the USSR "to initiate a gradual transformation of the party-state toward a somewhat more normal, or at least less abnormal, modern nation-state." And, in this effort, "Khrushchev married the themes of coexistence abroad with relaxation at home"—in contrast to Brezhnev's combination of "détente" with domestic orthodoxy.[1]

As I shall point out later in this chapter and argue in more detail in the next, it was the combination of the ending of domestic relaxation by Khrushchev's successors and the pursuit of a hard-line policy abroad, as indicated by the invasion of Czechoslovakia, that elicited the Soviet dissenters' critique of the Kremlin's foreign policy, to which much of this volume is devoted. Whether, and if so when, a reform movement broader in scope and clearer in vision than the one fitfully sponsored by Khrushchev will occur, no one can predict with assurance. The hope that it will occur, however, undoubtedly underlies the dissenting thought and action that we shall describe and analyze in the pages to follow.

Unfortunately, since 1968, the year when Soviet tanks terminated the Czechoslovak experiment in "socialism with a human face," the Democratic Movement has been the target of increasingly severe pressures and sanctions. These pressures were intensified in 1972, the high point of the oversold Nixon–Brezhnev "détente," and have remained unremittingly harsh ever since. Now it would, of course, be anachronistic to link the Warsaw Pact invasion of Czechoslovakia to "détente," and to the problems—such as increased contact between Soviet citizens and foreigners—to which "détente" gave rise. It seems clear, however, that the ferment in Czechoslovakia and the requirements of "détente" together spurred the Kremlin to tighten ideological and political controls, because both challenged the Kremlin's traditional monopoly or near-monopoly of political communication, one of the main pillars of its power. In contrast to Khrushchev, who had tolerated a measure of internal freedom of opinion, his successors obviously considered that Khrushchev's experiments in this area had been well-nigh subversive. It would not be too much of an exaggeration to say that theirs was a "neo-Stalinist" policy, though one free of mass terror and other Stalinist excesses.

It seems highly significant that improvement of official diplomatic relations between the United States and the Soviet Union after 1969 was accompanied not by any relaxation in the USSR (or in Eastern Europe either) of political and ideological controls, but, on the contrary, by increasing intolerance of nonconformity. Thus, in 1972, when then President Nixon visited Moscow, and some Soviet citizens still hoped that accommodation in foreign affairs would have a liberalizing effect at home, the KGB cracked down on internal dissent. This indicated that the conservative leadership of the Communist Party of the Soviet Union (hereinafter sometimes referred to as CPSU) regarded any equating of relaxation of tensions abroad with relaxation of controls at home as politically destabilizing. The Brezhnev party leadership apparently feared that "détente," with its connotations—at least for Soviet citizens insufficiently steeped in the Leninist "dialectic" approach to international politics—of the replacement of hostility by cordiality and unfettered communication across ideological frontiers, might undermine the party's authority. They seem to have reasoned that a positive image of "détente" might weaken the belief, still an essential component of the regime's arsenal of legitimizing claims, in the irreconcilable hostility of "imperialism" for "socialism." (The latter is still asserted to be a social system attainable only under the auspices of ruling Communist parties certified as "Leninist" by Moscow.)

Before proceeding further, it would be well to define what I mean by "dissent" and "democratization." The former term will be used in this book to refer to a broad range of articulated negative attitudes regarding political matters. These negative attitudes can be directed at political authority in general—anarchist doctrines come to mind—or at certain types of political systems, regimes, and structures; or they may involve criticism or condemnation of political actors, ranging from collective condemnation of whole groups of incumbents down to episodic attacks on individual officials. Other targets of dissent include political norms and rules, principles, doctrines, and ideologies.

Dissent has not only a negative aspect but, at least implicitly, a positive one. The ultimate objective of rational dissent and opposition is to correct mistakes, to right wrongs, or, in extreme cases, to protest against, and if possible eradicate, what is perceived as an intolerable evil. In general, its purpose is to effect changes in political structures, policies, and leadership in conformity with the dissenters' values and preferences.[2]

Opposition, and of course dissent, at least of a covert nature, are apparently common to all political systems even if in most polities they are considered "legitimate." However, the content and style of dissent in different systems, the ideological, administrative, and legal norms and rules governing it articulation and organization (in sys-

tems in which organized dissent is permitted at all), and the nature
of the relationships between authorities and dissenters vary enormously. In some political cultures open public debate and competitive party activity are regarded as legitimate, and legal provision is
made for their exercise. In others such modes of behavior are considered subversive, and their advocates—especially if they organize
to achieve their objectives—are likely to be severely penalized. Probably the most elegant formulation of the range of differences among
political systems in respect to the opportunities they provide for
opposition and dissent is that proposed by Robert A. Dahl. "All political systems," he writes, "in some respects constrain the expression, representation and satisfaction of political preferences." But
some, which he terms "hegemonies," "impose the most severe limits"
on these behaviors; they "prohibit organized dissent and opposition."
At the other end of the continuum are "polyarchies," which "impose the fewest restraints." In polyarchies, "most individuals are effectively protected in their right to express, privately or publicly,
their opposition to the government, to organize, to form parties,
and to compete in elections. . . ."[3]

It remains to indicate the sense in which the term "democratization" will be used in this book. It occurs frequently in, and is indeed
fundamental to, the thinking of the intellectual leaders of the Democratic Movement. They use it to refer to the transformation that occurs, according to Dahl, "when hegemonic regimes and competitive
oligarchies move toward polyarchy" and in so doing "increase the
opportunities for effective participation and contestation and hence
the number of individuals, groups and interests whose preferences
have to be considered in policy making."[4]

Dissent, once articulated and publicly disseminated, is an aspect
of political behavior, but unlike opposition, it is primarily a symbolic
rather than an organizational mode of behavior. Regimes such as the
Soviet that are very intolerant of opposition, however, tend to blur
the distinction between opposition and dissent and to repress dissenters with a severity approaching that which they apply to real
oppositionists. This observation is applicable to almost the entire
history of the USSR—especially, of course, the period of Stalin's
dictatorship—as well as to the other "Leninist" systems, although
Yugoslavia is to a considerable degree an exception to this rule.[5]

Probably not many Western students of Communist systems
would object to Leonard Schapiro's judgment that Communist parties, once in power, "have still not broken out of the self-defeating

system for the arbitrary suppression of all dissenting opinions and criticism which was imposed by Lenin on Russia in 1921."[6] However, it should be noted that the well-known dissident Roy Medvedev, who claims to be a Leninist (though I am inclined to characterize his views as more social democratic than Leninist), argues that the restrictive prescriptions set forth by Lenin in 1921 were intended only as temporary measures. According to Medvedev, Lenin's successors incorrectly interpreted Lenin's approach to intra-party dissent.[7]

One quite useful way of distinguishing what we refer to in this book as dissent from what in the USSR is regarded as "legitimate" expression of opinions and preferences is to reserve the term "dissent" for verbal behavior that, at any given time, is deemed by the authorities to be in violation of norms or policy directives. The validity of this approach tends to be confirmed by the pejorativeness of the few references that are to be found in Soviet reference works and in the press to what I here term dissent. Its exponents are called "persons who think differently" (inakomyslyashchie), and, so far as I can discover, it is usually said of them that they desire to "restore capitalism" in Russia or are hirelings of foreign intelligence services. Certainly it is made clear that dissent from the prevailing official view is beyond the pale of legitimate public discourse.[8]

Admission of the existence of conflicts of interest in Soviet society is rare, cryptic, and unspecific in published utterances carrying the signatures of the ruling oligarchy. It seems significant, therefore, that KGB chief and Politburo alternate member Yuri V. Andropov, in a speech delivered at the culmination of his "campaign" for election to the RSFSR Supreme Soviet in 1975, was apparently assigned the role of speaking on this subject. Defending Soviet "socialist democracy" against "bourgeois democracy," Andropov asserted that any Soviet citizen whose interests coincided with those of "society" would feel "the full scope of our democratic freedoms." But it was another matter, he said, if "in a few instances" these interests did not coincide. In such cases, he firmly asserted, the "interests of society as a whole" must take priority.

Andropov's remarks on the contrast between the Soviet and "bourgeois" versions of "democracy," on "détente," and on alleged foreign efforts to foist an alien and subversive "democratization" on the USSR, are highly relevant to the concerns of this book. His address was full of complaints about alleged efforts by "imperialism"—a code word for the "capitalist" West, especially the United States

—to stir up trouble in Russia by means of "ideological diversion" and other evil machinations. Among the tactics ascribed to the "imperialists" and the "opponents of relaxation of tensions"—typically, Andropov lumped these elements together—was that of "cloaking themselves in the garb of well-wishers of the 'democratization' and the 'improvement' of socialism."[9]

The security chief's little essay on political philosophy indicated that Moscow still deemed it necessary to prevent exposure of Soviet citizens to "bourgeois" ideas and, in general, to any influences not congruent with the images of reality propagated by the centralized Soviet political apparatus and communications networks. In particular, Andropov minced no words about rejecting any version of "democracy" incompatible with the standard Soviet model. Once again it was made plain that any tinkering with that model was still regarded by the Soviet leadership as a weapon of "imperialist" political warfare, capable of disorienting Soviet citizens by undermining their faith in Soviet "socialism." Given this premise, it is not entirely illogical to conclude that Soviet citizens whose political thinking does not fully conform to official specifications must be deemed to be under the pernicious ideological influence of hostile "bourgeois" sources.

Finally, it is appropriate to note here—although this point was not made by Andropov—that there is abundant evidence, including KGB harassment and criminal prosecution of dissenters, that Soviet citizens' contacts with foreigners tend to be regarded as evidence of political carelessness, unreliability, and even political "crime." This is especially so if such contacts result in dissemination abroad of information that undermines the credibility in the outside world of official myths and images.[*][10]

Brezhnev-era warnings, such as Andropov's, against allowing increased contacts with the West incident to "détente" to become channels for penetration of Russia by subversive Western political concepts are, of course, reminiscent of the centuries-long efforts on the part of previous Russian rulers to borrow the West's technology while shunning its culture. In a shrinking world, confronted

---

[*] In connection with Andropov's speech, it is ironic, and piquant to note that, according to sources I regard as thoroughly reliable, a leading Soviet dissenter reported a few years ago that Andropov, along with Marshall Ivan Yakubovski, Warsaw Pact military commander, was among the few highly placed Soviet political personalities who were willing—or more likely, perhaps—authorized—to enter into a dialogue of sorts with Soviet dissenters.

by problems transcending national and other traditional frameworks, Moscow's continued effort to maintain a largely closed society may seem doomed to failure. However, its eventual failure may still lie far in the future, for the impulses that sustain it seem to be central to the political beliefs not only of the Soviet political elite but of the Russian "masses" as well. They are rejected, it appears, only by a relatively "cosmopolitan" element of the Soviet intelligentsia. And even in the thinking of the intelligentsia, authoritarian and xenophobic dispositions apparently still remain strong and perhaps dominant, except for its most independent and venturesome members. Even where these sentiments are weak, fear of the consequences of open dissent exerts a powerful restraining influence.

Now of course it must be admitted that violation of the rules of the political game is penalized in all political systems. But Soviet citizens, owing to the absence of a legitimate political opposition and to other basic features of the Soviet system, have far fewer opportunities to influence the making of the rules under which they live than do the citizens of polyarchies. Moreover, unlike those in polyarchies, rules and norms in Soviet-type systems are subject to sudden changes or reinterpretations when the authorities so desire.

The opportunities available to Soviet citizens for the expression of political aspirations and preferences, then, are still very severely limited. Such opportunities, however, along with the range and quantity of material goods and services supplied by the regime to the population, have gradually increased since Stalin passed from the scene. Since the dismissal of Khrushchev from office by his fellow oligarchs in 1964, there has especially been increasing autonomy for professionals who could convince the pragmatic post-Khrushchev leadership of the value of their output to the economy and the polity. The same cannot be said of creative people whose work involves moral judgments and noninstrumental issues. Insofar as freedom to explore the moral, philosophical, and aesthetic realms was concerned, the period after the fall of Khrushchev saw a cutting back on what appeared to be promises made while Khrushchev was shaping policy. A revival of ideological fundamentalism in Moscow was spurred both by developments in Czechoslovakia—where ideological ferment had already, by the summer of 1967 (a year before the beginning of the Prague "spring"), attained an intensity that alarmed conservative elements in the Soviet elite—and, for reasons already suggested by the Soviet–American "détente" of the early 1970's.

Czechoslovak "democratization" raised the spectre of an alternative interpretation of Marxism, attractive to many Soviet intellectuals; "détente" threatened, in the absence of countermeasures, an influx of subversive, "bourgeois" ideas. Other unsettling influences, the most important of which was probably the failure of Khrushchev, and to a greater degree of his successors, to complete the process of moral regeneration symbolized by the term "de-Stalinization," were at work as well

Hence it is not surprising that in the late 1960's and early 1970's warnings were sounded regarding the potentially disastrous consequences of relaxing ideological vigilance. Thus, shortly after the Warsaw Pact invasion of Czechoslovakia, a CPSU Central Committee resolution reiterated, in boldface type, Lenin's statement, made a half-century earlier, that "any neglect of socialist ideology ...signifies...the strengthening of bourgeois ideology."[11] In the following months, Soviet—and especially East European—intellectuals were chided for excessive preoccupation with the evils of Stalinism, which, it was asserted, distracted them from the constructive tasks of the present.[12] And the CPSU's organizational journal published this statement late in 1973: "Especially relevant today is Lenin's statement that if the party's guiding, educational and organizational roles are weakened, this can only lead to the triumph of bourgeois counterrevolution."[13]

The atmosphere and circumstances of the late 1960's were such as to spark a tragic confrontation between a political leadership apparently increasingly concerned about challenges to its legitimacy, and the most critical and resolute members of the Soviet intelligentsia. Yet, so far as the vast majority of Soviet intellectuals were concerned, it appears that the established norms of relations between the regime and the intelligentsia continued to be regarded, even in this period, as at least bearable (if by no means satisfactory). The available evidence indicates that most moderately discontented intellectuals, including many of those who went so far as to engage in some form of overt protest, apparently decided, after regime admonitions to cease and desist, that the costs of resistance outweighed any possible benefits.

The greater part of the intelligentsia seems to have lacked the will and the desire to attempt to radically alter its relationship to the political elite, or to challenge what Franklin Griffiths has characterized as the dominance in Soviet politics of the "activity of the system as a whole" over its "subsystems" or components, such as groups, coalitions, and other "intermediate actors." However, Griffiths also postulates the existence of "conflicting tendencies... through which values are allocated, or policies are made and implemented, for Soviet society," an observation that, I believe, helps us to understand the often shifting pattern of relations between authorities and dissenters in the USSR.[14] In deciding whether to permit or suppress articulation of clashing tendencies—in other words, in distinguishing "legitimate" from "nonlegitimate" articulation—the supreme political leadership (which, of course, is itself often significantly divided in its preferences) is guided, Griffiths suggests, by its answer to the question: Do these conflicting tendencies reflect "antagonistic" or "nonantagonistic" "contradictions"? This distinction seems to translate into that between what we might call destructive and constructive criticism. It follows that if "lower participants" in the Soviet political process are to express their views, "the signaling of a favorable disposition from the upper levels" must occur.[15]

Few informed students of Soviet politics would reject Griffiths' finding that "where tendency conflict on issues accepted as legitimate in the Stalin era seems to have been largely confined to members of the political elite," it came after Stalin's death "to reach more deeply into the political structure."[16] Like many other analysts, Griffiths attributes this widening of political participation—though participation is still confined, of course, to narrow limits—to factors such as social, economic, and technological changes attendant upon the continuing modernization of the Soviet economy, internal division in the party leadership, and the post-Stalin reduction in terror. As a result of these factors, he observes, "The expectation has become widespread that it is possible within reason to dissent and live."[17] Finally, he believes that improvement in the military security of the USSR, by contributing to some decline in the expectation of war, has fostered expanded political participation. In conclusion, he cautiously forecasts persistence of these trends, despite the misgivings of the Soviet military and security police establishments.[18]

In view of the evident determination on the part of the dominant elements of the Soviet elite to essentially maintain the present oligarchical political system, with its centralized, hierarchical pattern of access to political participation, and to resort to coercion if necessary to preserve this pattern, it is not surprising that only a very small minority of Soviet citizens have dared to defy authority by openly dissenting from its commands. Although Soviet secrecy makes it impossible to assemble full and accurate information about the quantitative scope of dissent, all responsible observers agree that its overt manifestations were on a scale minuscule by comparison, for example, with protest in the United States against the Vietnam War. For each of the seven Soviet citizens who demonstrated against the Soviet invasion of Czechoslovakia in 1968 there were thousands, probably hundreds of thousands, of American demonstrators against the war in Vietnam. And although there were deplorable violations of the civil rights of some Vietnam War protesters, these were in many cases at least partially corrected by due process of law. But in the case, for example, of the Soviet Red Square demonstrators —as with all other trials in the USSR for "especially dangerous state crimes"—conviction and harsh penalties followed arrest as night follows day.[19]

According to L. G. Churchward, the author of the only comprehensive recent study of the Soviet intelligentsia, "perhaps only one in three or four hundred" of its members "will accept the risks involved" in addressing protest letters to political leaders, collecting signatures to petitions, and the like.[20] Churchward's estimate is not incompatible with Reddaway's count of "about two thousand" members of the "mainstream" of the Democratic Movement who had by 1970 "dared to identify themselves deliberately by name."[21] Reddaway added that the more visible members of the Democratic Movement were supported by "many thousands of sympathizers."[22] If one's estimate of the numerical dimension of Soviet dissent were to include not only the mainly high-status professionals referred to by Reddaway and Churchward, but also rank-and-file Jews, Crimean Tatars and Lithuanians, and to a lesser degree Germans (who have in recent years signed protest petitions, participated in demonstrations, and the like) one could easily arrive—as did Reddaway —at a figure of the order of magnitude of "tens of thousands" of so-called "prisoners of conscience" in Soviet labor camps and in exile.[23]

Closely related to the question of the quantitative dimension of dissent is the problem of its potential for persistence and possible future growth, to which I shall return toward the end of this book. At this point it may be appropriate to note that Churchward, on the basis of personal contacts with Soviet intellectuals, found evidence of what might be characterized as increasing disidentification with official ideological norms as currently interpreted and even of increasing alienation, especially among young academic specialists.[24]

Churchward's analysis is compatible with my own hypothesis that if the Soviet system proves to be distinctly unresponsive to intelligentsia aspirations generated by further modernization of the economy, tensions between the regime and the intelligentsia will intensify and dissent will become an increasingly serious problem.

Some Soviet intellectuals, including Andrei Sakharov and Alexander Solzhenitsyn, moved in the late 1960's and early 1970's from dissent that at least nominally accepted the system and took the form of respectfully petitioning the authorities for significant changes in policy to a position amounting to rejection of the legitimacy and viability of the Soviet system and even of Marxism–Leninism. Sakharov, in his famous 1968 "memorandum," characterized his ideological position as "profoundly socialist."[25] But in his interview on Swedish television in 1973 Sakharov, among other things, said that he no longer felt that he understood what socialism was. He characterized the allegedly socialist Soviet system as "an extremely monopolized form" of "that capitalist path of development found in the United States and other Western countries," with "maximum restraint, maximum ideological restrictions," etc.[26]

Solzhenitsyn, until quite late in his career, respected official protocol. In his nonfiction writings, at least, he refrained from explicit, fundamental criticism of the regime and its official creed until well after his expulsion from the Union of Soviet Writers in November 1969.[27] But in response to the slanderous press campaign unleashed by Moscow after he was awarded the Nobel Prize for literature in 1970, Solzhenitsyn retaliated. At first cautious and indirect he ultimately elaborated an open, sweeping, comprehensive critique, analyzed later in this book, which he addressed to the Soviet leadership in 1973. In the already written but previously unpublished *Gulag Archipelago,* he condemned root and branch the regime and its policies (including those of the mummified Lenin) and the secular religion of Marxism–Leninism with enormous power and passion.

One source of the "radicalization" of some dissenters' thinking, to borrow a term used by Albert Weeks in his survey of Sakharov's views, was the Soviet-organized military intervention in Czechoslovakia in August 1968.[28] It seems correct to stress the significance of Czechoslovakia as a precipitant of defiance for some dissidents and of despair and resignation for others. It is clear, however, that many other factors, some of them deeply rooted in the past, were at work. These included the curtailment of de-Stalinization, the violation of juridical norms in the trials of young protesters such as Yuri Galanskov and Alexander Ginzburg, and the frustration and bitterness generated by the failure of Khrushchev's successors to fulfill the hopes aroused by Khrushchev's reformist rhetoric. Nor should it be forgotten that disillusionment on a smaller scale had already been engendered by what appeared to some to be the hypocrisy of Khrushchev himself. This was observable particularly among younger dissidents, when beginning in 1966, the regime instituted a series of repressive acts. No wonder that they responded in the fashion that theorists of "relative deprivation" postulate as probable when, after improvement in expectations about "value capabilities," "expectations are frustrated by declining value output or repressive governmental action."[29]

Yuri Glazov has argued, convincingly I think, that the sources of the Democratic Movement can be traced to the combination of relative looseness of ideological control under Khrushchev and the courageous example set by Boris Pasternak's critical reexamination of the results of the Bolshevik revolution in his novel *Doctor Zhivago*. It must not be forgotten that *Doctor Zhivago* was the first major Soviet literary work to be published abroad. When repression began in earnest after Khrushchev's ouster, there was, for a time, a burst of spontaneous indignation among intellectuals who held dear the memory of Pasternak and who felt a need to demonstrate solidarity with his values—and with one another.[30]

Glazov emphasizes that Pasternak was the first Russian of stature to throw off the fetters of fear—an example that was followed, at least for a time, by a substantial number of established intellectuals as well as by hundreds and perhaps thousands of youths, such as the young poet Vladimir Bukovski. A minority, including Bukovski and the historian Andrei Amalrik as well as the young scientist Pavel Litvinov, Sakharov, and others, held on, but many were intimidated by the repression to which the authorities resorted after they overcame their initial shock and disorientation. According to Glazov, it is only in the light of Pasternak's influence that one can comprehend the meaning of the works of the significant writers of the 1960's, including Sinyavski—symbolically, he was a pallbearer at Pasternak's funeral—Solzhenitsyn, Amalrik, Joseph Brodski, Nadezhda Mandelstam, and others.

It is startling to compare the vitality and optimism of the protest movement of the late 1960's with the pessimism voiced, even by Sakharov, in the 1970's. In the 1970's, especially but not only in emigration, some former activists of the Democratic Movement produced postmortem-like accounts of their experiences, apparently forgetful of the prospects for positive political change that were enunciated in their statements of happier days, and were implied by the vigor of their actions. Even Glazov's account of the protest of 1968 seems to reflect such a pessimism, and of course the effect of Peter Yakir's "confession" in 1973, under KGB auspices, was shattering. Yakir had for years been a mainstay of the Democratic Movement; his "apostasy," as some dissenters called it, was depressing. Among Soviet leaders there was some nervousness about the increasing imminence of a new, post-Brezhnev era, and they looked back with anger and fear at what must have seemed the evil consequences of Nikita Khrushchev's ill-advised tinkering with the tried and true methods of governance perfected by Stalin—to which the post-Khrushchev regime had reverted, albeit in a more moderate, rational, and sophisticated form. But while some dissidents responded to repression with a deepened moral commitment, others, far more numerous, were intimidated and silenced, and still other dissidents emigrated under varying degrees of pressure or were forcibly expelled, like Solzhenitsyn who left the Soviet Union in February 1974. Still others, of course, disappeared into prison or forced labor camps or worst of all, were subjected to indefinite compulsory "treatment" in "special psychiatric hospitals," such as the notorious one at Chernyakhovsk in Western Russia, where General Peter Grigorenko was held for many years. These "hospitals," about which more will be said later (especially in Chapter 3), are administered by the KGB.[31]

We have not thus far given adequate attention to the wide diversity of dissent in the USSR. It would be very misleading to equate the Soviet Democratic Movement with the entirety of dissent in the Soviet Union. Indeed, as a number of analysts, both Soviet and Western, have pointed out, the Democratic Movement itself comprises a rather wide spectrum of perspectives, goals, and programs. Andrei Amalrik, in a well-known essay completed in 1969, hazarded the opinion that the "ideology" of the Democratic Movement was either an "eclectic fusion" of "genuine Marxism–Leninism," "Russian Christianity," and "liberalism" or was based on the "common elements in these ideologies." He added that although the "movement" had no clearly defined program, "all its supporters assume at least one common aim: the rule of law, based on respect for the basic rights of man."[32] Adherents of the first category, according to Amalrik, argued that the Soviet regime had perverted Marxism–Leninism for its own ends; a return to the true principles of the doctrine was, they felt, a necessary condition for curing the ills of Soviet society. To this category of "true Leninist" he assigned, for example, General Peter Grigorenko. Representatives of the second category advocated a "return to Christian moral principles," interpreted "in a somewhat Slavophile spirit, with a claim for a special role for Russia." Amalrik cited as a representative of this second subgroup within the Democratic Movement Igor Ogurtsov, the leader of the "All-Russian Social Christian Union," a group of dissident Leningrad intellectuals several of whose members were, in 1967 and 1968 trials, sentenced to exceptionally long terms in labor camps.[33] Until recently very little was known abroad about Ogurtsov's group because of the extreme secrecy exercised by the Kremlin toward them.

Amalrik asserted that believers in "liberal ideology" envisaged "a transition to a Western kind of democratic society," retaining, however, "the principle of public or governmental ownership of the means of production." To this subgroup, according to him, belonged Pavel Litvinov and, "with some reservations," Sakharov.[34]

Still another group, not, however, identified by Amalrik, were the "legalists" ("zakonniki"), who should be classified as a subgroup of the "Western liberals." They stressed the value of legal scholarship, with a view to inducing—or shaming?—the Soviet authorities into adopting a strict, literal application of Soviet and universal legal and constitutional principles and norms to specific cases. This approach, so far as I can determine, was first conceived by the mathematical logician Alexander Esenin-Volpin, but its most diligent and systematic exponent was and is the young physicist Valeri Chalidze.

The historian Roy Medvedev, a self-proclaimed Marxist–Leninist, developed a typology of the various currents of dissent similar to, though more elaborate than, the one contrived by the skeptical anti-Marxist Amalrik. In his important book on "socialist democracy," Medvedev discussed "non-party political currents" and various "currents" of opinion inside the CPSU, as well as "nationalist currents and groups." Medvedev, who according to well-informed emigrant sources almost single-handedly produced the voluminous *samizdat Political Diary (Politicheski Dnevnik)*, has consistently maintained that although Soviet leaders since Lenin have misinterpreted and misapplied the ideas and theories of Marx and Lenin, nevertheless the path to "socialist democracy" lies through reform within the system under the leadership of a reformed CPSU. He has chided some Soviet "Westernizers"—though not his friend Andrei Sakharov—for selfish "individualism," along with some of the major activists of the Democratic Movement, including General Peter Grigorenko and Peter Yakir, for what he saw as their self-defeating "extremism," which, he claimed, only aroused the hostility of the authorities.[35] Medvedev also introduced the concept of "ethical socialism," including within it "Christian socialism" both of which ideologies he saw reflected in Alexander Solzhenitsyn's writings.[36] He praised the efforts of the "legalists" (sometimes referred to as "constitutionalists") to "raise the level of legal consciousness" of our society, particularly such aspects of their activity as their effort to familiarize the Soviet public with United Nations documents on human rights.

As has already been indicated, differences of perspective, at any one period of time, among the small "circles" (kruzhki) that articulated dissenting opinion were perhaps matched, or exceeded, by the dissenters' diversity of outlook and mood over time. Particularly striking was the fading of the hopeful mood of the 1960's, at least to 1968 or 1969, and its replacement by pessimism and a sense of nearly total isolation, apparently affecting most dissenters by the early 1970's.[37] Some key dissenters, whose overall perspective had been, one might say, pragmatic—though underlying their protest was a strong moral impulse—came (Sakharov is a case in point) to adopt an attitude of stoicism in the face of adversity. Others felt so isolated and discouraged as to consider themselves fully justified in emigrating when this option became available. Solzhenitsyn, however, became increasingly defiant in the face of persecution.

In addition to the variants of democratic thinking I have mentioned, there is also a current of Russian chauvinist dissenting thought in the USSR that is repellent both to the talented and critically minded Soviet intellectuals who created the Soviet Democratic Movement and (of course) to Western constitutional democrats. However, this extreme nationalist, sometimes anti-Semitic, and even quasi-fascist trend, which differs more from all of the currents of "democratizing" dissent than the various elements of the latter do from one another, is important because of the covert support that, according to some reports, it receives from powerful elements of the political elite, and because, unlike the Democratic Movement, it apparently has some potential capability of becoming a mass phenomenon. A relatively mild form of Russian nationalism has found expression in the activities of the officially tolerated Rodina (Motherland) and Rossiya (Russia) clubs, and in articles by journalists such as Victor Chalmaev and S. Semanov in the youth magazine *Molodaya Gvardiya (Young Guard)*, some of which have sung the praises of Russian tsars such as Ivan the Terrible or of

nineteenth-century conservative thinkers such as Konstantin Le-
ontev, while others have interpreted the Bolshevik revolution from
a Russian nationalist point of view.[38]

The regime's tolerance of expressions of great Russian nationalism that are not embarrassingly frank contrasts sharply with its
malevolence toward the Democratic Movement, as well as with its
extreme suspicion of and at times severe sanctions against Jews,
Ukrainians, Lithuanians, Crimean Tatars, Germans, Armenians, and
the other non-Russian national minority members of the Soviet
"family of nations" who express what are considered "bourgeois
nationalist" sentiments. But in a political community whose leaders
still claim to be internationalists, and who claim to have found in
the Leninist nationality policy a universally applicable model for
resolution of problems of nationality, extreme manifestations of Russian chauvinism can be politically embarrassing, and on occasion
persons judged to have been exponents of such views have been
severely punished.[39] It should be stressed that disaffection and alienation among members of non-Russian nationalities, an extreme form
of which is expressed in advocacy of the secession of a given nation
from the USSR, probably represents the form of dissent potentially
most dangerous to the continued existence of the Soviet political
community as presently constituted.[40]

Perhaps Zbigniew Brzezinski has most forcefully evaluated the
political potential of the aspirations of non-Russians in the USSR
with his statement that "it is not inconceivable that in the next several decades the nationality problem will become politically more
important in the Soviet Union than the racial issue has in the United
States."[41]

Ironically, Article 17 of the Soviet Constitution grants to each of
the—at present fifteen—union republics of which the nominally fed-
erative USSR is composed "the right freely to secede" from the federation. In fact, of course, it is not only mere discussion of session
(as distinct from organized activity) that becomes the object of draconian sanctions, but even what in Canada or Belgium, for example,
would be regarded as totally inoffensive, indeed commendable, expressions of national pride and demands for equal access of all
ethnic groups to educational and cultural opportunities. Consider,
for example, the penalties inflicted upon the Ukrainian historian
and literary scholar Valentyn Moroz because he had the temerity to
criticize regime practices that in his opinion were destroying Ukrainian national identity.[42]

I believe that of all the many varieties of Soviet dissent only the Democratic Movement has produced analyses and recommendations which, if they received responsive consideration by the Soviet authorities, might facilitate rational and humane solutions to the domestic and foreign-policy problems confronting an increasingly complex Soviet industrial society. To be sure, some of the writings of some Soviet advocates of democratization are "painfully naive, simplistic, utopian, or abstruse."[43] But considering the mind-numbing impact of standard Soviet political indoctrination—to which all Soviet citizens, including the Amalriks, Sahkarovs, and Solzhenitsyns, are subjected—the high intellectual quality and lofty moral tone of many of the essays, petitions, and polemics produced by the best minds of the Democratic Movement are remarkable. Certainly the quality of this output is incomparably higher than that of the censored official press. Perhaps an even more striking contrast is that between the dull-witted but menacing authoritarianism manifested by prosecutors and judges in trials of dissenters and—in many cases, such as those of Vladimir Bukovski and Andrei Amalrik—the latters' cool defiance and lucidity of discourse.[44]

Of course, as has been indicated, the moral fervor and intellectual vigor of the Democratic Movement have far exceeded its numerical strength. Nevertheless there is impressive albeit somewhat inconclusive evidence that, for a time and in respect to important issues, the Soviet proponents of "democratization" commanded support among social strata whose continuing effective performance is vital to the optimum functioning of the political system.

At the meeting called in 1966 by the Union of Soviet Writers to discuss the issue of whether or not to publish Solzhenitsyn's novel *Cancer Ward*—the decision, of course, was negative—"Solzhenitsyn's detractors were subdued by the outspoken support of the majority of his fellow writers. . . . "[45] Sakharov, Roy Medvedev, and the physicist Valentine Turchin, in the long petition/recommendation they addressed in 1970 to the highest Soviet leaders, asserted that the "preponderant part" (podavlyayushchaya chast) of the Soviet "intelligentsia and youth" understood the necessity for democratizing Soviet society.[46] Nine of the twenty signers of a protest petition against the adoption in September 1966 of Articles 190/1 and 190/3 of the RSFSR Criminal Code—which the signers viewed as an unconstitutional blow at dissent—were full members or corresponding members of the enormously prestigious Academy of Sciences of the USSR.[47] And to provide just one more—and a very striking —example, consider Alexander Solzhenitsyn's statement, in a commentary written in 1969 but unpublished until 1974, that those Soviet people who rejected the official mode of thought "almost universally" believed that political freedom "and a multiparty parliamentary system" were "necessary for our society."[48]

Solzhenitsyn's testimony is impressive in several respects. Certainly he is most knowledgeable. And as a thinker who rejects much in the Western constitutionalist political tradition, he presumably would not admit its vitality and popularity unless he were convinced that it enjoys—or did enjoy—wide support in the ranks of the Soviet intelligentsia.

It should not be forgotten that for several years dissent was extraordinarily vigorous. Perhaps the dissenters' most important accomplishment was that for a few years they succeeded in breaching —albeit to a limited extent—the Soviet regime's monopoly of political communication, for the first time since the early 1920's.

Indeed, as one scholar has observed, democratic dissenters developed and for a time maintained with vigor an "alternative system of political communication," which performed such functions as "focusing attention on certain issues and circumstances that most people might find more comfortable to overlook." The same author even asserts that this "alternative communications network constitutes a skeletal political organization through which political action not controlled by the regime can be initiated."[49]

Today, of course, most of the former articulators of dissent— and many of their more active supporters as well—are in camps, or in exile; some are confined in prison psychiatric hospitals; and many of those who were fortunate enough to be well known and to command strong support outside the USSR have emigrated. Perhaps others will follow them to emigration. Only Sakharov, among the major figures of the Democratic Movement, was still active inside the USSR in 1976. Yet, as is noted in this book's last chapter, an abundance of dissident activity continues, especially in the religious and nationality areas. And thanks to the activities of the dissenters, thousands of Soviet citizens, to at least a limited degree, gained access to sources of information other than those controlled by their rulers, thus enjoying, however illicitly and precariously, one of the conditions that, as Robert Dahl has stipulated, must be institutionally guaranteed if a government is to be "responsive to the preferences of its citizens."[50]

This information-disseminating function was performed in varying degrees by all the unauthorized *samizdat* (literally, self-published) "publications," but most important were the underground periodicals, in particular the remarkable civil rights journal *Chronicle of Current Events (Khronika tekushchikh sobytii)*, which appeared approximately once every two months from April 1968 to November 1972. In addition, counterparts of the Chronicle were prepared and distributed by Jewish, Ukrainian, and Lithuanian groups, and there were such periodicals as *Demokrat*—which unlike almost all other *samizdat* sources advocated the formation of underground political organizations—*Seyatel (The Sower)*, the mouthpiece of an underground "Social Democratic Party"; *Svobodnaya Mysl (Free Thought)*, the neo-Slavophile journal; *Veche (Assembly); Pomiticheski Dnevnik (Political Diary)*, the "insider" bulletin circulated from 1964 to 1970, apparently by Roy Medvedev, to a few hundred liberal members of the Soviet intellectual establishment; *Obshchestvennye Problemy (Social Problems)*, an enterprise dominated by Valeri Chalidze; and many others.[51]

Samizdat and its authors challenged the regime's claim to speak for all Soviet citizens, thus setting a precedent with enormous potential for the future of the peoples now controlled by the Kremlin. This is indicated by the massiveness of the regime's effort to discredit and suppress dissent, despite the damage that, as the Politburo must have realized, repression would do to the Soviet image abroad. Repression, intimidation, and the emigration of many dissidents have gravely wounded the resistance movement in Russia. Whether its participants are to be mourned as martyrs or honored as political pioneers, however, they have already performed invaluable services to truth, and have demonstrated that concepts such as respect for law and democracy can have meaning even in a largely closed society. Not the least of their services, for which the West owes them an enormous debt, consists in the light that their for the most part eminently reasonable, high-minded judgments on Soviet foreign policy have shed on the calculations underlying the Kremlin's professed intention of "relaxing international tensions." The Soviet regime's incredibly harsh response to the refusal of many of the dissenters to be silenced was revealing. From this record we can derive both useful information and inspiration.[52]

2.

Dissenters and Foreign Relations

Development of Dissent on Foreign Policy Issues

THIS SECTION AND THE NEXT provide background for the detailed treatment to follow of dissenters' views on world affairs and in particular on Moscow's foreign policy. Here I shall delineate as clearly as possible the main stages of crystallization and articulation of Soviet democrats' thinking about foreign affairs, highlighting events that may have constituted landmarks in this process. In the subsequent introductory section I seek to construct a collective profile of democratic dissenters' perception of Kremlin world policy, focusing on a number of significant themes and attitudes common to the utterances of several leading dissenters.

It is, unfortunately, perhaps even more difficult to perceive a clear chronological sequence or pattern in the field of foreign policy dissent than in other protest areas. Dispositions to protest against various aspects of Moscow's activities abroad existed throughout the post-Stalin era. These dispositions were triggered into vigorous articulation by various events, at least until massive intervention in Czechoslovakia and the mini-terror that followed it intimidated all but the most committed critics. Let us recall, for example, the paradoxical year 1956; it began with Khrushchev's denunciation of Stalin's abuses of power, but near its end Khrushchev was to violently disillusion some Soviet citizens by military intervention in Hungary. Some citizens, especially some university students and other youths, whose hopes for liberalization at home and abroad had been aroused by the famous "secret speech," engaged in indignant protest, expressed in the slogan "Hands Off Hungary!"[1] Perhaps less was known in the USSR about the Hungarian intervention than about the invasion of Czechoslovakia twelve years later. Yet, judging from Cornelia Gerstenmaier's data on the rather large scale of student protest in 1956, and the lack of any indication of comparably massive protest, by students or other elements of the population, in 1968 (though 1968 witnessed the well-known open, public Red Square demonstration by seven intellectuals, for which there was no counterpart in 1956), Soviet steamrollering of Hungary may have elicited a far more massive protest, in terms of numbers, than the blow against Czechoslovakia.[2] But there does not exist a body of well-articulated statements condemning the Hungarian invasion, such as those protesting the Warsaw Pact operation against Czechoslovakia.

Two prominent dissenters, however, the mathematician Revolt Pimenov and the actor Boris Vail, sentenced to five years' exile in October 1970 for "slanderous fabrications derogating the Soviet system," had in the late 1950's and early 1960's served long terms in labor camps for their condemnation of the Soviet intervention in Hungary.[3] One *samizdat* author, in 1971, retrospectively connected Soviet suppression of the liberation movements in Hungary and Czechoslovakia, and also of the 1953 Berlin workers' uprising, seeing in all three, and especially in the Czechoslovak case, sources of a "moral/political crisis" which the Soviet leadership had not been able to overcome. This author also stressed the anomaly of Soviet violence against other Communists in Hungary and Czechoslovakia.[4] It is appropriate to hypothesize that severe repression of protest against the Hungarian invasion, as well as the fact that by the time the invasion of Czechoslovakia occurred the Soviet authorities had for some time been engaged in a determined campaign to stamp out dissent, helps to explain the comparatively limited support received by the 1968 Red Square demonstrators and other protestors against Soviet violence in Czechoslovakia.

Apart from the muffled protest against the Hungarian invasion and the heroic Red Square demonstration of August 25, 1968, along with less well known protest demonstrations that occurred concurrently, one can perceive a series of phases within the larger, overall dissent movement, extending from the late 1950's and early 1960's to the mid-1970's.

The first of the phases, or sub-movements, that will be identified might be termed anarcho-pacifism, or anarcho-democratic pacifism. It flourished in the late 1950's and early 1960's. This current of opinion, which was, as Amalrik pointed out, "directed not against the political regime as such but only against its culture," nevertheless had, under Soviet conditions, ominous political implications, in the opinion of the authorities. A number of its exponents, such as the poet Yuri Galanskov, were subjected to severe sanctions. In 1961, Galanskov was arrested for distributing the *samizdat* journal *Feniks (Phoenix)* and was confined for several months in a psychiatric hospital.[5] In 1966, Galanskov, had produced a *samizdat* journal, *Phoenix 66*, which, as he stated at his trial in January 1968, was intended by him to be a collection of articles on pacifism, but which, "under the influence of the trial of Sinyavsky and Daniel," was transformed into a much broader, more politically oriented journal.[6] Thus began the second phase of dissent marked by expanded scope, an increasingly political content, and efforts to generate support in the West for the civil rights movement at home.

In 1968, Galanskov, together with Alexander Ginzburg, another young intellectual (who had been arrested in 1960 for distributing the samizdat journal *Sintaksis (Syntax)* and subsequently was prosecuted, ostensibly for taking an examination for a friend, and sentenced to a year in a camp), was tried for compiling a record of the trial of the writers Andrei Sinyavski and Yuli Daniel. Publication of the Sinyavski–Daniel trial record abroad proved, of course, extremely embarrassing to the Kremlin, and Galanskov and Ginzburg received long sentences in labor camps. Because of the failure to provide Galanskov with adequate medical care—he suffered from a stomach ulcer—he died in a strict-regime labor camp in the fall of 1972.[7]

Postponing for a time examination of the peace propaganda and other activities of Galanskov and his friends and associates, let us briefly inventory the literature of the 1968 protest against the invasion of Czechoslovakia. Protests against the invasion were issued by two main groups of individuals: such Communists as Grigorenko, Kosterin, Pisarev, Yakhimovich, and Pavlinchuk; and a number of non-Communists, especially the seven participants in the Red Square demonstration (Larisa Bogoraz, Konstantin Babitski, Vadim Delone, Vladimir Dremlyuga, Victor Feinberg, Natalya Gorbanevskaya, and Pavel Litvinov), and also including Anatoli Marchenko, Yuri Gendler, Lev Kvachevski, Anatoli Yakobson, Boris Shragin, and others. We shall subsequently have occasion to refer to various aspects of the statements condemning the invasion of Czechoslovakia. Suffice it to say here that while the petitions and protests of both the Communist party members involved and the non-Communists raised a considerable number of issues, all of the statements essentially agreed on the grounds for condemnation. It was argued that the invasion was representative of a trend in Soviet political life in the direction of a revival of "Stalinism"; that it had struck a blow against democratization, freedom, and the rule of law both in Czechoslovakia and in the USSR; and that it was a violation of the principle, formally accepted by the Soviet Union, of noninterference in the internal affairs of other countries and of the right of nations to self-determination, and hence was contrary to generally accepted principles of international law.[8]

The surge of protest against the suppression of democratization in Czechoslovakia was only one manifestation of the blossoming of dissent against various Soviet foreign and domestic policies in 1968, following the political trials of late 1967 and early 1968 and other evidences of reactionary trends in Soviet political life. (It should, of course, be kept in mind that while developments at home in the 1966-68 period were discouraging to Soviet proponents of liberalization and democratization, the trend in Eastern Europe, particularly in Czechoslovakia, was, prior to the crushing blow struck by the Warsaw Pact forces' intervention, encouraging.) Thus 1968 also saw the issuance (in February) of the appeal to the Budapest Conference of Communist and Workers Parties, denouncing arbitrary political trials in Russia, and the publication of Andrei Sakharov's famous essay *Reflections on Progress, Coexistence, and Intellectual Freedom,* often referred to as Sakharov's "memorandum."

The appeal to the Budapest assembly not only protested arbitrary arrests and trials, imprisonment of dissenters, and other "illegal and antihuman actions," but also called attention to "discrimination against small nations," especially the Crimean Tatars, in the USSR. Its most important feature, however, indicated both by the fact that it was addressed to a foreign (though at this stage still a Communist) constituency and by its language, was the evidence it provided that some successful Soviet professionals had been so frustrated by regime indifference to their hitherto humble petitions as to violate, in the name of *glasnost* (publicity, or disclosure), the hoary taboo against airing domestic disputes before a foreign audience.[9]

As the sense of frustration and indignation among committed dissenters deepened in the period of 1968-70, this strategy of reaching out to foreign audiences, including non-Communist ones, was employed with increasing frequency and boldness and, it seems in some cases, with a sense of hopelessness and even desperation. The majority of dissenters, however, confronted by the determination of the Kremlin and the security police to silence dissenters whenever their protests seemed to challenge, in any way and even by implication, the legitimacy of the regime and its policies and the peace of mind of the powerful and privileged, abandoned the unequal struggle. They left the field to a small minority of deeply committed and incredibly courageous people, who consciously assumed the awesome risks involved when, in the language later to be employed by Alexander Solzhenitsyn for the title of an account of his experiences in battling the KGB, "the calf butted the oak tree."

Ironically, in the light of later events, Andrei Sakharov's program derived much of its impact from its author's stature as a major figure in the Soviet "military–industrial complex." Moved by concern about the threat of thermonuclear war, radioactive contamination of the atmosphere, and other problems related to the headlong pace of nuclear weapons development, Sakharov, "beginning in 1957 (not without the influence of statements made throughout the world by such people as Albert Schweitzer, Linus Pauling, and others)," began to feel a sense of personal responsibility for having helped to create these problems.[10]

Despite his deep concern about the nuclear arms race—to which by 1968 there had been added, among other things, indignation regarding increasing suppression of dissent, especially after the Ginzburg–Galanskov trial—Sakharov's memorandum was a basically optimistic (at least for the long term), rationalistic, and reformist essay. It set forth an internationalist perspective on major problems that Sakharov perceived as common to all of mankind. It advocated Soviet–American cooperation over a broad range of world problems, such as arms control and environmental questions, and expressed confidence in science as the main instrument of mankind's salvation. It was, at least ostensibly—and presumably sincerely—couched in the form of a respectful petition to the Soviet leaders, though it also expressed concern and even alarm at the growing influence in high policy councils of such "conservatives" as the head of the science section of the CPSU, Sergei Trapeznikov.[11] Concerned above all with the threat to the world of nuclear warfare, Sakharov toward the beginning of the memorandum asserted that "any action increasing the division of mankind, any preaching of the incompatibility of world ideologies and nations is madness and a crime."[12] Near the end, he foresaw that by the period 1980–2000 "convergence" of the American and Soviet systems, which would reduce "differences in social structure [and] promote intellectual freedom, science and economic progress," would "lead to the creation of a world government and the smoothing of national contradictions."[13]

As far as the post-Khrushchev Soviet political leadership was concerned, Sakharov's respectful petition was obviously embarrassing and unwelcome. It was not even mentioned in the Soviet press until February 1972, when it and its author were ridiculed as "utopian" in the Literary Gazette by that major weekly's hard-line editor, the veteran propagandist Alexander Chakovski. He also ominously asserted that Sakharov's ideas were grist for anti-Soviet propaganda in the West.[14] It should be kept in mind that although Sakharov's tract was courteous and moderate in tone, it also reflected an alienation generated by years of unsuccessful, and undoubtedly deeply frustrating, lobbying through appropriate Soviet governmental channels for a variety of arms control measures. (In this activity, Sakharov received some discrete support from the late distinguished physicist, I. V. Kurchatov.) On one occasion, Nikita Khrushchev, at a meeting with atomic scientists, praised Sakharov— widely known and honored for his role in the development of Soviet nuclear weapons—as a fine scientist, but told him and the other scientists present to leave the "tricky business" of foreign policy to him.[15] As the second volume of Khrushchev's memoirs puts it, Sakharov, like another famous Soviet scientist, Peter Kapitsa, "had misgivings about military research."[16]

Sakharov's stand on military policy had irked Khrushchev, and his 1968 memorandum aroused much greater Kremlin displeasure; but his views were also unsatisfactory to some Soviet dissenters. Thus, according to a manifesto purporting to represent the views of the "Estonian technical intelligentsia," Sakharov, although he deserved praise for his sincerity and moral courage, had far too much confidence in the capacity of science to solve the problems of mankind. Moreover, his petitioner's approach to the authorities, in the opinion of this group (of unknown, and possibly not Estonian but Russian, identity), was too timid. Rather than humbly petitioning, they asserted, he should have boldly demanded fundamental changes in the Soviet system. Above all, they maintained, he erred in not sufficiently stressing the centrality of moral values if Russia, and the world, were to be saved from imminent catastrophe.[17]

In denying that natural scientists alone held the key to resolving mankind's pressing problems, the "Estonian" manifesto corresponded to a major strand in the thinking of Alexander Solzhenitsyn. In his Nobel lecture, for example, Solzhenitsyn was to assert that "propaganda, and coercion, and scientific proof" were all powerless to transcend differences among political units in a world fragmented by virtue of clashing traditions but rendered interdependent—or, at least, shrunken—by technology. In such a world, he warned, "lack of mutual understanding carries the threat of a quick and stormy death." Here the great novelist of dissent, who has often emphasized, as did the "Estonians," the primacy of ethics in human affairs, declared that not science but art, in particular literature, could "create for all humanity one single unitary system of evaluation—for evil deeds and good deeds," thus undoing the attempts of governments to rule mankind by evil myths and fictions. Here also—and in this, at least, Solzhenitsyn was at one with Sakharov and other Soviet dissenters who had carried their cause to the court of world opinion—he proclaimed that there was no longer any such thing in the world as the "internal affairs" of any single, isolated country.[18]

There were also other major *samizdat* documents, such as the militant pamphlet by the pseudonymous "S. Zorin" and "N. Alekseev" entitled "Time Does Not Wait" ("Vremya ne zhdet") and the wide-ranging "Program of the Democrats of Russia, the Ukraine, and the Baltic Area" ("Programma demokraticheskogo dvizheniya rossii, ukrainy i pribaltiki"), both of which began to circulate early in 1969, as well as Andrei Amalrik's brilliant book *Will the Soviet Union Survive Until 1984?* All of these expressed opinions sharply at variance with some of the views set forth in Sakharov's memorandum. The first two, especially the Zorin–Alekseev pamphlet, were far more accusatory than Sakharov's calmly reasoned memorandum; the pair, in a neo-Marxist analysis of the Soviet system, compared the dominant, privileged political elite of the USSR to the upper *bourgeoisie* in capitalist societies. They painted a frightening picture of a militaristic "unified monopoly" straining to achieve world domination. The "Program of the Democrats" assailed Soviet "colonialism" and called for the granting to ethnic minorities of a real opportunity to exercise their constitutional right of self-determination. Both documents called for a "struggle" to force the Soviet leaders to restructure the political system along democratic lines, and the "Program" demanded a "rapprochement with the capitalist countries" as well as "political self-determination for the socialist countries."[19]

Andrei Amalrik's position differed from Sakharov's in two very important respects. First, Amalrik was far less optimistic about the prospects for democratic reform of the Soviet system and indeed for that system's survival than was the atomic scientist, and his scenario for the future of the regime's relations with foreign powers, in particular the People's Republic of China, was, by comparison with anything said by Sakharov, bleak. Amalrik assigned very high probability to a protracted and exhausting Sino-Soviet war, in the course of which both the Communist-ruled states of Eastern Europe and the non-Russian nationalities of the Soviet Union would break away from Russian control. However—and this is seldom mentioned in discussions of Amalrik's prediction—he also allowed for the very limited possibility that catastrophe might be averted or at least ameliorated by democratic reforms instituted by the regime.[20]

In his 1968 essay, Sakharov praised Roy Medvedev's as yet unpublished book on Stalin, *Let History Judge*. Sakharov admitted, however, that the Marxist Medvedev found elements of "Westernism" in his, Sakharov's, opinion. Although Medvedev joined forces in 1970 with Sakharov and the physicist Valentine Turchin in addressing to the CPSU leadership a set of reformist policy recommendations, along with predictions of the dire consequences for the future of failure to "democratize" Soviet political life, a rift later developed between Sakharov and the Medvedev twins.[21]

Nineteen sixty-eight was also, of course, the year marked by perhaps the most important event in the annals of the Democratic Movement, namely the distribution in April of the first issue of the *Chronicle of Current Events*. As I noted in the last chapter, *Chronicle* was not the first regular *samizdat* journal to appear, nor was it to be the last.

One could date from the *Chronicle's* commencement of four and one-half years of unbroken distribution the beginning of a third, organizational phase of dissent regarding Soviet domestic and foreign policies. Significant also were the formation of the Action Group for the Defense of Human Rights in the USSR, in May 1969, and of the Human Rights Committee (HRC) in November 1970. The 1969 Action Group (also called the Initiative Group, from its Russian name, Initsiativnaya Gruppa) probably originated as a result of the arrest of the major civil and human rights activist Peter Grigorenko a fortnight before.[22] To be sure, the impetus for the establishment of the *Chronicle*, the Action Group, and the HRC probably dates at least as far back as December 1965, when a group of intellectuals demonstrated in Pushkin Square in Moscow, displaying the slogan, "Respect the Constitution, the Basic Law of the USSR," thus setting a standard for future demonstrations.[23] But the Action Group and the HRC confronted the Soviet authorities with a new, potentially formidable challenge. They had launched types of protest activities which the authorities obviously regarded as infringements upon their traditional monopoly on the formulation and enunciation of public policy, both domestic and foreign.

The Action Group, on May 20, 1969, addressed a letter to the United Nations Commission on Human Rights requesting it to investigate violations of "basic human rights" in the USSR.[24] The U.N. did not act upon or even acknowledge this and a series of additional requests from the Action Group, but the Soviet security police responded vigorously. Hard upon the founding of the association—a more accurate term than organization for this loose aggregate—its members found themselves being interrogated and otherwise harassed by the KGB.[25] By mid-1973, fourteen of the Action Group's fifteen founders had been subjected to such forms of "extrajudicial repression" as minatory "prophylactic chats" with KGB officers or judicial repression by means of sentences to labor camps. And some were committed to special psychiatric hospitals. The fifteenth, the biologist Sergei Kovalev, remained unmolested longest of all.[26] However, Kovalev was finally arrested in December 1974, ostensibly for connections with a Lithuanian *samizdat* journal and with the *Chronicle*.[27] He was tried in Vilnius, the capital of Lithuania.

A year after his arrest Kovalev was sentenced to ten years of forced labor and exile. During his detention his friends and even his wife were refused permission to visit him. Andrei Sakharov and other friends who succeeded, despite official obstructionism, in getting to Vilnius and who wished to attend his trial—which according to Soviet propaganda to the outside world was "open" and "legal" —were forcibly prevented from doing so by the police. In the meantime, the Soviet people received no information at all on Kovalev's trial and harsh treatment or on the activities of Sakharov and others on his behalf.[28]

As Reddaway notes, the members of the Action Group were not "cranks, but intelligent, mostly professional men and women with an average age of somewhat under forty."[29] They included Peter Yakir and Victor Krasin, both of whom were to plead guilty to charges of anti-Soviet agitation in late 1973 in a trial mildly reminiscent of Stalin's notorious show trials, as well as the poetess Gorbanevskaya, the brilliant Ukrainian mathematician/biologist Leonid Plyushch—later to become one of the most tormented victims of post-Stalin repression—the eloquent translator/critic Anatoli Yakobson, and the mathematician Tatyana Veilkanova.

The smaller Human Rights Committee was founded by Andrei Sakharov along with his fellow physicist Andrei Tverdokhlebov and Valeri Chalidze. In 1971 the very distinguished algebraist Igor Shafarevich was elected a member. Boris Zuckerman and Alexander Volpin, both of whom emigrated in 1972, acted for a time in the capacity of "experts" for the HRC. Alexander Solzhenitsyn and Alexander Galich were elected honorary corresponding members of the HRC. In late 1972 Chalidze, after accepting invitations to lecture on Soviet legal practices at several American universities (he resigned from the HRC before leaving the USSR) was, by a ruse, deprived of his Soviet passport and of Soviet citizenship, and was refused permission to return to the Soviet Union. In 1973, Tverdokhlebov having resigned, the physicist Gregory Podyapolski joined the HRC and, together with Sakharov and Shafarevich, addressed various appeals to the Soviet authorities, and in some cases to the international public, on behalf, for example, of "persons prosecuted in connection with their convictions" and "ruled mentally ill and sent for compulsory treatment, mainly to special prison hospitals."[30]

In June 1971 the HRC formally affiliated with the International League for the Rights of Man, headquartered in New York. The affiliation, like all of HRC's activities, was conducted openly and publicly. The HRC maintained that it was not a "public organization," in the sense in which that term is applied in the USSR to such mass organizations as the trade unions and the Communist Youth League, but rather a "collective of authors." Above all, it maintained —especially in documents drafted mainly by Chalidze—that its activities in no way violated or conflicted with Soviet law. The Soviet authorities subjected the HRC and its individual members to an amazing variety of threats and harassments—including dismissal from work, cutting off of telephone service, and calling Chalidze into offices of the Moscow procuracy—the closest Soviet equivalent to district attorney in United States, at highest level, equivalent to U.S. Attorney General and KGB. But they did not, for a long time, arrest or prosecute any of them. Presumably this relative forbearance was a function of the high domestic and international status of

HRC's members, foreign support for them, and the scrupulous and sophisticated respect for the letter of Soviet and international law which they displayed.

It should be noted, however, that in an essay distributed by the International League for the Rights of Man in June 1972, Alexander Sergeevich Esenin-Volpin, shortly after emigrating, expressed fear that Chalidze might be arrested if he did not receive firm support from abroad. Indeed, much interest had already been displayed by the KGB in a visit paid to Chalidze by a representative of the Flemish Committee for the Defense of Human Rights, who was arrested in March 1971. Clearly Volpin's belief that the threat to Chalidze was "grave" was not without foundation.[31]

During the period when Chalidze was the most active member of the HRC its activities were largely of a scholarly, seemingly almost academic character. After Chalidze's departure in November 1972 for the United States, where he was deprived of his Soviet citizenship, Sakharov, who was thenceforth to bear the main burden of its work, turned increasingly to widely publicized protests against what he and his colleagues regarded as illegal and inhumane violations of the rights of individuals. Some of the committee's later protests have also been concerned with such group rights as emigration (in the cases especially but not exclusively of members of the Jewish, German, Crimean Tatar, and other nationalities) and the right to return to one's native country. Increasingly in the years after 1972, Sakharov; his second wife, Elena Bonner, also a vigorous champion of civil rights, whom he married after having become a widower; and members of his wife's family were subjected to enormous pressures and numerous grievous deprivations.

A final and still unfolding phase in the clash between dissenters and regime over foreign policy can be said to have begun in 1972. With the blossoming of what the Kremlin's spokesmen termed "relaxation of tensions" and of what in the West was hailed as "détente," Moscow was more than ever determined to crush dissent. This determination was doubtless shaped by a sense that it was urgent to emphasize that "relaxation of tensions" did not herald an era of "East–West" ideological coexistence or any weakening of ideological control and discipline at home. Increased harshness seemed to be required toward Soviet citizens who challenged authority. But there were countervailing considerations, flowing from the need, in an era of still limited but gradually increasing scientific and technical cooperation with "capitalist" societies, to avoid needlessly antagonizing elements of foreign public opinion sympathetic to the Democratic Movement, or to Soviet Jews and other Soviet citizens who wished to emigrate. In this complex situation, the Soviet authorities applied harsher measures than before to dissidents without strong foreign support or other political resources; but in a considerable number of cases, especially but by no means exclusively those of dissidents of Jewish ancestry, they in effect gave dissidents the choice of emigration or imprisonment. There were of course a number of individuals, such as Sakharov and Solzhenitsyn, for whom special strategies had to be devised.

As far as dissenters were concerned, none of the alternatives offered by the regime seemed enticing. This was a period of intensified effort to stifle dissent, and of substantial if by no means complete Kremlin success in this effort. Dissenters like Sakharov, Solzhenitsyn, and some others, who still had the courage to continue to resist and the international stature and foreign support to ensure them a high probability of staying out of prison, were losing whatever hope they might earlier have had that the Soviet authorities would voluntarily institute the domestic and foreign policy reform that dissenters had advocated for years. A process of growing disenchantment and intense moral indignation, in large part a response to the inhumanity displayed toward the least fortunate victims of repression such as Bukovski, Moroz, and others, was reflected in growing militancy in the tone of the writings of some dissenters. It was reflected, in particular in the attacks of Solzhenitsyn and Sakharov on a version of "détente" that in the opinion of the two men might amount to capitulation by the West to a Soviet Union bent on world domination. Probably to repair damage to its image abroad resulting from publicity about cases publicized by Sakharov and others, the regime in recent years has permitted some victims of repression to emigrate, although its policy has still been highly selective.

Despite the increasing dangers involved in dissent, it has not ceased and, as I shall argue in a later chapter, it appears it never will. Efforts to create new forms and vehicles of struggle have continued, both by dissenters inside the USSR and by members of the increasingly numerous emigrant dissident community of Europe and North America. The existence of an influential emigrant community may have enhanced the survival capability of dissenters still in the Soviet Union, and also offset the damage done to the morale of those remaining behind by the in some cases enforced and in other cases voluntary departure of key civil rights activists.

To anticipate somewhat treatment of topics that will be discussed more fully later, I note here that in the summer of 1974 Valentine Turchin established in Moscow a branch of the international civil rights association, Amnesty International. Turchin had followed up his already mentioned collaboration of 1970 with Andrei Sakharov and Roy Medvedev in recommending democratization to CPSU leaders by refusing, in the fall of 1973, to join in the organized hounding of Sakharov. Subsequent to his action of setting up the Soviet Amnesty International branch, Turchin, despite his outstanding qualifications as a physicist and data processor, was condemned by official action to unemployment.

In June 1975, Turchin and Roy Medvedev were interviewed by two *London Observer* correspondents. Later, in connection with the KGB's 1975–76 drive to smash Amnesty's activities in Russia, he was severely harassed and as of late January 1976, he reportedly had been told that criminal charges were being prepared against him.[32]

In 1974, Solzhenitsyn established in Switzerland the "Russian Social Fund," financed by royalties from his writings, for the purpose of sending aid to the families of political prisoners in Soviet forced labor camps. The well-known human rights activist Alexander Ginzburg bravely accepted the responsibility of serving as representative of the fund in the USSR.[33]

An event of great potential significance was the founding, and the publication in late 1974, of the first issue of the emigrant quarterly *Kontinent*. Edited by the well-known writer Vladimir Maksimov, who had recently emigrated, and graced by a distinguished international editorial board, the journal began to publish quarterly in Russian and German with the intention of appearing later in French, Italian, and English. Among the contributors to the first issue were authors living outside the USSR—Andrei Sinyavski and Eugene Ionesco based in Paris, Joseph Brodski in the United States, Solzhenitsyn in Switzerland—along with Sakharov and another living in Moscow. Ionesco, Solzhenitsyn, and Sakharov contributed inaugural statements. Among the roles attributed by Solzhenitsyn to *Kontinent* were those of carrying on the suppressed efforts of *Novy Mir* to express opinions not subordinated to the official ideology and "becoming the true voice of Eastern Europe."

Sakharov stressed the mission of explaining to Western readers the "historical phenomenon" of life in the "socialist" countries, which, he pointed out, could not be understood from the window of a tourist bus or from the controlled press. The new journal opened with an appeal for unity against totalitarianism, and for "unconditional democratism," "unconditional religious idealism," and "unconditional nonpartisanship." However, as Alfred Erich Senn noted in reviewing the first issue, *Kontinent's* editor, Maksimov, "contributed to the further division of the dissidents" by his response to a question put by the immigrant Polish journal *Kultura*. Asked if Valeri Chalidze and Roy Medvedev had objected to *Kontinent's* (in Senn's words) religious bent, Maksimov replied that according to Chalidze and Medvedev the Soviet system needed only "certain corrections," whereas "in our view, nothing short of fundamental reforms will change the situation or remove the evil which is deeply imbedded in the system itself."[34]

Perhaps it should also be noted that the Soviet authorities seem in 1974 and 1975 to have intensified their long-standing campaign to discredit the exiled emigrant community. An aspect of this tactic noted by Senn was publication by the KGB-connected press agency *Novosti* of an English-language anthology of Soviet attacks on Solzhenitsyn. More recently there has been a spate of attacks on Radio Liberty and its emigrant staff, some of them on a level comparable to the most virulent Stalin-era Soviet cold war output.

Another major joint project of dissenters in emigration and in the homeland, this one having a much stronger representation of the latter, was the already mentioned publication *Out from Under the Avalanche*. Finally, be it noted that Solzhenitsyn's visit to the United States in the summer of 1975, especially his addresses (sponsored by the American Federation of Labor and Congress of Industrial Organizations), dramatized, as nothing else had, the moral issues involved in "détente" and the dangers to the West of permitting euphoria generated by the joint Soviet–American space spectacular of July to distract attention from unyielding terrestrial realities.

I do not mean to imply by the foregoing that I fully share Solzhenitsyn's criticism of "détente" and of United States foreign policy. Solzhenitsyn was correct in alerting Americans to the despotic and imperialistic impulses still dominant in Soviet politics. But it would be unfortunate if his impassioned rhetoric were to distract attention from the most important common task facing all governments and peoples in our era, namely that of finding ways

to achieve a degree of international political cooperation commensu-
rate with the ever-increasing interdependence of nations resulting
from the relentless advances of science.

A Thematic Overview

We turn now to a survey of some salient themes common to
much of the corpus of democratic dissenters' thought in the field
of foreign affairs. Though it varies in tone and stance—ranging from
respectful petitioning to unqualified condemnation and defiance—
this body of opinion is generally characterized by logical argument
and by moderation in expression. Essentially it constitutes an extension to international affairs of the dissenters' aspirations for a
freer and more humane and democratic political life at home. Thus
the dissenters' views on foreign affairs have been characterized by
the same attributes of moral concern and idealism, perhaps verging
at times on naiveté, and by the same combination of rational/em-
pirical and normative/didactic elements that one finds in their reactions to the Soviet domestic scene. And, as is also true of the
judgments passed by participants in the Democratic Movement on
"internal" affairs, there is so much individuality in their foreign
policy analysis that to generalize about it is inevitably to distort
it, at least to some extent.

In general, the dissenters' critique of Soviet foreign policy has
sought to evaluate it in terms of moral and intellectual standards
applicable to all states, regardless of ideological pretensions. Soviet
democrats evaluated the international behavior of "socialist," and
also "capitalist" governments not in terms of what the respective
policy makers claimed to be doing, and still less in terms of the
ideologies that theoretically guided the behavior of the governments
in question, but rather by examining the details and consequences—
or, in modern social science jargon, the "outputs"—of policy decisions. Their objectivity is indicated, among other things, by the
fact that they did not hesitate on occasion to condemn American
or British foreign policies as well as Soviet ones. Their condemnation
differed, of course, from the echoing of the official CPSU line demanded, as the performance of a civic duty, by the official Soviet
political culture. When dissenters criticized the policies of Western
states they did so not as members of manipulated collectives but

as independent individuals. For example, in 1965 Yuri Galanskov staged a one-man demonstration in front of the United States Embassy in Moscow protesting American military intervention in the Dominican Republic.[35] And in 1968, Andrei Amalrik and his wife, Gyuzel, carried out a two-person demonstration against the British policy of supplying arms to Nigeria for use against the Biafran rebels.[36]

But a more striking manifestation of this universalist and objective aspect of the dissident approach to world affairs is represented by statements juxtaposing the domestic or foreign policies or both of the USSR with those of various non-Communist nations, and applying common moral standards to both.

Thus, Vladimir Bukovski, during his 1967 trial for allegedly slandering the Soviet state, pointed out that freedom of speech—formally guaranteed by the Soviet Constitution—was, in practice, throttled in the USSR, while "in the bourgeois countries there exist Communist parties that make it their deliberate purpose to undermine the regime."[37] During this same trial Bukovski boldly compared suppression of dissent in Spain and in Russia. In so doing, he pointed to what he termed "the touching unanimity of fascist and Soviet law." For these and other statements in the same vein Bukovski was reprimanded by the trial judge, who asserted that for a "comparison between Soviet policies and those of foreign bourgeois countries" to be made in a Soviet court was an "outrage."[38]

Authors more controlled in their expression than Bukovski, such as Andrei Sakharov, Roy Medvedev, and others, also penned bold and systematic comparisons of the performance of the Soviet and Western social and political systems that incurred the displeasure of the Soviet authorities. Sakharov, both in his well-known 1968 essay and in the lengthy set of recommendations that he, Roy Medvedev, and Valentine Turchin addressed to the CPSU leaders in 1970, unfavorably compared Soviet expenditures on education and Soviet performance with respect to labor productivity, the development and use of computers, and other areas, with the American record.[39] Like Bukovski, Sakharov, at least retrospectively, compared the Soviet Union with a "facist" polity by asserting that even greater evil had been inflicted on the world by Stalin than by Hitler.[40] He also, more mildly, criticized America by contending that there were similarities between harassment of dissenters in the Soviet Union in the 1960's and the earlier phenomenon of "McCarthyism" in the United States.[41]

In the 1968 essay Sakharov attributed to the United States "direct responsibility" for the "tragic" situation in Vietnam, but balanced this criticism by attributing to the USSR the major share of responsibility for the "tragic" situation of the Middle East.[42] He urged that the "international policies" of the two "leading superpowers" be based on "unified and general principles," which could be "guaranteed" by international control over observance by all signatories of the Universal Declaration of Human Rights, adopted by the United Nations in 1948 but never ratified by the Soviet Union.[43] Further examination of this last recommendation, which of course underlays the activities of Sakharov, Valeri Chalidze, and other participants in the work of the Human Rights Committee, and of related human rights issues will be left for later consideration (pp. 94-104). Similarly, discussion of the implications of the comparison between Soviet and United States approaches to international relations that underlay the warnings voiced by dissidents on the dangers for democracy in a world of unqualified acceptance of the Soviet version of "détente" belongs to a later chapter.

The orientations identified above are associated, and logically linked, with one of the most significant themes of the dissenters' critique of Soviet conduct in international affairs. This is the argument best developed by Sakharov but supported in various ways by other dissidents, that a necessary condition for world peace and for the maximization of mankind's welfare is a Soviet foreign policy squarely based on the democratization of the Soviet domestic political structure. As Sakharov, Roy Medvedev, and Turchin asserted in their 1970 message to Soviet leaders, "all negative phenomena in our foreign policy are closely connected with the problem of democratization...." "Great disquiet," they added, "is caused by the absence of democratic discussion of such questions as arms aid to a number of countries...."[44] In a more positive vein, the three authors asserted that "democratization will facilitate a better public understanding of our foreign policy and remove from it all its negative features."[45]

As was to be expected of its scholarly and fair-minded authors, "Manifesto II," as the 1970 document is sometimes called, was not directed against Soviet policy alone. Like Sakharov's 1968 memorandum, it was also sharply critical of much in Western, and also in Chinese Communist, policy. (Later, Sakharov, for one, was to reject the extremely negative view of Communist China held by most Soviet democrats, at the time "Manifesto II" was prepared and still held by Solzhenitsyn in late 1973 when he addressed his well-known message to top Soviet leaders.) Indeed, the 1970 statement was still, on the whole, couched in terms presumably calculated to avoid unnecessarily irritating the masters of the Kremlin.

One argument presented in favor of democratization by the three authors was the democratization would "strengthen progressive Communist forces in the entire world." (in view of the differences of opinion, later to be revealed, between Sakharov and Roy Medvedev, the language may be presumed to have been proposed by the latter.)[46] The trio also warned that if a "course toward democratization" were not taken, the USSR would "gradually be transformed into a second-rate provincial power."[47] From these examples of the document's contents—and indeed, it seems to me, from its whole tenor—a good case could be made that its authors were writing as loyal and patriotic citizens. However, this document, like so many other expressions of democratically oriented dissent, recommended a line of policy so liberal, indeed so implicitly radical in the contemporary Soviet context, as to inevitably, one must judge, seem objectionable if not downright subversive to an aging, conservative Soviet leadership. What other interpretation is possible in view of the similarity of much of its contents to the Dubcek program of democratic reforms in Czechoslovakia, for which the Politburo, or at least its dominant majority, had, by its August 1968 invasion and subsequent measures, so clearly demonstrated its abhorrence? It should also be remembered that not only did "Manifesto II" propose an end to all jamming of foreign radio broadcasts, free sale of foreign books and periodicals, and amnesty for political prisoners, but it also recommended gradual elimination of the internal passport system, one of the most important control instruments in the hands of the regime. It urged facilitation of "the possibility of creating new publishers by public organizations and groups of citizens," "nomination of several candidates for each office in elections for Party and government organs at all levels," restoring the "rights of all nations forcibly resettled under Stalin," and several other measures the effect of which would certainly be unsettling, to say the least, to the Soviet "establishment."[48]

Not surprisingly, a linkage between internal democratization and an enlightened foreign policy is a pervasive theme in much of the dissenters' public output. At this point, some attention will be devoted to one more source of relevant statements, the remarkable work *A Book about Socialist Democracy (Kniga o sotsialisticheskoi demokratii)*, by Roy Medvedev. It would be inappropriate to attempt here a full-scale analysis of this impressive, wide-ranging study—which, though it is written from an ostensibly "Leninist" point of view, is in my opinion permeated by a spirit that might better be characterized as social democratic or "Bukharinist,"[11] or at any rate sufficiently non-Stalinist to be considered "revisionist" by the present Soviet rulers.[49]

Suffice it to say that in a chapter entitled "Socialist Democratization and the Foreign Policy of the USSR," Medvedev, while expressing disapproval of the "bourgeois" political system of the United States and arguing that in the West only the Communist parties could provide dynamic leadership for the coalitions he considered necessary if socialism and democracy were to triumph (especially in Western Europe), also pointed out that "antidemocratic actions" inside the USSR, such as the trial of the writers Sinyavski and Daniel in 1966, the press campaign against Solzhenitsyn, and the invasion of Czechoslovakia, "checked the development of the world revolutionary process" and of the Communist movement, diminished Soviet influence abroad, and played into the hands of "bourgeois propaganda."[50] Much in Roy Medvedev's writings is puzzling and even distasteful to those (this author included) who believe that, with all its faults, Western-style constitutional democracy is the least harmful to human liberties of all forms of government. However, it seems certain that adoption by Moscow of the program he advocates for Soviet domestic and foreign policy would have a positive impact, not only because it would facilitate closer American–Soviet cooperation than now seems on the horizon, but because it might spur reexamination of the global premises of American foreign policy. The United States might, if the USSR began to practice the socialism and internationalism that Medvedev preaches, be forced—if only to remain competitive—to accentuate the internationalist and altruistic components of its own policies abroad.

Of course, my speculation assumes that Medvedev-style foreign policy recommendations are feasible for the USSR—a very large and at present unprovable, but nevertheless highly interesting hypothesis. It should be added that such speculation is relevant not only to Roy Medvedev's recommendations but also to those of Sakharov and other Soviet democrats. Any loosening up of the rigid pattern of Soviet politics—and, one surmises, any genuinely symmetrical movement on the part of both the Soviet Union and the United States toward the kind of mutually beneficial cooperation advocated by Sakharov and implicitly, despite his forbidding ideological language, by Roy Medvedev—could have highly beneficial and stimulating effects in both societies and throughout the world.

However, a potent implication of the advocacy of democratization by Soviet democratic dissidents—and it is well to recall the evidence presented earlier of the wide support for their views by Soviet intellectuals, experts and professionals—is that, at least in terms of political institutions and processes, a more profound change would have to occur in the Soviet policy than in the American if the domestic and international goals envisaged by men like Sakharov were to be attained. "Leninists" such as Roy Medvedev insist that "socialism" is the only desirable pattern of economic organization for the whole world. This is a prescription to which, at this time, only a small minority of Americans would probably be receptive. However, Medvedev's insistence that socialism without democracy—a concept which he obviously interpreted in a fashion light years removed from the existing Soviet model—is no socialism at all but a perversion thereof makes his views, if not as objectionable to the Soviet authorities as those of Solzhenitsyn or Sakharov—partly, one guesses, because of the Marxist terminology in which they are presented—as offensive, perhaps, to the present Soviet political leadership as they presumably are to most sectors of American opinion. The Kremlin's disapproval of his "democratic Leninism" was indicated by his expulsion in 1969 from the CPSU "for convictions incompatible with the title of party member." But it is significant that expulsion was not voted by his local party organization, the membership of which apparently shared them to some degree, but rather followed action by the district committee superordinate thereto.[51] Regime displeasure is certainly indicated by the fact that, as of 1976, according to sources I consider completely reliable, he had not had any regular employment for some five years; he reportedly makes ends meet by doing free-lance work and with the aid of his wife's income and of well-wishers abroad who are permitted to send him small sums of money.

A corollary of the points just made regarding the implications for political change inside the Soviet Union of the dissidents' proposals, is that when Soviet reformers urge—as did Sakharov in his 1968 memorandum and subsequently—that world peace and welfare require "convergence" of the "socialist" and "capitalist" systems they mean, in effect, that the Soviet system must move in the direction of becoming a polyarchy rather than that polyarchies must be transformed into hegemonies. The pupils of Stalin who still rule Russia are, of course, aware of this. That is why the recommendations of Sakharov—and of Roy Medvedev as well—met with no response, except, of course, with as negative a one as the Kremlin deemed appropriate on the basis of calculations of the possible costs and benefits of limited, as opposed to extreme, sanctions.

Problems and Proposed Solutions

Soviet dissidents, of course, share the deep concern of all informed and enlightened people about the dangers to the welfare and indeed the survival of mankind posed by the arms race and by the threat of war between the great powers in an era of nuclear weapons. The dissenters' views on war and peace cannot be fully understood without keeping in mind the continued adherence of Kremlin propaganda, even in an era of "relaxation of international tensions," to the claim that Moscow and its supporters possess the only reliable formula for eventually banishing war from the world. namely, the replacement of "capitalism" by Soviet-style "socialism." Typical of the official CPSU propaganda line on this pivotal topic is an editorial published by the CPSU theoretical journal *Kommunist* in June 1972, shortly after the Nixon-Brezhnev meeting of the preceding month, which had inspired much optimism in wide circles of United States public opinion about prospects for improved relations with Moscow. Greeting "the development of a new international situation more favorable to the cause of peace," the editorial nevertheless warned that as long as "capitalism" existed, the USSR must redouble its military/political efforts in the never-ending struggle for security, and for the expansion of its international influence.[52]

In sharp contrast to official orthodoxy, Soviet Democratic opinion on world affairs, while often critical of specific Western policies (such as U.S. policy in Southeast Asia), has on balance cast the USSR and Communist China in the roles of chief disturbers of world peace. (This is, of course, an understatement so far as the views of Solzhenitsyn are concerned, which were expressed with enormous intensity during the novelist's American visit in 1975.) In particular, the dissenters, in diametrical opposition to the official view, tend to regard the influence of Soviet ideology as baneful. Again in contradiction to official doctrine, some dissenters tend to look with favor upon the heresies (from the official point of view) of East–West "convergence" and ideological coexistence.

YURI GALANSKOV AND HIS CIRCLE

Striking indications of the dissenters' lack of confidence in the peaceful intentions of the Soviet government (and, it must be added, of all other existing governments), were contained in the series of poems and prose statements by a group of young radical intellectuals, including Yuri Galanskov, Natalya Gorbanevskaya, and others, disseminated in the 1960's in the *samizdat* journals *Phoenix-61* and its successor, *Phoenix-66*. Not surprisingly, Galanskov, the major figure of the group—at least in terms of the political relevance of his ideas—began his activity in the belief that, as Pavel Litvinov put it, "it was the duty of every honest individual to do his utmost to bring about the gradual revival of the true aims" of the Bolshevik revolution.[53] Galanskov offered an anarchopopulist and pacifist, and also a "New Left," interpretation of the Bolshevik heritage. As Litvinov, who knew him well notes, Galanskov believed that "socialist and Communist propaganda might gradually alter the appearance of the whole world, and end wars, hunger and social inequality."[54] Already in *Phoenix-61* he had, especially in his *Human Manifesto (Chelovecheski Manifest)*, revealed anguished concern over the danger of nuclear war. In the *Human Manifesto* he urged his readers not to trust "ministers, leaders and newspapers" but to "demolish the rotting prison of the state," in language that bore a striking resemblance to that of Dimitri Pisarev, another young Russian radical, who had written similar denunciations of the Russian "establishment" a century before Galanskov.[55]

In 1966, turning from poetry to political propaganda, Galanskov set forth a plan for a broadly based international movement for peace and disarmament. His vehicle was a remarkable tract entitled "Organizational Problems of the Movement for Complete and General Disarmament and Peace Throughout the World" ("Organizatsiyonnye problemy dvizheniya za polnoe i vseobshchee razoruzhenie i mir vo vsem mire"), disseminated in *Phoenix 66*.[56] In the introduction to this work Galanskov acknowledged that his plan for a mass pacifist organization with its own journal challenged the "totalitarian" state's monopoly of political organization, which, he asserted, had outlived whatever usefulness it might once have possessed. Hence, he went on, he was subjecting himself to the danger of arrest—a supposition that the KGB verified in January 1967.

In the essay itself, Galanskov argued that it was unforgivably naive to trust governments, diplomatic negotiations, and treaties to make more than the most limited contribution to peace and disarmament. In fact, he averred, official negotiations and agreements were harmful, since they created the illusion of progress toward peace and thus disoriented public opinion. Real disarmament, the key to eliminating the danger of nuclear war, could be achieved, he asserted, only as the "social-psychological product of the economic and moral development of mankind in the direction of economic justice and moral improvement."[57] This, in turn, depended upon organized propaganda and activity in all countries, among all strata of society. Furthermore, argued Galanskov, it was fatuous to depend on the United Nations, as it was (and is) constituted, to conduct such an effort. The U.N., he argued, was really only "an organization of unified authority"; what was needed was an organization (which could theoretically, give a free hand, function within the U.N.) with "immunity" and "autonomy."[58] It is interesting, incidentally, that the inspiration for Galanskov's article seems to have come, in part, from an article by the Nobel Prize-winning American chemist Linus Pauling, in the November 1964 issue of *UNESCO Courier,* from which Galanskov quoted extensively.

Perhaps the most striking features of the martyred Galanskov's writings (as noted earlier, he was to die in a forced labor camp, apparently because of the authorities' failure to provide him with proper medical care) were their radical internationalism and, above all, their insistence upon the absolute necessity of openness and disclosure—the principle of "glasnost," of laying the facts before the public, both at home and abroad—along with, of course, distrust for bureaucracy and officialdom, whether "socialist" or "capitalist."

Galanskov's radical pacifism was not cited at his trial or otherwise used against him by the Soviet authorities. For example, it was not mentioned in the highly distorted press coverage of his (and Ginzburg's) trial in 1968. But the authorities' silence regarding the very core of Galanskov's program does not, of course, indicate that they approved of it. More likely, it resulted from the conviction that to lend any credence to the young radical's ardent desire to promote peace would undercut the effort so assiduously pursued by the secret police to cast him in the role of an agent of Western "imperialism."

We may never know how widely shared the views of Galanskov and his collaborators were, but the regime's harsh reprisal against this eloquent and determined spokesman of the Soviet equivalent of the Western "New Left" of the 1960's indicates that their views were rather popular among young Soviet intellectuals. It is interesting that Galanskov, in a withering attack on the orthodox writer Mikhail Sholokhov, asserted that the Soviet intelligentsia's negative reaction to the Sinyavski-Daniel trial proved that the "absolute majority" of Soviet intellectuals were on the side of freedom.[59] The indignation aroused by the repression of Galanskov, Ginzburg, Vladimir Bukovski, and other protesters in 1966 and 1967 gave powerful impetus to the efforts made in 1967 and 1968 by dissidents still at large, and willing to pay the price of open resistance to bring the cause of the Soviet Democratic Movement to world attention. Clearly as Galanskov believed, there was wide support for the democrats for a time, especially in Moscow and Leningrad.

It is not surprising, then, that some among those friends and associates of Galanskov who were still at large after the arrests of 1967 should have protested the act of violence committed by the USSR and its Warsaw Pact allies in 1968. Among the Red Square demonstrators—as has been already noted—were Gorbanevskaya, who had contributed to *Phoenix 61* and *Phoenix 66*, and Litvinov, who had compiled the record of the arrest, interrogation, trial, and sentencing of Galanskov and his friend Alexander Ginzburg. Since considerable attention has already been given to the significance of the Czechoslovak "spring" for the Soviet democratizers, and to their despair and indignation over Moscow's aggression, these topics will not be discussed here in detail. Suffice it to say that Czechoslovakia—a glaring example of aggression, brazenly and successfully conducted, and following hard upon other convincing evidence of the Kremlin's determination to crush resistance to its hegemony, both inside the USSR and within its East European domain—was a watershed in the unequal struggle between the dissenters and the authorities. After Czechoslovakia, only men and women with exceptional inner resources of conviction and principle, as well as "outer" resources of reputation and status, had the stomach for further open struggle or any reasonable expectation, if they continued to dissent, of remaining outside of jail, labor camp, or psychiatric cell.[60]

Almost certainly, the discouragement and apathy that afflicted many members of the dissident community after Czechoslovakia was substantially due to the almost complete failure of ordinary Soviet citizens to offer any visible support to those who publicly criticized the invasion. The meager available evidence indicates that "the people" passively approved of invasion as a defensive measure against an alleged foreign threat, or, at any rate, remained apathetic. Even among some Soviet liberals there seems to have been a belief that the Red Square demonstration, in particular, was an imprudent, if not an irresponsible, action. Some, however, clearly shared the views of the well-known civil rights activist Anatoli Yakobson, who wrote that "these seven demonstrators undoubtedly saved the honor of the Soviet people."[61] And, there is reason to believe that feelings of shame and guilt aroused by the Soviet occupation of Czechoslovakia constituted one factor impelling some Soviet citizens to seek to emigrate from the USSR.[62]

SAKHAROV'S POSITION

If Yuri Galanskov's approach to the fateful problems of our crisis-torn world, which I have outlined above, can be characterized as a radical anarchopopulist one, Andrei Sakharov's position comes as close, probably, as is possible for that of anyone reared under Soviet conditions, to Western, especially American liberal, internationalism. His is an orientation that I confess I find extremely attractive and persuasive. Despite the moral idealism underlying his basic perspectives—similar to that of virtually all Soviet dissenters, so far as is known—his foreign policy prescriptions, as has been indicated above, were, for a surprisingly long period, pragmatic and for the most part rather moderate. That is to say, they were couched in terms as compatible as he could make them with established Soviet doctrine. Thus, in his March 1971 "memorandum" (as he entitled it) to Soviet leaders, Sakharov proposed the establishment of an "International Council of experts on the Problems of Peace, Disarmament, Economic Aid to Needy Countries, the Defense of Human Rights, and the Protection of the Environment." This "consultative" organ, as Sakharov characterized it, might, he suggested, be placed "within the framework of the United Nations."[63]

Recommending that this body be accorded "maximum independence of the interests of individual states and groups of states"

—how, he did not explain—Sakharov also argued that it should be set up in such a fashion as to "take into account the wishes of the main international organizations."

In view of the well-known aversion of the Soviet leaders—or, for that matter, of sovereign governments generally—toward anything smacking of "interference" in their internal affairs by international organizations, I must say I find somewhat unrealistic Sakharov's above-mentioned stipulation on the "independence" of the council of experts, and even more so, perhaps, his proposal that an international pact must be signed obliging legislative and governmental organs to examine the council's recommendations and openly proclaim their decisions with respect to them.[64]

The recommendation for the council of experts was repeated in Sakharov's June 1972 "Postscript" to the above "memorandum," where he stressed the particular importance he attached to it.[65] Thus, despite his increasingly somber mood regarding Kremlin policies, both domestic and foreign, Sakharov continued well into 1972 to propagate idealistic and internationalist but also moderate prescriptions against the possibility of international conflict and war and the conditions that threatened to produce these supreme evils. Other recommendations in his 1971 communication to Soviet leaders—as in the case of his 1968 treatise, of course, no response was forthcoming from the Politburo—were of a piece with his proposal for a council of experts. These recommendations included, one for a unilateral announcement by the USSR that it would not be the first to use weapons of mass destruction, and one urging that provision be made for allowing inspection teams "to visit our territory for effective arms control."[66]

Sakharov's attitude toward Communist China should also be surveyed here, both to introduce discussion of views common, for a time at least, to a number of prominent dissident thinkers and as a further indication of the continuity in the noted scientist's foreign affairs posture between 1968 and 1971.

In his 1968 essay, Sakharov cited "the regimes of Stalin, Hitler and Mao Tse-tung" as the worst examples of "demagogic, hypocritical, and monstrously cruel police regimes."[67] He somewhat vaguely recommended, as his remedy against the dangers he perceived as emanating from Maoism, help to the Chinese people "from the world's democratic forces," and he foresaw "a growing ideological struggle in the socialist countries between Stalinist and Maoist forces, on the one hand, and the realistic forces of leftist

Leninist Communists (and leftist Westerners) on the other," leading to "a deep ideological split on an international, national and intraparty scale."[68] He also expressed confidence, in his relatively optimistic 1968 essay, that this struggle would bring about the establishment in the USSR and other socialist countries of a multiparty system and other democratic transformations.[69]

But in 1970, Sakharov (together with Roy Medvedev and Valentine Turchin) had referred to a "menacing" danger from "Chinese totalitarian nationalism," which could be countered only "if we increase or at least maintain the technological and economic gap between our country and China, if we add to the number of our friends in the world at large, and if we offer the Chinese people the alternative of cooperation and aid."[70] Reading the foregoing, one is tempted to speculate on the extent, if any, to which the Politburo's "détente" policies since 1969 have been influenced by such warnings as the one by Sakharov.

In 1971, Sakharov continued to believe that "our chief foreign policy problem is our relations with China," and his prescription for dealing with this problem remained much as before, though he now added a recommendation that the USSR "avoid all other possible complications in our foreign and domestic policies, and implement our plans for the development of Siberia."[71] What he said about Siberia, of course, bears some—but only a very limited—resemblance to Solzhenitsyn's later recommendations regarding that territory.

Sakharov failed to mention China in his June 1972 "Postscript," however, and in his interview with the Swedish television correspondent Olle Stenholm in July 1973 he indicated that he wished to "correct" what he had said earlier about that country, which now, he declared, he "would not blame for aggression," and which he compared to Russia at the stage of development the latter had reached "in the 1920's and the beginning of the 1930's." He now judged China to be "directed more toward revolutionary self-assertion both internally and in the outer world than, for example, with achieving prosperity for her people and expanding her territory."[72]

In the context of other themes, already prominent in the June 1972 "Postscript," the softened stance toward China clearly indicated that the noted scientist no longer regarded the policies of Mao's China, still less those of the United States, as constituting the major threat to world peace, but rather the secretive, militaristic policies of his own country's rulers. This interpretation gains support from the emphasis in the 1972 "Postscript" on the "militarization" of the Soviet economy. Among other pertinent statements, Sakharov asserted there that it was necessary to point out that "in no country does the share of military expenditures with relation to the national income reach such proportions as in the USSR (over 40 percent)."[73]

Throughout the series of messages he addressed to the Soviet leaders in 1968-72, Sakharov pleaded for, and with an increasing urgency demanded, freedom of access on the part of Soviet citizens to information originating abroad, reduction of restrictions on contacts between Soviet citizens and foreigners, and, especially in 1971 and subsequently, freedom for Soviet citizens to emigrate and, if they desired, return to their homeland. These topics, along with Sakharov's views and those of other dissidents on relations between the dominant Russian and the minority, non-Russian nationalities of the USSR, will be reserved for later treatment.

In his July 1973 interview with Olle Stenholm of the Swedish TV, Sakharov began by referring to significant changes in his focus of attention that had occurred since 1968. In particular, he stressed his loss of confidence in any special virtues of Soviet "socialism," and its replacement by a vivid sense of the defects of the Soviet system, especially its lack of freedom and its inequality, along with a realization of its "very strong internal stability." Immediately following his observation on the power and stability of the Soviet internal regime, Sakharov, in response to a question as to what "outside forces" could do to influence internal Soviet development, said, "We have a very poor understanding of what the foreign world is doing. Possibly the foreign world will soon accept our rules of the game. That would be very bad."[74] In the same passage, Sakharov referred to the possibility that the West, in its relationship to the USSR, might be engaging in "capitulation"—in effect, in selling out the interests of its peoples.

After the Stenholm interview Sakharov was called in for a "discussion" with—meaning an admonition by—Mikhail P. Malyarov, First Deputy Procurator General of the USSR and apparently in recent years the real head of the Soviet procuracy (somewhat equivalent to the office of Attorney General in the United States). Malyarov began by stating that the conversation between him and Sakharov was "intended to be in the nature of a warning," and he asserted that the physicist had been "seeing foreigners and giving them material for anti-Soviet publications."[75] In particular Malyarov stressed the harmful consequences of the publication of Sakharov's statements in the emigrant Russian-language magazine *Posev*. He even asserted that Sakharov was "beginning to be used not only by anti-Soviet forces hostile to our country but by foreign intelligence," thus going far beyond the insinuation made earlier by Chakovski, mentioned earlier in this chapter (see p. 28).[76]

In his mid-August 1973 interview with several foreign correspondents, Sakharov spoke of the "very great danger" to the world of Soviet-Western rapprochement if it were to take place without democratization in the USSR, which, he stated, "would be dangerous in the sense that it would not really solve any of the world's problems and would mean simply capitulating in the face of real or exaggerated Soviet power." Such a development, he asserted, "would contaminate the whole world with the antidemocratic peculiarities of Soviet society" and would "enable the Soviet Union to bypass problems it cannot resolve on its own and to concentrate on accumulating further strength," with the result that "the world would become disarmed and helpless while facing our uncontrollable bureaucratic apparatus."[77] Sakharov placed these forebodings, however, within a framework of continuity with his earlier thinking with his statement that his basic premise of 1968 still held true, "namely that the world faces two alternatives—either gradual convergence with democratization within the Soviet Union, or increasing confrontation with a growing danger of thermonuclear war."[78] But he was saying, in effect, that rapprochement without democratization in the USSR would be even more dangerous than no rapprochement at all. This is indicated by the further development of his warning about the consequences of "capitulation"—among other things, he referred to the USSR as "a country wearing a mask that hides its true face" and "a neighbor, armed to the teeth"—and also by his endorsement of the Jackson Amendment (to the trade bill then under consideration by the United States Congress) "as a minimal step that would be significant not only by itself, but also as a symbolic expression of the view that rapprochement must involve some sort of control to insure that this country will not become a threat to its neighbors."[79]

In September 1973, Sakharov, refuting official Soviet press charges that he opposed relaxation of tensions, reiterated his contention that "a supposed détente not accompanied by increased trust and democratization" was "a danger."[80] And in October he appealed to the Congress to pass the Jackson Amendment, arguing that it constituted "a defense of international law" and, among other things, that failure to pass it would "be tantamount to total capitulation of democratic principle in the face of blackmail, deceit, and violence."[81]

ANDREI AMALRIK'S VIEWPOINT

At this point it is perhaps appropriate to recall that Sakharov was not the only, nor the first, major Soviet dissident to express the view that the Soviet regime and its leaders constituted the chief threat to world peace, or to argue that achieving a mutually satisfactory relationship with Moscow would, for the West, be extraordinarily difficult if not impossible without democratization of Soviet political life.

In fact, the position arrived at by Sakharov in the second half of 1973 and subsequently maintained by him had, to a large extent, been reached by Andrei Amalrik in 1969. In a fairly detailed discussion of the triangular relationship between Communist China, the USSR, and the United States, Amalrik had argued that the primary, irreconcilable antagonism was between China and Russia. But he also devoted considerable attention to what he obviously regarded as misguided and inept American efforts, beginning during the presidency of Franklin D. Roosevelt, to achieve "an agreement and eventual partnership with the Soviet Union." Although this first step had led to the "division of Germany and the whole of Europe and to a decade of 'cold war,'" asserted Amalrik, the Americans continued, "both in the Khrushchev era and today," to hope to reach an agreement with Moscow, "together to solve the problems of the world."[82]

Amalrik criticized past American policy toward China—which, he asserted had played into Stalin's hands by supporting Chiang Kai-shek against Mao. He urged the United States to seek good, cooperative relations with China—which, apparently, in contrast both to Sakharov's views up to 1972 and to Solzhenitsyn's even later, he considered to be a somewhat less aggressive power than the USSR—and at all costs to resist any Soviet blandishments.

Particularly interesting, in this connection, was Amalrik's statement that "a rapprochement between the United States and the Soviet Union would make sense only after serious steps toward democracy were taken in the USSR. Until such time, any agreements on the part of the Soviet Union will be motivated either by fear of China or by an attempt to preserve the regime...or by the desire to use American friendship to install or maintain Soviet influence in other countries."[83] He added that such a "friendship" would bring the United States nothing but the "same sort of troubles that arose from the cooperation between Roosevelt and Stalin," since, after all, "genuine rapprochement must be based on similarity of interests, cultures and traditions, and on mutual understanding"—none of which as yet existed.[84]

Again in distinction from Sakharov and Solzhenitsyn, Amalrik considered that the main threat to world peace consisted, not in a possible U.S.—Soviet nuclear holocaust but in a conventional war between Russia and China (a position that he has apparently modified or abandoned, judging by his latest article, to be commented upon presently). Of course, when the *samizdat* essay in which he dealt with this and related topics began to be circulated, tensions between the two giant Communist powers were at their height, and Amalrik's orientation may have been influenced thereby.

Even the precarious freedom Amalrik had hitherto intermittently enjoyed was snatched from him by his arrest in May 1970 and sentence to a forced labor camp in the bitterly cold Magadan region of Northeastern Siberia, where so many of Stalin's victims perished —immediately followed, upon completion of this sentence, by another three-year term. Probably because of protests from fellow historians, especially in France, Amalrik's second forced labor sentence, which probably would have killed him if he had had to serve it out, was commuted to three years' exile—still in the Magadan area, but under relatively mild conditions. In May 1975, Amalrik completed his second sentence and returned to Moscow. He defied the Soviet authorities' order that he leave the capital; for a while he was able to remain with his wife in the couple's Moscow apartment. In retaliation for her sheltering her husband, however, the authorities threatened to evict her. Amalrik denounced as "hypocrisy" the order that he leave Moscow, in view of Soviet agreement, at the Helsinki Conference on Security and Co-operation in Europe, to help reunite members of separated families.[85] Subsequently he took up residence in a town near the capital, and he was reportedly permitted brief visits to Moscow from time to time.

The world learned in October 1975 that Amalrik's spirit was unbroken and his mind still sharp. In a provocative article published on the *New York Times* Op-Ed page, he criticized United States policy toward Russia for allegedly trying by a "Dr. Spock" approach to mollify the Kremlin. Such an approach, argued Amalrik, pleased the Soviet leaders, for it asked nothing in exchange for substantial American concessions, and it aroused "a degree of contempt" in Moscow. The only proper United States policy toward the USSR, Amalrik argued, was one based upon American humanitarian and libertarian tradition, firmly and patiently applied within a long-range perspective.

Stressing the capacity of Soviet leaders to "set themselves distant goals and also to wait patiently," Amalrik declared:

> *If the U.S. sets itself the objective of establishing truly friendly relations with the USSR and wants to be assured of their durability, then it must strive for the transformation of the closed Soviet system to an open one. The awakening of the Soviet people to human rights is a force working in this direction.*

Apparently anticipating criticism on the ground that his prescription would endanger Soviet–Western arms control negotiations, Amalrik denied that "détente" was the alternative to war. He argued that "the cold war, being a form of sublimation of hot war, was not less effective than "détente" in averting a real war because peace depended, and still depends, on the balance of nuclear power."[86]

Hard upon publication of Amalrik's article, his viewpoint was criticized by Professor Marshall D. Shulman of Columbia University, perhaps the most eloquent American analyst and advocate of arms control. Gently chiding Amalrik for what he considered his underestimation of the dangers inherent in the current arms race, Shulman urged priority attention, "whatever the nature of the Soviet regime," to reversing "the present drift toward more unstable and less controllable military technologies, toward larger and more widely spread military technologies." He also warned that giving priority to transforming the Soviet system would be a self-defeating policy that would strengthen neo-Stalinist forces in the USSR.[87]

I would argue that both Amalrik and Shulman made valuable contributions to public enlightenment: the former by stressing the need for long-range commitment to democratic principles, the latter by his insistence on the urgency of arms control if there is to *be* a future, and by his balanced presentation of the tormenting complexities of the current world situation and the need for a multifaceted approach to their resolution.

SOLZHENITSYN'S PROGRAM

Alexander Solzhenitsyn is a less systematic political thinker than either Sakharov or Amalrik. As an artist and moralist, he thinks mainly in terms of the dichotomous concepts of absolute evil and absolute good. Moreover, to the extent that he has directly and explicitly addressed himself to political issues, he has more often concerned himself with domestic than with foreign-policy problems, at least until 1973, when he became involved in what is sometimes characterized as a debate with Sakharov and Roy Medvedev over Soviet–American "détente." Before discussing that remarkable trialogue, we should note that, despite Solzhenitsyn's preoccupation throughout most of his career with literary matters, his activities, and more especially the Soviet authorities' interpretation of their significance, had made him an important factor in Soviet-Western relations long before his 1975 trip to America. As far as Solzhenitsyn's own attitudes toward the West were concerned, they were always characterized by an ambivalence that has apparently persisted. On the one hand, he has consistently championed the Western liberal value of freedom of expression, especially artistic expression, as in his famous letter to the 1967 Congress of the Union of Soviet Writers denouncing Soviet censorship. On the other hand, he long ago made it clear that he did not, as he said in 1967, regard "abroad" as "some higher authority whose opinion was very much cherished." No, said Solzhenitsyn, "for my entire life, I have had the soil of my homeland under my feet; only *its* pain do I hear, only about *it* do I write." (Italics in original).[88]

But the Soviet ruling bureaucracy, in a campaign of ostracism, harassment, vilification, and suppression that reached its screaming crescendo in February 1974, when the writer was literally ejected from his beloved Russia, after first being threatened with death by KGB agents, insisted on depicting the intensely patriotic Solzhenitsyn as an enemy agent. Official harassment forced Solzhenitsyn, in his struggle for survival, to learn how to present his case to world public opinion. But even after he had become as master strategist in the international communications arena, Solzhenitsyn by no means sought to curry favor with Western public opinion. Thus, in his first major address to a world audience, the Nobel Lecture on Literature, written in 1970-71 and released in 1972 (about a year after its completion), Solzhenitsyn referred to the "spirit of Munich" as "an illness of the will of prosperous people."[89] Here also Solzhenitsyn called attention to the danger of "blockage of information," warning that "within a soundproofed and silenced zone"—an obvious reference to such countries as the USSR and Communist China—"any treaty whatsoever can be reinterpreted at will—or better still, just forgotten."[90] Here too, in language reminiscent of that used earlier by Galanskov, he criticized the United Nations Organization for being, in reality, "a United Governments Organization, in which governments freely elected are equated with those which have imposed themselves by force," and for never having tried to make obligatory for governments, as a condition of their membership in the U.N., adherence to "the best document of its twenty-five years— the Declaration of Human Rights"; thus, he asserted, it has consigned the little people "to the will of governments they did not elect."[91] Solzhenitsyn also criticized scientists for never having "made a clear attempt to become an independent motive-force for humanity," and he expressed the view that only world literature could save humanity from lies and misunderstandings and, ultimately, from violence."[92]

In a startling press conference with the American journalist Frank Crepeau and the Frenchman Alain Jacob—of the Associated Press and Le Monde, respectively—in August 1973, a week after Sakharov's interrogation by Malyarov, Solzhenitsyn informed the world that if he were to suddenly die, it would be obvious that the Soviet secret police had done him in. Having thus made it more difficult than if he had remained silent for the Soviet authorities to do away with him or otherwise retaliate against him, Solzhenitsyn paid warm tribute to Western public opinion and communications media for having "saved many of our persecuted." He stressed, in this connection, that it was "important to understand that the East is not at all indifferent to protests from public opinion in the West. On the contrary, it has a deadly fear of them. . . ." But he chided Western public opinion, not only for lacking awareness of the gratitude of persecuted fighters for freedom in the USSR, but for failure to appreciate the heroism required to conduct a moral/political struggle against the seemingly overwhelming power of a mighty police state.[93] He also had high praise for Andrei Sakharov's activities— though he expressed mild disagreement with Sakharov's policy proposals, which, however, he characterized as constructive—and words of admiration and compassion for General Grigorenko and for Amalrik, Bukovski, and many other persecuted dissenters. He ridiculed those in the West who equated political repression in Greece, Spain, and other countries with what Solzhenitsyn—convincingly, in my opinion—argued was an infinitely more powerful, brutal, and dangerous system of repression in Russia.

Solzhenitsyn's arguments just summarized reflect his attitude toward the role of the West in the relations between the Soviet regime and dissidents, and indeed toward relations between the West and Soviet power generally. His criticism of the West, one infers, was the product of disappointment rather than hostility.

In his September 1973 letter to the Norwegian newspaper *Aftenposten,* printed in the *New York Times* under the title "Peace and Violence," in which he proposed the candidacy of Andrei Sakharov for a Nobel Peace Prize, Solzhenitsyn reiterated and further developed some of the themes enunciated in his Nobel Lecture.[94]

In "Peace and Violence," Solzhenitsyn denounced Communist regimes for practicing violence against their subjects and for instigating terrorism abroad. And he berated the "hypocrisy" of Western leftists who protested against repression in South Africa but remained silent, for example, about Moscow's crushing of freedom in Czechoslovakia. He denounced what he regarded as the false antithesis between "stormy" war and peace, when in fact war was only one form of violence, and the true comparison was—he maintained—between all forms of violence, taken together, and genuine peace. Thus, he argued, terrorism, too easily condoned by liberal, pro-socialist Western public opinion and not condemned by the United Nations, as well as the violence and intimidation imposed on their citizens by Communist governments, was just as dangerous to the world as the more massive, easily observable forms of violence represented by "a shot fired on a national frontier or a bomb dropped into the territory of another country." Here Solzhenitsyn referred again to "the spirit of Munich" in the West, "the spirit of compromise and concession," and asserted that there could be no real coexistence without renunciation of violence everywhere.

If Solzhenitsyn, in the statements mentioned above, had implicitly condemned the West for moral and political irresolution, weakness, and confusion in the face of an array of threats from Communist powers and their accomplices, he was later, in 1974, after his violent expulsion from his homeland, to explicitly and sharply attack Soviet political leadership as constituting a moral threat to freedom in the world. At the same time he continued to criticize Western policy for running the risks he saw as inherent in what, judging from parts of his spring 1974 letter to *Aftenposten*—a follow-up, in effect, to "Peace and Violence"—he regarded as a "dé-tente" perilously resembling "another Munich." Another significant theme in this letter was Solzhenitsyn's statement that the danger to the West flowing from acts of violence in the USSR—such as the repression visited upon his former research assistant, the gifted young scholar Gabriel Superfin (he had assisted Solzhenitsyn in as-sembling material for the *Gulag Archipelago*)—threatened world peace more than any possible expansion of East-West trade could strengthen it.

In his interview with CBS correspondent Walter Cronkite in Zurich on July 17, 1974, Solzhenitsyn reiterated his belief that Western public opinion, provided it were resolutely expressed, could exert a powerful influence on the Soviet authorities. And he offered as proof, on this occasion, the granting of exit visas to the dancers Valery and Galina Panov after seemingly endless delay and, more generally, the easing of emigration restrictions. But he was, as be-fore, sharply critical of "détente" as he saw it developing. The ongoing relaxation of East-West tensions, he asserted, had not ame-liorated either the world situation or the internal regime in the USSR. Once again he insisted that repression in Russia was not a mere "internal affair" of that country but a matter of concern to the world as a whole, in view of the fact, as he saw it, that the USSR—like the People's Republic of China—sought to impose its political system on the whole world. He also expressed the opinion that Soviet su-periority in nuclear weapons presented an increasing threat to the security of the free nations of the West.[95]

But one cannot fully understand Solzhenitsyn's attitude toward the role, situation, and destiny of the West, or his warnings regarding the dangers inherent in East-West "détente," without studying his remarkable *Letter to the Leaders of the Soviet Union*, addressed to the Communist hierarchs in September 1973 and published in the West, in both Russian and English, some six months later.[96]

This thoughtful and powerful work of diagnosis and prescription consists of a brief introduction and seven sections. Its integrating concept is the mortal danger, to mankind generally, to the peoples of the USSR in particular, and especially to the Russian people, Solzhenitsyn's own people and his main concern, of policies Solzhen-itsyn perceives to be based on false ideological preconceptions. While Solzhenitsyn's critique of ideology and its nefarious conse-quences is directed above all against Marxism, it is by no means confined to Marxism, but extends to the whole modern Western concept of material and technological progress and economic growth.

However, the immediate danger, which Solzhenitsyn regards as the most pernicious fruit of an "exact adherence to the precepts of Marxism–Leninism," is a Soviet war with Mao Tse-tung's China, which in his opinion would destroy both Russia and Western civilization.[97]

In the introduction and first section of the essay message, Solzhenitsyn sardonically praises the Kremlin for its brilliant politico-diplomatic strategy, which, he argues, has reduced Europe and even America to overwhelming inferiority relative to the might of the USSR—but only to leave the latter face to face with "a country of almost a billion people, such as never before in history has waged war."[98] Like Amalrik, whom he praises for prophetic vision for which the Kremlin rewarded him with ruin, instead of naming him one of its expert advisers, Solzhenitsyn paints a horrifying picture of a protracted war with China. Such a war would, he predicts, cost Russia no less than sixty million lives, destroying in the process the "last root" of the Russian people, which would for practical purposes cease to exist on the earth.[99] Such a war could be prevented, asserts Solzhenitsyn, by abandoning the bitter and fruitless dispute with China over which government, that of the USSR or China, is the only true exponent of Marxism–Leninism.

In the third section of his essay, Solzhenitsyn launches into a discussion of the "impasse" which Russia shares, he says, with all economically advanced countries. In this somewhat confusing section he rejects the values of technological advance and economic growth in favor of zero growth and a conservationist policy, which reminds one somewhat of the doctrines advocated in the West by, for example, the biologist René Dubos. Then, in the fourth section, the novelist makes his most important positive proposal, namely, that the state "transfer the center of attention and the center of national activity (the center of settlement, the center of aspirations of youth) from distant continents, and even from Europe, nay even from the South of our country, to its Northeast."[100] Herein, in a footnote to the passage just quoted, Solzhenitsyn offered an observation that perhaps attracted more attention in the West than any other part of this famous "letter," when he wrote that "of course, such a relocation will sooner or later lead to our removing our control over Eastern Europe. Also, there can be no question of holding any borderland nation within the territory of our country, by force."

According to Solzhenitsyn—and this was the central theme of the fifth section of his letter—transferring the center of activity of the country would require an overall shift of attention and energies from external to internal tasks. Among Solzhenitsyn's recommendations for achieving this objective were the abolition of compulsory collectivization of agriculture, the abolition of the government trade in vodka, which he castigated as immoral and ruinous to his people's health, and the abolition of compulsory military service, along with other measures intended to greatly reduce military expenditures. He justified drastic cuts in military expenditures on the ground that apart from the China problem the USSR had achieved ample security for a long time to come, and as for that threat, developing the Northeast and pursuing a nonideological policy would be Russia's best possible defense.[101]

In the last part of the fifth section of his essay, and in the sixth, Solzhenitsyn returns to the subject of Marxist ideology—adherence to which, he asserts, leads the Soviet authorities to squander the Russian people's resources on useless ventures in the Mediterranean and other distant parts of the globe, while neglecting internal development, including education, and leaving the vital Northeast unexploited. He warns the Soviet leaders that if war did break out on the Sino-Soviet border it might be too late to develop a healthy national consciousness. You have seen, he says, how mighty America lost to little North Vietnam because the United States has a very weak national consciousness.[102]

In the last section of the letter Solzhenitsyn recommends, as the required political instrumentality for effecting the changes necessary, in his opinion, for the salvation of his beloved Russian people, an authoritarian polity. His rather vague and perhaps contradictory political prescription was presented in a context of criticism of Western democracy and of the failure of the struggle for democracy in Russia—which indicated, he suggested, that for Russia the democratic path was "either incorrect or premature."[103] Perhaps, he submitted, Russia was destined to live under an authoritarian system. But he insisted that an authoritarian order did not necessarily imply arbitrariness and caprice. On the contrary, if purged of ideology and extreme centralism it could be a good system, capable of eliciting support from the people and of carrying out necessary reforms. Among the numerous proposals Solzhenitsyn offered in this extraordinary document, one of the most interesting was that some of the consultative and participatory functions of the soviets, which, he asserted, had lapsed in June 1918, should be revived.[104] Also very important, and perhaps in contradiction to the authoritarian elements in Solzhenitsyn's program, was his exhortation to the Soviet leaders that they permit freedom of expression, including freedom of publication, in the arts, in philosophy, in the social sciences, etc. This was in harmony with other recommendations that he offered for a free and competitive marketplace in ideas; thus he urged not that Marxism be prohibited, or that the orthodox religion be given state support, but that these and other world outlooks be allowed to freely compete for public support. He sarcastically argued that those who believed in Marxism—including paid, professional Soviet propaganda officials—could prove their sincere devotion to the doctrine by propagating it voluntarily in their spare time.[105]

It is almost impossible to accurately summarize and fairly evaluate this amalgam of analysis and exhortation, of libertarian and authoritarian elements. I do not believe that Solzhenitsyn should be classified as a "reactionary" or even as a nationalist—certainly not as a chauvinistic one—on the basis of his now-famous message. It stands, rather, in the Slavophile tradition, with its priority on moral values and national traditions as against political institutions. One can, however, justifiably question its realism—despite Solzhenitsyn's repeated claims that he was dispensing realistic advice—in view of the obvious aversion of the Soviet leaders to giving up such props of their legitimacy and power as the official creed of Marxism–Leninism and the institution of collectivized agriculture, to mention only two of the many elements of the Soviet system that Solzhenitsyn asked the Kremlin to restructure or discard.

In any case, some of the most basic points in Solzhenitsyn's program are not directly relevant to our focus on the interrelationships between dissent and official Soviet foreign-policy practice and doctrine. As far as that issue is concerned, Solzhenitsyn, like most dissenters—including Amalrik and Sakharov—was clearly telling the Soviet leaders, and the world, that the West was not an enemy of the Soviet people, still less the main enemy, as official doctrine has not ceased to maintain. Like Sakharov, he also denounced as enormously harmful Moscow's pursuit of a policy predicated on the assumption, inherent in official Soviet doctrine, of an inevitable struggle between Soviet "socialism" and Western "imperialism." In these and other important respects, Solzhenitsyn's position, though less clear, coherent, and systematic than that of Sakharov, was compatible with and reinforced the views of the noted physicist. In other important respects, however—obviously on the problem of China, but also on the potential capacity of science to solve mankind's problems, and, equally clearly, on the issue of democratic versus authoritarian political principles—the views of the two giants of non-Marxist Soviet dissenting thought differed drastically. And, as the analysis to follow of their triangular exchange of opinions after the fall of 1973 will indicate, the views of both Sakharov and Solzhenitsyn on Soviet foreign policy, Soviet–American relations, and the methods and measures necessary for restructuring those relations differed drastically from those offered by the revisionist Marxist Roy Medvedev.

Let us first examine Sakharov's responses to Solzhenitsyn's program, as well as other expressions in 1974–75 of Sakharov's views on war and peace and related topics, before going on to an examination of Roy Medvedev's "Leninist" rejoinder.

SAKHAROV'S RESPONSE

In a fourteen-page essay dated April 3, 1974, Sakharov subjected Solzhenitsyn's program to friendly but penetrating and at times sharp criticism.[106] Sakharov began by paying high tribute to the "exceptional role of Solzhenitsyn in the spiritual history of our country, manifested in his uncompromising, exact, and deep presentation of the sufferings of people and the crimes of the regime, unparalleled in their massive cruelty and secrecy." Thus he proclaimed his solidarity with Solzhenitsyn's moral values. However, both in his general remarks near the beginning of his commentary and in the course of a careful, point-by-point analysis that forms the heart of his reply, Sakharov took issue with some of the central arguments and proposals offered by his great colleague in the struggle for freedom in Russia and the world.

Sakharov boiled down Solzhenitsyn's program to the following points, which are here presented in abbreviated form:

1. Rejection of official support of Marxism—or, as Sakharov paraphrases Solzhenitsyn, "separation of Marxism from the state."
2. Refraining from support for foreign revolutionaries.
3. Putting an end to tutelage over Eastern Europe and renunciating the forcible holding of the national republics in the Soviet Union.
4. Agrarian reform, on the model of the Polish People's Republic. Sakharov parenthetically notes that on this point this is his own interpretation at Solzhentsyn's position.

5. Development of the Northeast—without large-scale fac-
   tories, in order to avoid pollution. Sakharov interprets
   Solzhenitsyn's plan as one requiring settlement by "com-
   munes of volunteer enthusiasts," and notes that its main
   purpose is to assure the defense of the Russian nation against
   China.
6. Cessation of the sale of Russian natural resources to foreigners, and "economic isolationism, in supplementation of
   military, political, and economic isolationism."
7. Disarmament, insofar as permitted by the Chinese threat.
8. Democratic freedoms; liberation of political prisoners.
9. Strengthening of the family; freedom of religious instruc-
   tion.
10. Retention of the party, but with an increased role for the
    soviets; a combination of an authoritarian order and free-
    dom of conscience.[107]

Sakharov asserted that Solzhenitsyn's program was a source of
"serious concern" to him, but he qualifiedly accepted its first four
points, especially the third, concerning Eastern Europe and the
non-Russian minorities—noting, however, that Solzhenitsyn dealt
with the nationality problems raised by point three only in a footnote.
In an earlier part of his commentary he had taken the novelist to
task for what he regarded as an unwarranted emphasis on the
sufferings of the Russian people, when in fact the non-Russians had
experienced all of the sufferings that the Russians had, in addition
to the impact of genocidal measures directed against them alone.[108]

As for Solzhenitsyn's proposal to let Marxism sink or swim, un-
aided by state subsidies and the labor of millions, Sakharov had
already expressed the view that Solzhenitsyn attributed far too much
significance to ideology as a factor in Soviet official policy. In fact,
he argued, Soviet society and policy were characterized by "ideological indifference and pragmatism," with ideology serving as a
facade for a flexible policy, which, however, was combined with
"traditional intolerance for dissent." In his analysis of the "ten
points," Sakharov briefly reiterated this position.[109]

Calling points five and six "central" to Solzhenitsyn's program,
the physicist asserted that Solzhenitsyn had grossly exaggerated the
danger of war with China—while admitting that he, too, had earlier
been under a similar misapprehension—and, at length and very
vigorously, he criticized Solzhenitsyn for anti-Western isolationism.
The only legitimate form of isolationism, said Sakharov, amounts

to refraining from "foisting our socialist messianism on other countries, to put an end to secret or open instigation of discord on other continents, to stop exporting deadly weaponry."[110] Sakharov thus touched once again on one of his most frequent charges against Kremlin world policy—an accusation, be it noted, that he shared with Solzhenitsyn and other dissenters. But, in contrast to Solzhenitsyn, Sakharov argued that none of the basic problems of the Soviet Union, or of other countries either, could be resolved "at the national level." Even to fulfill Solzhenitsyn's hopes for the development of Siberia—putting aside what he regarded as the great writer's unrealism in appearing to want to reject the use of the most advanced technology—Sakharov considered that "the international cooperation of the United States, the German Federal Republic, Japan, France, Italy, England, India, China, and other countries" would be absolutely necessary. And, he insisted, not only problems of disarmament, but a long list of others, could not be resolved—and indeed the continued existence of mankind would not be possible—without international cooperation in the application of science and technology.[111]

Although Sakharov assigned centrality in Solzhenitsyn's program to the Nobel laureate's plan for the autarkic development of Siberia, he perhaps most deeply differed from Solzhenitsyn in respect to the USSR's prospects for eventually creating a democratic political order. He objected strongly to what he regarded as the novelist's incorrect assertion that Russia, during the period of monarchical rule, had, in spite of all the defects of its political and social order, preserved its "national health," at least until the twentieth century. And he deplored Russia's heritage of "a servile, cringing spirit, combined with contempt for foreigners and people of alien race or creed," which he characterized as "the greatest misfortune," rather than as "national health."

Sakharov here came out unqualifiedly for the universal applicability of democratic institutions, asserting that "only under democratic conditions is it possible to develop a national character, capable of reasonable existence in a constantly changing world." Moreover, added Sakharov, there was no reason to believe that the development of democracy in Russia was in principle not possible, although he did admit that there were obstacles thereto which could not be overcome in a short period of time.[112] Linking foreign and domestic factors and returning to the theme of "convergence," which had figured prominently in his 1968 essay and had never been repudiated by him, Sakharov asserted that rapprochement with the West, which "must, in fact, play the part of the first stage in convergence," would "be accompanied by movements toward democracy in the USSR, partly voluntary and partly compelled by external economic and political pressure." In this connection, he cited as of particular importance "a democratic solution to the problem of freedom of emigration from the USSR and return," not only for Jews, but for Russians, Germans, Ukrainians, Lithuanians, Turks, Armenians, "and all others," and he declared that to the extent that this problem was resolved it would be impossible to preserve other undemocratic practices, it would become necessary to raise living standards to Western levels, and conditions for the free exchange of people and ideas would be realized.[113]

Finally, Sakharov returned to the subject of Solzhenitsyn's "nationalism." Among other things, he asserted that Stalin and his successors had resorted to "the call for patriotism," and that Solzhenitsyn was therefore not really asking the Soviet leaders to change their policies very much insofar as the novelist's program rested on national patriotic foundations. It might be said, he granted, that Solzhenitsyn's nationalism was of a defensive character. But, Sakharov warned, in view of predispositions "in a significant part of the Russian people and a segment of the leaders of the country" toward "Great Russian nationalism linked with a fear of falling into dependence on the West and of democratic transformations," Solzhenitsyn's "mistakes" could be dangerous.[114]

It should also be noted, in this connection, that Sakharov had earlier, in criticizing Solzhenitsyn's views on China, hypothesized that "exaggerating the Chinese threat" was "one element of the political game of the Soviet leadership;" and he had suggested that to be, in effect, taken in by this tactic constituted a disservice to "the cause of democratization and demilitarization," success of which was so vital and necessary for the USSR and the whole world.[115]

These portions of Sakharov's masterful analysis were apparently intended to combat what Sakharov regarded as sentimental, mythic, and—at least from the point of view of Sakharov's rationalist, logico-empirical, and thoroughly internationalist perspective—politically harmful elements in Solzhenitsyn's thinking.

However, the physicist concluded his critique on a positive note, calling Solzhenitsyn, despite the "mistaken aspects of his world outlook," "a giant in the struggle for human dignity in today's tragic world."[116]

SAKHAROV'S 1975 MANIFESTO

In June 1975, Sakharov completed a seventy-six-page political essay that constitutes his most systematic and comprehensive analysis to date, particularly in respect to the nature of the Soviet internal regime and the relationship between the Soviet system and Soviet-Western "détente." Entitled "Concerning the Country and the World" ("O strane i mire"), this new work was obviously intended to alert the West to the illusions and dangers that Sakharov perceived as likely products of Western ignorance and naivete regarding the intentions, capabilities, and politico-military techniques of the Communist "totalitarian" powers.[117]

Though couched in the precise, restrained language that the world has come to associate with its author, "Country and World," as Sakharov himself says near its beginning, was, in contrast to his famous "memorandum," primarily devoted not to "optimistic futurology" but to "the dangers, errors, and dramas of the day, to everything that lies between dream and reality."[118] Overall, this is a far more somber work than any of Sakharov's previous statements. Its relative pessimism, and the harshness, in comparison with Sakharov's previous works, of its criticism of Soviet domestic and foreign policies, can undoubtedly be attributed in part to its author's deep grief and indignation over the repression inflicted by the Soviet rulers on many of his close friends and associates and fellow participants in the campaign for human rights in the USSR. However, its note of deep concern obviously also reflects Sakharov's general estimate of the course of world politics in recent years.[119]

Sakharov offers approximately a page of additional comments in the new essay on the views of the Solzhenitsyn-(mathematician Igor) Shafarevich wing of Soviet dissent. Noting that Solzhenitsyn had "clarified and more precisely defined" his position, and that therefore he saw no reason for prolonging the discussion, Sakharov nevertheless reiterated his opposition to what he characterized as efforts to limit the path toward a "rebirth" of Russia to "religious or nationalistic ideology," or to "patriarchal strivings in the spirit of Rousseau. Rather, he insisted, there must be "democratic reforms, involving all aspects of life."[120] It should be noted, however, that Sakharov at a number of points in this essay cites Solzhenitsyn's *Gulag Archipelago* as a source in support of his characterization of the oppressive nature of Soviet "socialism." And the general tenor of Sakharov's findings, arguments, and prescriptions in this essay, particularly on the danger to the West of Soviet policies and the need for vigorous Western resistance to Soviet imperialism, closely resembles the positions taken by the novelist.

"Country and World" comprises, besides a brief introduction, five sections and a seven-page conclusion. The first and by far the longest section, "On Soviet Society," is followed by sections entitled "On Freedom of Choice of Country of Residence," "The Problem of Disarmament," and then "Events in Indochina and the Near East." The fifth and last section is entitled "The Liberal Intelligentsia in the West: Its Illusions and Its Responsibilities."

In his twenty-eight-page first section, Sakharov paints a grim picture of what he characterizes as a "state capitalist" society, in which inordinate concentration of power leads to such consequences as extreme intellectual conformity, a militarized economy, and mass poverty. Perhaps the most noteworthy features of Sakharov's description of the Soviet internal regime are his refutation—convincing to this writer—of the official Soviet image of a socialist welfare state and his long, detailed discussion of the repression of dissent. The latter presents both a description of the main features of the system of repression and moving accounts of the experiences of numerous individual victims of persecution.

A highlight of the section on freedom of choice of country is Sakharov's defense of the Jackson Amendment against criticism that it constituted interference in Soviet internal affairs, or was—in this connection he referred to a statement by President Ford—actually harmful to the cause of Jewish emigration and economically damaging to the United States. Sakharov asserted that the amendment was an expression of the "best democratic and humanistic traditions of the American people." He argued at some length that it in no way interfered in Soviet domestic affairs. This was impossible, he insisted, as the USSR was bound by several international pacts on human rights, including the right to emigration. Moreover, he argued, the right to leave the USSR was especially significant "as a guarantee of fulfillment of other human and civil rights."[121] Sakharov proceeded to express the opinion that the cause of what he referred to as a temporary decline in emigration both Jewish and non-Jewish, was not interference in Soviet affairs, but rather "the lack of unity of the Western countries." He thus related this issue to a central theme of the essay which he more fully and forcefully developed in some of its other parts, especially in the recommendations for concerted Western action contained in the concluding section.

Concluding his discussion of emigration, Sakharov thanked Senator James Buckley of New York, with whom (—as he also indicated toward the beginning of the essay—) he had met during the Senator's visit to the USSR, for accepting from him a list of six thousand Germans from Kazakhstan who desired to emigrate to the German Federal Republic.[122]

In Chapter 3 of this book, dealing with problems of arms control and disarmament, Sakharov, while characterizing the Brezhnev–Nixon and Brezhnev–Ford arms control agreements as "very important," also found fault with them on technical grounds, such as, in his opinion, the "insufficient attention" given "to problems of control." He recommended, in this connection, "a perfected system of control, including on-the-spot inspection."[123] He also expressed anxiety lest the USSR gain an advantage over the West owing to the superior throw-weight of its missile launchers, and he urged an agreement giving both sides equality in this respect. In addition, he urged further reduction of arms by both sides, with a view to the eventual prohibition of nuclear weapons. In particular, he prescribed complete prohibition of MIRV's (independently targeted multiple reentry vehicles—, as part of a set of measures designed to reduce and ultimately put an end to "strategic instability."[124] It should be emphasized that Sakharov made it clear in this study that he—unlike Solzhenitsyn and Roy Medvedev—perceived little or no diminution in the threat to mankind posed by nuclear war, and that he considered it his duty to do all in his power to warn of the danger and urge measures to reduce it.

But the most notable feature of Sakharov's discussion of strategic questions was his emphasis on their relationship to such factors as Western "disunity" (razobshchennost) and "illusions," and the "closedness" (zakrytost) and "totalitarian character" of Soviet society. Reliable progress in resolving arms control questions, he strongly contended, could be achieved only by "strengthening international trust," and this objective, in turn, depended on changing the above-mentioned conditions and on "facilitating exchanges of persons and information as the basis of international trust."[125] An important point raised in Sakharov's discussion, in this chapter, of the relationship between the peculiar characteristics of the Soviet system and arms control, as well as "relaxation of international tensions" in general, was his argument that reduction in the "militarization" of Soviet society would be damaging to the Soviet elite. In this connection, he asserted—as he had earlier—that one reason for the fall of Khrushchev was his attempt to reduce military expenditures.[126] Against this background, Sakharov warned that for the West, "one-sided disarmament," or lack of firmness in negotiating with the Kremlin, could, by upsetting the existing strategic balance, have disastrous consequences.[127]

Two points dominate the noted physicist's discussion in Section IV of the problems of Southeast Asia: namely, the baleful influence of Soviet—and also Chinese Communist—support for local Communist aggression, and the evil consequences of what he perceives to have been the lack of American and, in general, Western resolution in dealing with that aggression. For example, Sakharov believes that the "tragic development of events" in Indochina might have been prevented by the exertion of political pressure on the USSR with a view to preventing Moscow's supplying arms to North Vietnam. Like Solzhenitsyn in his June 1975 address in Washington, Sakharov foresees many years of harsh suffering for the people of South Vietnam. The depth of his concern over what he regarded as a serious American defeat in Southeast Asia is indicated by his statement that "what today threatens Thailand may tomorrow, albeit in other guises, become the fate of the whole world."[128]

The most striking feature of his discussion, also in Section IV, of the Arab–Israeli conflict was his reference to a 1955 statement on Soviet policy in the Middle East made to a group of scientists in the Kremlin by "a highly placed official" of the Soviet government. This official, reports Sakharov, told the scientists that henceforth Soviet policy would exploit Arab nationalism with a view to creating difficulties for the European countries in the matter of their oil supply, thus making them more manageable. He adds that today, with the world economy disorganized by the fuel crisis, the insidiousness of Soviet policy concealing the destructive aims of its petroleum diplomacy by its rhetoric about "defending the just cause of the Arab peoples," stands revealed.[129] And he asserts that, in view of the fact that American diplomacy may have deprived Israel of victory over Egypt in October 1973, the United States and the European countries bear responsibility for Israel's fate.

Here again he sees in united action by the Western nations the only hope of averting disaster, and he recommends, if necessary, a temporary embargo on Arab oil, along with other measures, such as a firm demand to the Soviet government and to other states to stop supplying arms to its clients.[130]

In the fifth and last section, Sakharov warns against what he sees as the dangerous consequences of the Western liberal intelligentsia's predilection for what he calls the "leftist mode" of thinking. One aspect of this tendency, he avers, is a fear of being regarded as behind the times. This, combined with ignorance of conditions in Communist-ruled lands and the effects of "socialist pro-Soviet or pro-Chinese propaganda," along with outright bribery of some writers and politicians, can lead to the holding of naive, irrational, and extremely dangerous views. The dangers, as Sakharov sees them, of the dominance of "leftist" or "leftist-liberal" intellectual fashions include forgetting the "global threat emanating from the totalitarian countries," and the possibility of weakening the defense of the rights of all men, in the East as well as in the West. He believes that many of the day-to-day cares of the ordinary man in the West are insignificant by comparison with the global issues which he has identified. Westerners will be convinced of this, he asserts, if they are ever forced to live under a regime similar to that of Russia or China, but then it will be too late. In this latter connection, Sakharov sharply criticizes those in the West, including Communists, who, he has heard, profess to believe that if socialism were to come to power in countries more advanced than Russia and China, it would be a kind of "socialism with a human face." These "typical left-liberal arguments," says Sakharov (he calls them "Slavophilism in reverse"), are refuted by history, for thus far socialism everywhere has "meant a one-party system, the power of an avaricious and incompetent bureaucracy, the expropriation of all private property, the terror of the Cheka [secret police committee] or its equivalents," and other evils.[131]

Sakharov saw Portugal as an example of a country threatened by enslavement by Communism; among other things, he noted that the Portuguese Communists were evidently receiving support from Moscow and that Communists were very strong in the Portuguese secret police. He expressed hope, however, that Portugal might escape the fate apparently threatening it and called on "world public opinion" to do everything possible to help Portugal escape "tragedy."[132]

In the final pages of Section V Sakharov touched on several other problems and offered a number of recommendations, such as united action by all elements of all Western countries in defense of

human rights. Here, as in other parts of this section, he criticized
"left-liberal intellectuals," in this instance for indifference to the
plight of victims of political persecution in socialist countries and
for unwillingness to see the seamy side of "socialism," in spite of the
information contained in the relevant works of Robert Conquest,
Alexander Solzhenitsyn, and Roy Medvedev and in scores of other
historical works.[133] But he finds some consolation, nevertheless, in
the lifting of the "fog of disinformation" about the Soviet Union to
which events of recent years in particular dissenters' protests emanating from socialist countries, have contributed.[134]

Sakharov concluded this remarkable essay, the poignancy and
power of which cannot be conveyed by any summary, with two
sets of recommendations—intended, respectively, for the Soviet
Union and for the West and, to a lesser degree, for the "third world."
The reforms he suggested for the USSR are of great interest. Detailed discussion of these proposals would be inappropriate here because of our focus on foreign affairs, and because they overlap considerably with Sakharov's earlier recommendations. For example,
Sakharov proposes a law granting "freedom to strike," something
that he had not previously recommended, and which exists in no
"Leninist" system. It is also noteworthy that in connection with a
recommendation for partial decollectivization of agriculture, Sakharov emphasized the psychological significance of "work on the
land," which, he said, had once given a sense of meaning to the lives
of millions of people that was now in danger of completely disap-
pearing.[135] And it is important to note that Sakharov again linked
Soviet domestic and world affairs by stating that a major purpose of
the twelve-point reform program he proposed for his own country
was "liquidation of the danger which our country, as a closed,
totalitarian police state, armed with superpowerful weaponry," presents to the whole world.[136]

His message to the West includes seven points, some with sub-
points. The two most important of these appear to be the repetition
of his urging the West to adopt a unified and coordinated, as well
as "far-sighted, decisive, and altruistic" strategy, and his recommendation that one of the central tasks of a unified strategy be a
program of pressures on the USSR and Eastern European Communist-ruled states to open up their societies. He expresses anxiety
lest, owing to lack of vigor on the part of Western governments, the
Communist regimes will be able to offer meaningless, self-serving
formulas in place of real change. The results of the Helsinki Con-

ference on Security and Co-operation in Europe seem, judging by available evidence, to have justified this fear. Admittedly, some of Sakharov's proposals in the field of international freedom of information, such as his demand for a lifting of the United Nations ban on freedom of television broadcasting by satellite, would be regarded with extreme disfavor by the Kremlin and by other governments fearful of the dysfunctional effects of free access to information on the part of their citizens.

It should be noted, too, that Sakharov emphasized here, as in earlier parts of this manifesto, that the United States, as the strongest Western nation, must assume the "heavy responsibilities" of the leadership that, he said, is required for unity.[137] Also of interest is Sakharov's advice to the West to render large-scale assistance to the underdeveloped countries, coupled with his urging the latter to be reasonable in their demands, and in particular to stop their practice of voting jointly with the "totalitarian states" in the United Nations. This practice, he asserts, could destroy an institution on which (together with other international organizations) "rests our common hope for a better future."[138]

In a final section, the eminent scientist mingled foreboding and hope, pointing out that the future might be even more tragic than the past, or it might be "more worthy of man." Or, he adds, there may be no future at all. The outcome, he asserts, depends on us all: on our wisdom, our freedom from illusions and prejudices, our willingness to work, and our "active decency and human breadth." Thus ends a noble work of mind and heart, reflecting in its somber aspects the effects of harsh trials at the hands of the powerful but frightened Soviet bureaucracy, but also reflecting the breadth of human sympathy and the moral fervor that one associates with the best traditions of the Russian intelligentsia.

ROY MEDVEDEV'S ANALYSIS

Roy Medvedev is perhaps, at least in terms of the continuity of his views over time, the most consistent major Soviet dissident thinker. From August 1973 on, Sakharov and Solzhenitsyn, presumably in full awareness of the possible consequences of their actions, courted confrontation with the Soviet regime by expressing opinions that the authorities could scarcely fail to consider subversive.

More intolerable still, they defiantly proclaimed to the world their increasingly sharp criticism of Soviet foreign and domestic policies in the numerous press conferences that Sakharov, in particular, held with Western newsmen. Medvedev, on the other hand, steadfastly pursued his well-established course of moderate criticism from a Marxist perspective in a series of *samizdat* essays, in which he presented an updated version of a critique of Soviet institutions and policies that might be characterized as Leninist in symbols and democratic in content.[139] Of course, judging by the unresponsiveness of the Soviet authorities to Roy Medvedev's criticism and proposals, and by his continued lack of employment (mentioned earlier), his views were also considered highly objectionable by the political leadership.

Of most immediate concern to us here, however, is Medvedev's criticism of Sakharov and, especially, of Solzhenitsyn. In general, Medvedev's negative reaction to many of the views and policy recommendations of Sakharov and Solzhenitsyn—significantly qualified, however, as we shall see, in respect to various aspects of the views of the two men—flowed logically enough from the fact that while their positions had changed substantially, his orientation had remained unaltered.

Roy Medvedev's long (twenty-one large pages) October 1973 essay was probably the deepest, most perceptive, and most objective analysis of the relationships between relaxation of East–West tensions and prospects for Soviet internal political development that has appeared in the USSR. Indeed, in terms of logical structure and coherence it compares favorably with the best Western analyses.

Unlike Sakharov, Solzhenitsyn, and for that matter, so far as I am aware, all other Soviet dissenters, Medvedev displayed a keen awareness of the constraints, requiring concessions on both sides, under which presumably both Soviet and non-Soviet statesmen labored in the process of bargaining for a mutually agreed-upon "relaxation of tensions." Admitting that "détente"—which he clearly regarded as a positive trend, since in his view it was a necessary condition for arms limitation and hence "for the acceleration of peaceful economic development on all continents"—had unfortunately been accompanied by intensified police pressure on Soviet dissenters, he hypothesized that suppression of dissent might have been the price demanded by CPSU Central Committee "rightists" for agreeing to support the "détente" policy favored by the majority faction in the party leadership. Soviet "hawks," he noted, were concerned over relaxation of international tensions because such relaxation inevitably affected "the sphere of ideological relations," in which, according to Medvedev, the responsible officials involved were less competent and less capable of adapting to the new situation than their counterparts in the economic, foreign-policy, and foreign-trade fields. All that the "responsible ideologists" were capable of recommending as closer contacts developed between the USSR and the West, was to demand such traditional policies as tightened "ideological discipline," intimidation of dissenters, and the like.[140] He observed that under Soviet conditions, where "the more moderate and soberly disposed politicians sit in the same central committee together with outright reactionaries, and a struggle proceeds behind closed doors" among "various groups," a "cooling" of the internal political atmosphere occurs.[141] Medvedev's language was obscure, but he seemed to be saying that as long as "reactionaries" retained significant leverage in the Soviet power structure they could veto or at least obstruct liberalization measures.

Medvedev criticized Solzhenitsyn for having, in his Nobel Lecture, unfavorably compared Soviet treatment of dissidents with the Union of South Africa's treatment of blacks, and also Sakharov for asking the United States Congress to require Soviet concessions on emigration in return for improving the terms of Soviet–American trade (he also deplored Vladimir Maksimov's attack on Willy Brandt for allegedly "selling out" Western democracy by his "Ostpolitik" [Eastern Policy]). However, he was not unsympathetic to such dissenters, who, he pointed out, had been under "intense and continuous pressure and were subjected to unwarranted abuse in the press and in oral propaganda and, moreover, had felt keenly the arrests of their less well known colleagues and friends...."[142]

It is important to note here Medvedev's belief that—to his obvious regret—the regime's campaign to curb dissent, in the years since 1968, had been largely successful. Among its results, he pointed out, had been the silencing of "a considerable number of people, who wanted to and could have said a great deal but who were not prepared to risk their seeming freedom or the welfare of their dear ones." He also expressed the view that the regime's exploitation of the statements and testimony of Yakir and Krasin— after their "recantation" in 1972—had contributed to the "demoralization" of dissent circles, and that the easing of emigration policies for Jews and, "on an experimental basis," for other nationalities had also helped to weaken the democratic forces. But he concluded his discussion of this topic by asserting that the main factor in restraining dissent was the ability of the state, in a system lacking democratic checks and balances, to exert pressure on dissenters in its capacity as virtually the society's sole employer—a point Yuri Glazov also emphasized in his works cited in Chapter 1 (see p. 15).[143]

Having discussed the enfeeblement of the forces working for democratization and the growing influence of reactionary, rightist groups in the ideological and cultural life of the USSR, Medvedev rhetorically asked how these trends could be reversed. Noting the relative weakness, both in the party apparatus and within the intelligentsia, of "progressive" and "democratic" tendencies, along with the "obvious political passivity of the working class," he concluded by an implicit process of elimination that reform could come only "from above." He rejected—as had Sakharov and Solzhenitsyn in various of their writings—both the likelihood and the desirability of "a mass movement capable of leading to significant political changes."[144] But, he reiterated his previously voiced conviction that "systematic democratization" of Soviet society was long overdue, and that in its absence popular discontent over such problems as bureaucratization, inefficiency, insufficiency of information, and, in general, the USSR's "lagging in many respects behind the West" would increase—although he thought the regime could continue to successfully control it.[145]

Under these circumstances, he noted, it was natural to think of pressure from abroad as a means of inducing internal change. He agreed that their international reputation and the help they received from abroad had saved Sakharov and Solzhenitsyn from the harsh reprisals demanded by "right-wing circles in the Soviet leadership," and that pressure from American as well as international public opinion had helped end American "interference" in the Indochina war. Nevertheless, he argued that Western pressure on the Kremlin, while it could sometimes exert a constructive influence, could not force a country as powerful as the USSR to make significant changes in its domestic policy.[146] In fact, he warned, pressure from the American Congress to spur emigration from the USSR, for example, would worsen, not improve, prospects for emigration and would also damage Soviet–American relations. It might also, he argued, adversely affect prospects for including in the forthcoming Soviet constitution—which, it was planned, was to replace the 1936 constitution—provisions for broadened civil rights.[147]

Moreover, he asserted, most Western statesmen, representing "the ruling classes of their countries," were not really interested in the "development of socialist democracy in the USSR" or in promoting progress in that country. Hence, he argued, Soviet dissenters should appeal not to the Nixons but to left-wing circles, including "socialist and Communist parties, the progressive intelligentsia, and various leftist public organizations."[148]

Reiterating his belief that relaxation of tensions, bringing with it increased trade and international cooperation, was "important as such," Medvedev insisted, in conclusion, that no Western ultimatums could induce liberalization in the USSR. On the contrary, he argued, outside pressure, by inhibiting the ongoing process of gradual reduction of the USSR's isolation from the external world, might have undesirable effects. Relaxing international tensions was, he asserted, "a very important preliminary condition," although not the only one —he did not present a list—for "the development of the democratization of Soviet society." Furthermore, under conditions of "détente," "international public opinion" could exert maximum influence on "the internal politics of big countries."[149] Finally, he insisted, democratization in the USSR must, after all, emerge from within Soviet society itself. While the current regressive tendencies in the USSR were alarming, they did not exclude the possible emergence of other tendencies as a new generation's leaders came to power.[150]

In his careful, sober analysis, Roy Medvedev, as we have tried to show in our summary, balanced hopeful perspectives on the future against the depressing present. He weighed measured praise for the courage exhibited by non-Marxist dissenters against the possible harm their indignant moralizing might do. And, above all, he contrasted sober political realism, as he saw it, with an impatience and anger bred—as he recognized—of frustrations resulting from the policies of an irresolute, divided Soviet leadership.

Now it should be noted that, although in the essay summarized above Roy Medvedev presented a by no means rosy picture of the prospects for Soviet internal political development, at least in the forseeable future, he did assess the prospects for world peace rather optimistically. Not only did he express the view that a substantial relaxation of international tensions had already occurred, owing to the efforts of both the Soviet and major Western governments, but he did not register any alarm regarding the likelihood of a war between the Soviet Union and either the United States or China.

One finds in Medvedev's review of *Gulag Archipelago* an interesting combination of praise for the "tremendously powerful blow" dealt by Solzhenitsyn to "Stalinism and neo-Stalinism" with a vigorous rebuff to Solzhenitsyn's criticism of Lenin and to his rejection of the whole Bolshevik tradition. However, it will not be discussed here, since it does not directly relate to foreign affairs.

Medvedev on Solzhenitsyn. In his nineteen-page polemic of May 1974 in response to Solzhenitsyn's *Letter to the Soviet Leaders*, which reached the West in October of that year, Medvedev made a number of important statements about international questions. Overall, his reaction to Solzhenitsyn's *Letter* was similar to Sakharov's but much more negative. He bluntly termed Solzhenitsyn's essay "a disappointing document," and he characterized it as an "extreme and even grotesque" expression of views held by many people in the Soviet Union.[151] Like Sakharov, he rejected Solzhenitsyn's highly negative views on scientific/technological progress as unrealistic or harmful, and he took a decidedly negative view toward the novelist's recommendations regarding Siberia.[152] Also in common with Sakharov, but at great length and employing his usual "Marxist" language, he criticized the authoritarian aspects of Solzhenitsyn's program, asserting that the novelist rejected for the USSR "not only a socialist perspective, but even democracy," which was, he affirmed, "the only reasonable alternative and the sole possible path of genuine progress for all the nations of our country."[153]

While it would be inappropriate here to expatiate on Medvedev's treatment in this essay of the central theme underlying all of his writing, namely, the indispensability of democratization in the USSR if socialist ideals were to be fully realized, mention should at least be made of a startling proposal that he offered, albeit in semi-hypothetical language. Asserting, near the end of the article, that he still hoped that the incumbent CPSU leaders might undertake decentralizing and democratizing reforms, he added that he did not exclude at least the limited possibility of the appearance in the Soviet political arena of "a new socialist party," which could "form a loyal and legal opposition to the existing leadership and could facilitate the renewal and the reinvigoration of the CPSU."[154] He expressed the hope that such a party, which he predicted would differ from all existing social democratic and Communist parties, "could base its ideology on only those propositions of Marx, Engels, and Lenin that have withstood the test of time and, not being bound by existing dogma, would develop scientific socialism and Communism in correspondence with the imperatives of the present epoch, taking also into account the historical path traversed by our country."[155]

This guardedly hopeful conjecture capped a long discussion of what Medvedev criticized as Solzhenitsyn's false hope that traditional religion might replace Marxism as the integrating perspective of Soviet society. In his complex analysis, Medvedev asserted, among other things, that although religion might for some time gain increasing influence in Soviet Russia, it was essentially an aspect of a past that could never be restored. He criticized official Soviet discrimination against religious believers, however, particularly in view of the fact that "all the religious organizations in the country have long since ceased to interfere in the political life of society."[156]

Medvedev accused Solzhenitsyn of mistakenly regarding Marxism as a dogma (verouchenie); he admitted that it had been presented as such, by Soviet leaders, media and schools, in Solzhenitsyn's youth and his own, but he insisted that Marxism was in reality a "science." To be sure, as had happened with other sciences, errors had been committed in the course of Marxism's development, but these errors could and should be corrected.[157]

But perhaps the most fundamental point in Medvedev's criticism of Solzhenitsyn's program—applicable also, though to a lesser degree and implicitly rather than explicitly, to Sakharov—was his insistence that the future structure of Soviet society must be built on its already established socialist foundations. There could be no turning back either to "ancient orthodoxy, or to capitalism." There must be a movement forward "from primitive bureaucratized variants of socialism and false socialism to socialism with a human face," asserted Medvedev, becoming the first Soviet author, so far as I know to use that odious (in the eyes of the Soviet authorities) metaphor, reminiscent of the "Prague spring."[158]

Medvedev rejected Solzhenitsyn's belief—expressed, it will be recalled, in a footnote of his Letter—that, as Medvedev interpreted it, it would be desirable if the "border nations," with the exception, perhaps, of the Ukraine and Belorussia, were to be separated from the USSR. The novel feature of his discussion of the nationality problem was that, although he, like Sakharov, was critical of Solzhenitsyn's excessive emphasis on the Russians, in contrast to Sakharov he argued that the Russian people had not been accorded appropriate opportunities to develop their own national and cultural distinctiveness. In this connection, he suggested that a capital for the Russian Soviet Federated Socialist Republic (RSFSR), separate from the USSR capital, be established.[159]

In a two-page section entitled "The Military–Industrial Complex and the Threat of War," Roy Medvedev said that he agreed with Solzhenitsyn that the threat of war with the West had, as Medvedev put it, "almost" disappeared. He also asserted, however, that he could in no way agree with the novelist that "the Western world, as a significant force, had ceased to oppose the USSR," and he pointed out that not long ago the danger of a thermonuclear war had been "a reality." The diminution of this threat he attributed to the "equalization of strategic nuclear potential," which had also led to the relaxation of tensions and to increased trade and economic cooperation and cultural exchanges, "consolidating the relaxation."[160]

He criticized the "military–industrial complex," both in the United States and in the USSR, and asserted that in the latter the influence of "military–industrial circles" on basic political decisions had increased since the death of Stalin, though not sufficiently to prevent a further relaxation of tensions. In this connection, he argued that the USSR was militarily strong enough to permit a reduction in the resources allocated to defense.[161] Bringing his favorite theme into play, he broadly implied that democratization within the USSR would foster a reduction of military expenditures, since the Soviet forces in Eastern Europe no longer served primarily as a shield against possible external aggression but, rather, performed the function of maintaining Soviet influence in that region against indigenous forces.

While he granted that there was a greater danger of war with China than with the West, he largely rejected the Amalrik–Solzhenitsyn scenario of the looming menace of a war with China, mainly on the ground of overwhelming Soviet military superiority *vis-a-vis* China (which was perhaps implicitly inconsistent with his expressed belief that in the relations between the USSR and the West tensions had relaxed as Soviet strength grew). He pointed out also that, owing to geographic and other conditions, it would be irrational and impracticable for either the Chinese or the Soviet government to inaugurate such a war.

He concluded his calm discussion of the China problem, so central to Solzhenitsyn's and (to a somewhat lesser degree) Sakharov's concerns, with an expression of "full agreement" with the former that from the Soviet side everything possible should be done to avoid war with China, adding that the USSR was strong enough, *vis-a-vis* China, to undertake substantial arms cuts. Finally, he asserted that "it must be kept in mind that 'détente' in the West serves to diminish the danger of war in the East."[162]

One other point in this, perhaps the most "liberal" of Roy Medvedev's works, should be mentioned since it bears on Andrei Sakharov's central theme of "convergence." In the course of his discussion of the numerous democratizing reforms he considered necessary in the USSR, Medvedev also asserted that "in the developed capitalist countries," economic progress "demanded" "a broadening of state regulation in the sphere of the economy and in many other fields of social life, including nationalization of the most important branches...of industry," and he cited the views of "even such an economist as Galbraith" as "symptomatic" in this connection. Thus, if Medvedev could at all be called a believer in convergence—a term he does not use—he, in contrast to Sakharov, would apparently expect, for its realization, changes in the West perhaps at least as fundamental as those he prescribes for his own country.[163]

This raises questions in the context of other aspects of Roy Medvedev's thinking, such as his resolute unwillingness to repudiate or even critically reexamine the role of the Bolsheviks in 1917 and his "plague on both your houses" approach to East–West relations. One wonders, at the very least, how realistic it is to advocate the institution of opposition and dissent in the Communist systems while at the same time, in effect, tacitly approving the further advancement throughout the world of what both official Soviet doctrine, and Medvedev himself, choose to regard as the "socialist" revolution.

CONFLICT AMONG THE DISSENTERS

In view of such considerations, it is not surprising that Solzhenitsyn, in his Stockholm press conference of December 12, 1974, asserted—among other critical remarks—that Medvedev had written what the novelist labeled an ostensibly favorable, but in essence hostile, review of *Gulag* "in order to save Lenin and the idea of Communism."[164] And unfortunately, sharp acrimony and even bitterness, at least on the part of Solzhenitsyn, appears to have developed between Solzhenitsyn and Roy Medvedev during 1974. Although Medvedev's reaction to the second volume of *Gulag* was characterized by a mixture of praise and criticism that aroused Solzhenitsyn's ire, he nevertheless supported the exiled writer's charge that the orthodox, Nobel prize-winning pillar of the Soviet establishment, Mikhail Sholokhov, was not the real author of *And Quiet Flows the Don*, the novel that won him fame.[165]

In June 1975, Dr. and Mrs. Sakharov, and shortly thereafter Roy Medvedev together with the physicist Valentine Turchin, held press conferences with *London Observer* correspondents Dev Murarka and Robert Stephens. For the most part, the Sakharovs covered ground familiar to followers of their activities. However, some points made by the blunt and coolly confident Medvedev deserve special attention. For example, as reported by Murarka and Stephens, Medvedev had by this time come round to the view that the West, in pursuing "détente," should seek certain concessions, such as greater freedom of movement for foreign correspondents and free sale of foreign newspapers to Soviet citizens, which Medvedev thought could be secured by intelligent negotiation. And in response to a question as to what he would do if he were made head of the Soviet government, Medvedev replied that he would make sweeping personnel changes, with a view to achieving efficient administration. He would also, he said, make many other major changes, including giving the green light to the starting up of small, private service businesses and to the establishment of commercial publishing houses to provide healthy competition for the media controlled by the party. According to the *Observer*, Medvedev asserted that if Sakharov came to power he would not know what to do, as his views were more negative than positive and more moralistic than intellectual. As for Solzhenitsyn, whom he almost ignored, Medvedev remarked that if he, with his "religious" ideas, attained power the results would be "dreadful."* In arguing his case for "within-system" reform led by Marxists, who alone could be understood by the relevant elements of Soviet society, Roy Medvedev likened today's Marxist reformers to the Protestant religious reformers of the sixteenth century.

Despite Medvedev's criticism of Solzhenitsyn and Sakharov, he and, more emphatically, Turchin agreed with them that vigorous

---

* It should be noted here that according to sources I consider reliable, Medvedev said after the *Observer* interview that it had represented him as more negative in his comments on Sakharov's views than in fact he was—though he still insisted that Sakharov, for whom he professed great esteem, was not a good forecaster of Russia's future.

Western support was necessary if dissent in the USSR were to have any chance of surviving. There was also substantial agreement among all four participants in the two interviews on the current weakness of dissent, the intensity and resourcefulness of repression, and the stagnant state of Soviet society. Still, the picture painted by the Sakharovs and by Turchin was a more somber one than that perceived by the doggedly optimistic Medvedev. Sakharov refrained from criticism of other dissenters and from offering reform proposals; it is clear that he regarded the defense of endangered colleagues as the absolute priority task of Soviet dissenters and their foreign supporters. He mentioned, for example, his friend and associate in the civil rights movement, the biologist Sergei Kovalev, who in December was to receive a staggeringly severe sentence for alleged anti-Soviet activity. He chided Western opinion leaders both for having failed to protest Stalin's crimes vigorously when they occurred and, in the post-Stalin era, for failing to build a fire under the feet of Western politicians that would, in turn, impel them to pressure Soviet leaders to stop persecuting dissidents.

Medvedev, for his part, indulged in speculation on possible outcomes of the forthcoming Twenty-fifth CPSU Congress and on other topics obviously regarded as trivial, under the circumstances, by the Sakharovs. He predicted, and considered it desirable, that Brezhnev would retain leadership, and that he might well be joined in the top echelons of the party by a number of younger men. He even expressed the opinion that the youngish (late forties) Central Committee secretary, Konstantin Katushev—a major enforcer of Soviet policy in Czechoslovakia—or KGB head Yuri Andropov would better understand the problems of the Soviet intelligentsia than could older leaders such as Mikhail Suslov or Andrei Kirilenko. Although he denied that there was any "dialogue" of any kind between the Soviet leadership and dissidents, it is perhaps understandable, in view of such speculations on his part about high politics, that some Western specialists on Soviet affairs occasionally toy with the notion that Roy and Zhores Medvedev might be spokesmen for a reformist faction in the party elite. However, information passed on by trustworthy Western sources in contact with Roy Medvedev in 1975 convinced me that while his potential influence might be considerable, and may have been of some importance in the past, when he was single-handedly producing the important *samizdat* journal *Political Diary,* he was for the time being completely isolated politically. Indeed, as he himself pointed out to visitors, he was, unlike Sakharov and other major figures, not even criticized by the official press but completely ignored, as if he did not exist. And yet this stubborn, uncompromising man continued his lonely struggle in the conviction, apparently, that one day his country would be governed by men inspired by a vision of socialism vastly different from the Stalinist model—improved, to be sure, but not fundamentally altered—under which his people were forced to live.[166]

One very important claim made by Medvedev in the above interview, which perhaps helps to explain his relative optimism, was his assertion that his book, *Let History Judge*, was not available in the special libraries of anti-Soviet works maintained by the CPSU Central Committee to acquaint officials going abroad with the views of "ideological enemies." Solzhenitsyn's *Gulag*, the works of Maksimov, the emigrant journal *Kontinent* and others were available. According to Medvedev, party cadres were not allowed to read his book because being written in "Marxist language," it might—unlike the non-Marxist works of Solzhenitsyn and others—"change their views."

A more radical and certainly a more extreme criticism of the Soviet regime than any ever penned by Roy Medvedev was proclaimed from a professedly Marxist position by the Soviet mathematician and former political prisoner Leonid Plyushch in a press conference in Paris early in February 1976. In addition to confirming in detail reports of the horrors of his detention in a psychiatric institution for two and a half years beginning in mid-1972, Plyushch asserted that he had "proved" in his works circulated before his arrest that "state capitalism" not socialism existed in the USSR, where, he said, the "abstract capitalist" was the state, with the Soviet bureaucracy as its servant. While as reported in the *New York Times* his remarks touched mainly on the internal regime rather than on foreign policy, they had obvious foreign policy implications. For example, he called on the Communist parties of France, Italy, and Britain "to continue to press Moscow for the release of political prisoners in jails and mental institutions." He urged releases of V. Bukovski, V. Moroz, and the Crimean Tatar leader, Mustafa Djemilev, who had reportedly been on a hunger strike for seven months.

Certainly his reported contention that the Soviet authorities used "particularly cruel tactics against Marxist dissidents" and that "it is the internal enemy that the Soviet powers fear most" bore a resemblance—in concept if definitely not in tone—to some of Medvedev's statements.

Credit for securing Plyushch's release has been given not only to protests by foreign mathematicians, and to the efforts of such international organizations as Amnesty International, but also to interest displayed in his case by the French Communist Party. This reminded the world again of the complexity of the links between Soviet dissent and international politics, and also of the helpful role that vigorous foreign pressure can play for the benefit of dissenters.[167]

In the eyes of the party bosses, of course, the negative appraisal of Soviet foreign policy, disseminated by men whose views I have described, had to seem subversive and had to be dealt with sternly. Their criticisms were certainly incompatible with the official image, which, despite hailing "relaxation of tensions," continued to denounce "imperialists" and their alleged sinister plots against the USSR. Of course more hostility was displayed toward Sakharov and Solzhenitsyn for their sharp criticism of Soviet expansionism and their appeals for Western resistance thereto, than toward Medvedev. For this and other reasons, Roy Medvedev and his exiled brother, Zhores, who has since late 1973 made a number of statements supporting Roy's position, have been criticized, by some very harshly. Thus, the prominent and influential writer Vladimir Maksimov—whom Solzhenitsyn, in his interview with Crepeau and Jacob, had listed as one of the Soviet authors he most respected—in an angry open letter released in November 1973, attacked Roy and Zhores Medvedev for their failure to wholeheartedly support Sakharov and Solzhenitsyn. Among other things, Maksimov saw in the Medvedevs' "failure to understand" Solzhenitsyn's statement on "peace and violence" evidence of "calculated political slyness," and he accused them of ingratitude to Sakharov and Solzhenitsyn in "trying to discredit" their views despite their having been chiefly responsible for securing Zhores' release from detention in a psychiatric hospital in 1970.[168] Maksimov also expressed the opinion that Sakharov's appeal to the United States Congress had enabled many "sufferers" to emigrate from the USSR.

The Moscow cyberneticist and friend of Solzhenitsyn, Mikhail Agurski, also criticized the two brothers in a similar vein, characterizing them as having assumed perhaps the "most conservative" position among members of "the Soviet opposition."[169] But Valeri Chalidze, although he too, also in an open letter, stated that "the spirit" of the Medvedevs' statements was "alien" to him, nevertheless deplored the "thesis," which he attributed to some critics of the Medvedevs, "that uniformity of opinion is necessary among dissenters."[170] Chalidze, however, in support of Sakharov, expressed his "profound satisfaction" over adoption by the House of Representatives of the Jackson–Vanik amendment, linking the issues of concessions to the USSR in trade with America, and Soviet easing of restrictions on emigration. Maksimov's angry response to the Medvedevs' stance was to prove more representative of the opinion of dissenters, especially those in emigration, than Chalidze's moderation. Even the gentle Sakharov asserted that "the Medvedevs, with their pragmatism, have opposed themselves to those who today are waging a moral struggle for man's right to live and think freely."[171] And apart from the angry reaction of Solzhenitsyn, especially to Roy Medvedev's views on "détente," the vehement, contemptuous criticism of Roy in a long article on the protagonists of the "détente" trialogue by the former Soviet journalist Vadim Belotserkovsky, who had left the Soviet Union in 1972, is worth mentioning.[172]

As an outsider, however, I feel that the disputes among the three are less important than their common defiance, especially, but not only, characteristic of Sakharov and Solzhenitsyn, of a regime incapable of countenancing the expression of independent opinion, especially in the sensitive field of foreign affairs. It is regrettable, in my opinion, that Solzhenitsyn has been characterized, in some Soviet emigrant and non-Soviet comment, as "reactionary," largely on the basis of portions of his *Letter to the Leaders*.[173] While it is clear that from the point of view of adherents of Western democratic values the approaches of Medvedev and Solzhenitsyn, both to domestic and to foreign problems, are less appealing than is Sakharov's outlook, all three men, in my opinion, deserve our respect for their contribution to the cause of freedom. And one might hope that Soviet dissidents, both inside the USSR and in emigration, would stress the common elements in the thought and struggles of their most outstanding fellows, at least until such time as the common danger to them all, represented by a still enormously oppressive and unresponsive regime, begins to diminish. In any case, the flaring controversy, especially in emigrant dissent circles, reminds us that Soviet dissent is far from a homogenous body of thought, and also, alas, that the strains of life in emigration tend to exacerbate ideological conflicts. There seemed to be developing, in 1974 and 1975, both inside the USSR and in the emigrant dissenter community, a division between what might loosely be termed the Solzhenitsyn group and another collection of individuals, including Pavel Litvinov, Boris

Shragin, Valeri Chalidze, and others, whose views were similar to those of Andrei Sakharov. Paradoxically, Solzhenitsyn and his followers pursued a line that could be considered both more anti-Western and, in a sense, more militantly pro-Western than the Litvinov–Chalidze one. With respect to the future of Russia, Solzhenitsyn and—with varied nuances—his friends, such as Igor Shafarevich and Mikhail Agurski, sought salvation for their homeland in the revival of national traditions. The continuators in emigration of the struggle to reform the USSR along polyarchical lines, while they honored Solzhenitsyn and his associates for their contribution to the liberation struggle in Russia, nevertheless appeared to regard them as proponents of a romantic messianic outlook, inapplicable to the problems of the modern world.[174]

ISSUES IN SOLZHENITSYN'S CRITICISMS

So far as foreign affairs, and particularly America's relations with Soviet Russia, were concerned, Solzhenitsyn, in a series of addresses and statements beginning on June 30, 1975, in Washington, D.C., embarked on a vigorous campaign to warn the American people against the dangers of a false "détente" with Moscow. Especially after his July 21 statement asserting that if President Ford went to Helsinki to sign the document prepared for the thirty-five-nation meeting concluding the Conference on Security and Co-operation in Europe, he would be joining in the "betrayal" of Eastern Europe, Solzhenitsyn apparently achieved a powerful impact on American public opinion.[175]

In any case, Solzhenitsyn's criticism of the planned European "summit" meeting seems to me to have been justified. He was, more effectively than ever, raising the very important issue of the asymmetrical nature of "détente," in which the Soviet side reaped substantive benefits—in this case a measure of legitimization of its dominance in Eastern Europe—while in return the West got only, as the *New York Times* lead editorial of July 21 pointed out, such meaningless promises as "a reference to the possibility of border changes by peaceful agreement."[176] More than anyone else, Solzhenitsyn had dramatized the danger of accepting a propaganda spectacle as evidence of a real change in East–West relations, when in fact the Kremlin was relentlessly pursuing its anti-Western power drive. Perhaps it wa fitting that Solzhenitsyn, the artist and victim of Soviet terror, had issued such a clear call to the West not to be taken in by the Kremlin's latest exercise in international symbol manipulation.[177]

At this point a word of comment may be approriate on President Ford's refusal to receive Solzhenitsyn, which reportedly was based partly on Secretary of State Kissinger's opinion that a Ford–Solzhenitsyn meeting would be "disadvantageous" "from the foreign policy aspect."[178] The ineptitude displayed by the Ford administration in the Solzhenitsyn affair was amazing, and may have been a factor in the widespread press criticism of the Helsinki conference. It must have struck many Americans as absurd, and even shameful, that their government seemed to be practicing a form of self-censorship to avoid offending the Soviet rulers, while that country's controlled press continued day after day to blacken the image of America. Perhaps, instead of displaying such solicitude for the feelings of the Soviet leaders, Mr. Ford and his counselors would have been better advised to have heeded the words of Solzhenitsyn, who in his June 30 Washington address pointed out, in my opinion correctly, that "the Communist rulers respect only firmness and despise and ridicule those who continually give in to them."[179] And as a lead editorial in the *New Republic* pointed out, "A meeting between Gerald Ford and Alexander Isayevitch Solzhenitsyn would have been the most convincing of semaphores signaling...that we have not forgotten all that has happened to this man (and to millions of others)—his year in Soviet slave labor camps, his defiance of Soviet authorities...and his determination to inform the world of what he has witnessed and endured."[180]

The Kremlin's mood seemed, if anything, to turn increasingly sour and even harsh in the months after Helsinki. The hollowness of the human rights pledges made in the conference's Final Act was indicated, for example, by renewed measures against Sakharov, which will be discussed later, in connection with Soviet policy in the field of international communication and cultural exchanges. Repressive measures against other dissenters proceeded and if anything were intensified, though at the same time a number of minor dissidents, not charged with serious political offenses, were permitted, or perhaps forced, to leave Russia. In a letter published in the *New York Times* of October 7, 1975, Pavel Litvinov reported that two friends and associates of Sakharov, the biologist Sergei Kovalev and the physicist Andrei Tverdoklebov, were facing trial for their unorthodox opinions, while another well-known dissenter, Vladimir

Osipov, had just received the unusually harsh sentence of eight years in a labor camp for "having sent copies of the *samidzat* journal *Veche* abroad and having permitted his writings to be published in emigré journals in the West."

The *Times* also reported that "despite the recent summit conference at Helsinki, which dealt in part with freedom for news correspondents to carry out their work, they still live under the threat of expulsion or exclusion"—although the writer of the above words also noted a tendency in the USSR and Eastern Europe "to avoid direct confrontations with foreign correspondents and to adopt many of the tactics of Western press-agentry."[181] And in October and November, new measures against Andrei Sakharov, discussed in some detail in a later chapter of this work, provided further evidence that Helsinki had not wrought any major change in Soviet attitudes toward human rights or freedom of expression.

Perhaps the most revealing indicator of the perspective and calculations underlying the Kremlin's behavior was a very long article by the CPSU apparatchik and Academician Georgi Arbatov entitled "Maneuvers of the Opponents of Detente." Arbatov, head of the prestigious USA Institute and considered to be one of the more reasonable, enlightened members of Moscow's foreign policy establishment, hailed the Helsinki conference as a "symbol of a new stage in the development of international relations, the stage of détente in which reason triumphs." He devoted most of his space, however, to harsh criticism of "groups" and "forces" in the United States that, he asserted, had organized a "campaign" against "détente," and more particularly against the results of the Helsinki conference. Interestingly enough, Arbatov failed to specify the identity of the organizers of this "campaign." One wonders if this failure was motivated, in part, by the fact that George Meany, president of the American Federation of Labor–Congress of Industrial Organizations, was one of the major American critics of "détente," a fact that the Soviet authorities did not care to advertise.

Arbatov asserted that the organizers of the alleged anti-Helsinki enterprise expected the USSR to "pay" for Western "concessions," such as regularization of East–West frontiers "above all by one-sidedly yielding in matters concerned with internal affairs." Taking the offensive, though with a weak case, Arbatov pointed out, as if it were evidence of Soviet liberalism, that more American writers were translated in the USSR than Soviet writers were in America, and he asserted, falsely, to my knowledge, that it was far easier for

American citizens to get visas to visit the USSR than for their Soviet counterparts to come to America. But he failed to note the crucial fact that the only Soviet citizens permitted to travel abroad are those cleared by the KGB—which is especially strict in issuing exit visas for travel to "capitalist" countries.

Arbatov vigorously and at length accused American "opponents of relaxing tensions" of seeking to turn Helsinki into a weapon for interfering in the internal affairs of the "socialist" states—in violation both of the Helsinki Final Act and of pledges made by the United States when it established diplomatic relations with the USSR. Anyone who entertained such hopes, or thought that Helsinki had opened the doors to dissemination in the Soviet Union of "racist" and "pornographic" materials or of "subversive, anti-Soviet propaganda" was deluding himself, wrote Arbatov. But so also, he hastened to add, were those who thought that putting an end to the "cold war" meant "terminating the ideological struggle." That struggle, he stated, was "objectively grounded" and would "continue under the conditions of peaceful coexistence." Thus, echoing Lenin, Stalin, and Brezhnev, Arbatov in effect reiterated the old "heads I win, tails you lose" formula which asserts the Soviets' right to do all in their power to transform "capitalism" into what Moscow chooses to call "socialism," while declaring the "internal affairs" of the "socialist" states out of bounds for the West. In addition to raising this issue, Arbatov waxed wroth about Watergate—ignored by Soviet propaganda when it had suited Moscow's interest to keep silent— and other American "political scandals," including the revelations of bugging and wiretapping and other surveillance of dissenters! Assuming a lofty moral attitude, he asserted that before it lectured others on such matters America should first put its own house in order. And, as was to be expected, he expressed confidence that Soviet foreign policy would continue to win ever new successes, since it was wise and just and "had the future on its side."[182]

Arbatov's exercise in polemics, it should be noted, stopped well short of expressing pessimism about "détente." Rather, it sought to cast Moscow in the role of advocate of a constructive policy, geared to the "basic interests of the peoples involved," and its critics as hypocrites and even warmongers. But if it constituted yet another in a long series of such efforts it was also a warning, both to the West and to the Soviet reader, that the Kremlin was taking serious account of growing resistance to its "détente" strategy abroad, and was prepared, if need be, to toughen its own stance still further and put the blame for consequent heightened world tensions on Western "militarist circles." Doubtless the self-contradictory, sophistical, and at times exasperated character of the Arbatov piece reflected the complexities of the Kremlin's policy. Moscow was obviously seeking to have its cake and eat it too, as indicated by its effort to simultaneously exploit Western weaknesses in Southern Europe, the Mediterranean, and Africa, while maximizing the benefits of expanding trade with the West. And there was evidence, undoubtedly taken into account by the politically dexterous Arbatov, of continued debate in Soviet ruling circles as to just what "mix" of "coexistence" and revolutionary violence should govern Soviet policy at this stage of the "world revolutionary process."[183]

3.

Individual and Group
Rights and Foreign Affairs

PERHAPS NO ASPECT OF DISSENT in the USSR poses more arduous problems of evidence and interpretation than that to which we now turn. Indeed, our task might seem hopelessly difficult if it were defined so broadly as to involve a full investigation of the doctrines and practices to which, under Soviet conditions, such terms as "human rights" or "civil rights" refer. Such a full-scale effort would be inappropriate in view of the focus of this book on foreign relations, and also because a good deal has already been said in earlier sections of this essay on such concerns of the Democratic Movement as freedom of information, or "glasnost." Throughout the history of the Soviet dissent movement this has been perceived both as one of the major goals of the dissenters' struggle for human rights, and as an indispensable means for achieving all such rights.[1]

Regardless of the apparently unconditional guarantees of rights to freedom of speech, freedom of the press, and even—and this, in view of what we know of Soviet police and judicial practice, is truly mind-boggling—"freedom of street processions and demonstrations" set forth in Article 125 of the Soviet Constitution, "authors of legal texts and legal practitioners interpret this article differently," as Chalidze notes.[2]

And, Chalidze continues:

> In the USSR, in accordance with the notion of a uniquely correct state doctrine, information is divided into correct and incorrect.

91

> *By incorrect information the authorities mean that kind of infor-
> mation which, although not false, is better not mentioned, or in-
> formation whose mention in the opinion of the authorities, is
> untimely. Correctness of information is also evaluated by the au-
> thorities from the viewpoint of what aim is being served by that
> information. Thus one propaganda pamphlet states: "Bourgeois
> propaganda may in certain cases libelously utilize actual facts and
> reliable statistical data."*[3]

To be as fair as possible to the Soviet "side" of the argument
over freedom of expression, let us examine what appears to be a
typical presentation of the official Soviet doctrine on this subject.[4]
E.P. Prokhorov, in the cited study, equates the "bourgeois" conception of freedom with "acting as an individual wishes" and with
pure "arbitrariness" (proizvol). This conception is juxtaposed to the
"correct" one, derived, says Prokhorov, from Spinoza, Hegel, and
Lenin (limited mention is also made of Marx), according to which
"knowledge of necessity is the foundation of freedom."[5] "Necessity,"
in turn, is equated with action on the basis of Marxism–Leninism,
"the most advanced scientific world outlook," which "reflects the
interests of progressive social forces." Prokhorov denies that this
"Marxist conception" fails to provide for freedom of choice; on the
contrary, he maintains, citing Lenin, that there is abundant freedom
to consciously participate in the revolutionary struggle, so that "social progress may proceed optimally."[6] He goes on to present standard Soviet arguments according to which the only free press is the
Soviet press or one that harmonizes with it. According to Prokhorov,
in Article 125 of the Soviet Constitution—which, it will be recalled,
was long known in the USSR as the Stalin constitution—"is expressed
the spirit of the Marxist understanding of freedom of the press."[7]
Unlike Chalidze, who denies that the guarantees set forth in this
celebrated article should be regarded as subject to the proviso "that
they be exercised in accordance with the interests of the working
class and with a view to strengthening the socialist system," Prokhorov, by italicizing the key words, quoted above, of the Preamble,
emphasizes their relative, provisional character. And he adds that
the "definition" of various freedoms contained in this article "strictly
flows from the Leninist conception."[8] As if concerned that he has
still not clarified his meaning, Prokhorov adds that "a truly free press
in our epoch is a press expressing the class interests of the workers,
and proceeding from party positions. . . ."[9] Perhaps it would not be
digressive to note that the Portuguese Communists appear to have
adopted a position identical with that of Prokhorov, as was indicated

in their efforts in the spring and summer of 1975 to muzzle all non-Communist media in Portugal.

Before commenting, briefly, on Prokhorov's treatment of the problem of freedom of expression under "socialism," let me say that on the basis of wide reading in Soviet political literature I regard it as fully representative of official thinking in its field. Its authoritativeness is indicated, incidentally, by the fact that it appeared in a series published under the auspices of the CPSU Central Committee's Academy of Social Sciences.

In "Leninist" political systems, policy making is governed—according to party statutes and other authoritative documents—by the doctrine of "democratic centralism." Since this hierarchical doctrine requires that the decisions of higher party bodies are binding on lower-ranking ones, it is clear in theory—and also, as Soviet history shows, in practice—that "party positions" are defined by the Kremlin. Thus, it seems clear, freedom of the press (and other freedoms also) is equated with acceptance of and support for decisions and interpretations made by rulers or leaders, such as Stalin, Malenkov, Khrushchev, and Brezhnev and his colleagues. How, one may ask, do these men arrive at the "recognition of necessity" which, according to Soviet Marxism, is the basis of freedom? How, for that matter, did Marx, Engels, or Lenin? If leaders differ among themselves in their effort to resolve the problems facing the monopolistic and monolithic party and the society it governs, what help do they get, in resolving their differences, from "Leninism"? Who, among the rulers or for that matter among the citizens of a "Leninist" state —except, ultimately, those who have the will and the capacity to apply power—can decide what is "necessary"? One might suppose that the competence of scientists and experts, or, for that matter, information and judgment generated by wide, free, and open debate, or both combined, might be a better basis for defining "necessity" or the judgment of "history" than the opinion of a Stalin, or even of a handful of "collective" leaders.

Since the official Soviet approach to politics purports to be based upon historical knowledge, as is indicated by the prominence in the dominant ideology of the doctrine known as historical materialism, one might suppose that a full, critical account of the historical context in which, presumably, official doctrines have developed would be provided in Soviet theoretical literature. But, as Roy Medvedev proved in *Let History Judge,* his monumental study of Stalin's (to use Medvedev's term) crimes, and as other Soviet dissenters have amply demonstrated, Soviet official historiography is but an instrument of official whitewash and cover-up. In this connection, it is interesting that Prokhorov not only does not face up to any of the problems I have noted—and of course a full critical examination of his study would raise many others—but does not even mention Stalin. Yet, in effect, he expresses approval of Stalin by his laudatory reference to the provisions of the 1936 constitution, adopted, it will be recalled, at a time when Stalin was confronting Soviet citizens, including such of his former favored colleagues as Nikolai Bukharin and Gregory Zinovev, with the "necessity" of abject submission to his interpretation of Leninism, on pain of death.

There are, indeed, many questions to be considered in evaluating the official Soviet concept of freedom of expression. For example, I have said nothing about censorship and, except by tangential implication, nothing about the contradiction between official claims of wide, nay, nearly universal citizen support of party policy and the well-known proclivity of the Soviet rulers to employ police power to resolve ideological problems, as in the cases of many well-known Soviet dissenters. But perhaps enough has been said to indicate, at least with respect to one important sector, the authoritarian dogmatic, and arbitrary nature of a doctrine that its disseminators insist on calling "scientific." When one reads such material, one understands better the reports of some Soviet emigrants that they came to dissent at least in part because acceptance and echoing of official doctrine seemed an intolerable insult to their intelligence.

To be sure, the satisfaction that can be derived from perception of the defectiveness of Soviet ideological formulas is not without its drawbacks. It is easy to forget that the stridency and mendacity of the official creed do not preclude the pursuit by Soviet leaders of shrewd, pragmatic policies—which are, of course, asserted to have flowed logically from "scientific" ideological principles.

The Dissenters' Approach to Human Rights

The dogmatic, a priori official Soviet thought pattern, a sample of which has just been examined, is rejected by men like Sakharov, Volpin, Litvinov, and other Soviet democrats in favor of modes of thought in most cases heavily influenced by the critical, rational, experimental ethos of modern science. To be sure, all prominent Soviet dissenters are strongly moralistic or "normative" in their approach to politics, and hence they invoke scientific modes of thinking within a framework of moral indignation. This indignation is engendered by what they regard as official crimes, especially those committed by Stalin, and by the failure of the Soviet regime since Stalin's death either to permit honest, unhampered discussion of the horrors of the past or to institute reforms of sufficient scope and depth to remedy defects inherited therefrom, or even to do everything possible to assure that the evils of the past would not recur. This indignation impelled democratic dissenters to feel obliged to speak out against hypocrisy and injustice, and to demand that the authorities disclose adequate, accurate information about all major aspects of public policy. The demand for disclosure (glasnost), especially of legal proceedings against such dissenters as Alexander Ginzburg and Yuri Galanskov, became, of course, a central aspect of the Democratic Movement.[10]

A characteristic formulation of the Democratic Movement's aspiration for freedom of information and expression was the almost invariable appearance, on page one of the *Chronicle of Current Events*, probably the most significant and influential of all *samizdat* sources, of the text of Article 19 of the United Nations' Universal Declaration of Human Rights.[11]
The text of this article reads as follows:

> *Everyone has the right to freedom of opinion and expression; this right includes freedom to hold opinions without interference and to seek, receive and impart information through any media and regardless of frontiers.*

It is clear from the text of Article 19 that, by associating the *Chronicle's* mission therewith, its compilers were claiming for themselves and for Soviet citizens generally broad rights of access to information originating abroad and of communicating to foreigners information, and presumably interpretation thereof, about internal Soviet affairs. It will be convenient to organize the discussion that follows largely in terms of the articulation in a variety of *samizdat* sources of aspirations and demands and criticisms compatible with Article 19, though of course it cannot be demonstrated that it or the *Chronicle* inspired any particular statement cited.

ZHORES MEDVEDEV'S ANALYSIS

By far the most systematic, comprehensive, and carefully documented analysis by a Soviet dissenter of the problem of freedom of information and related questions is the major study by the biochemist and gerontologist Zhores Medvedev, written as two separate *samizdat* studies in the 1960's in the USSR but never published there. Indeed, it is evident that Zhores Medvedev's authorship of these studies, which deal respectively with international scientific cooperation and with the related subject of the secrecy and security governing correspondence between Soviet and foreign scientists, led to his commitment, and confinement for two and a half weeks in May and June 1970, to a psychiatric hospital, from which he was released only after a campaign on his behalf by prominent Soviet and foreign scientists and intellectuals had generated embarrassing publicity worldwide.[12]

In the section of the Medvedev papers devoted to Soviet restrictions on freedom of information there is a brief chapter on problems associated with the Universal Declaration on Human Rights. At the outset, Medvedev notes that the text of the Declaration has never been published in Russian in the USSR and particularly that, even though that country "associated itself with the United Nations Human Rights Year program for 1968," the Declaration was not—as he had hoped when he wrote the above—discussed in the Soviet general press. Soviet international law textbooks did, however, contain some "arbitrary" discussion of it, including the surprising claim that the USSR had championed the Declaration when it was debated by the U.N. in 1948. In fact, it was "adopted and drafted in a satisfactory form not due to, but in spite of, the attitude of the delegation of the USSR."[13]

Medvedev notes that at about the same time as Andrei Vyshinski was utilizing his not inconsiderable talents in seeking to block, and pervert the Human Rights Declaration, the USSR Supreme Soviet and the corresponding subordinate governmental bodies issued a decree effectively prohibiting contacts between Soviet citizens and foreigners, except those arranged through the USSR Ministry of Foreign Affairs. (Hairdressers, news venders, and some other categories of employees were exempted.) As a result of this decree and the attitudes and policies associated with it, he points out, "a dread grew up, or rather was intensified, of any contact with foreigners," "remnants" of which survived Stalin's death. The decree was never repealed, he observes, though with increased "contacts, letters and journeys" to and from foreign countries, its "practical enforcement" became, he states, "impossible." But, he adds, "there is still no legal foundation for taking trips abroad," and arranging for foreign travel is still "primarily an administrative question."[14] Thus Zhores Medvedev identified, and condemned, barriers interposed by the Soviet authorities to what according to Western theory is probably the most basic, influential kind of communication potentially available to Soviet citizens, namely, "primary," face-to-face contacts with foreigners.[15]

Continuing his painstaking analysis of restrictions on personal contacts with foreigners—he also criticizes, witheringly, the evil effects of the internal passport system, but the subject is not immediately relevant here—Medvedev points out that both in tsarist Russia and, up to 1929, in the USSR, it was easy to obtain a "foreign" passport for travel abroad. That state of affairs, despite considerable relaxation in practice since the death of Stalin, had, when he wrote, been by no means fully restored, and, I should add, is probably further from restoration than when his book was published. In fact, it remained necessary, in order to travel abroad, to submit to "a humiliating procedure" of investigation and checking of the applicant's professional, personal and political record by the KGB and by a section of the CPSU Central Committee.[16]

Zhores Medvedev, it is important to note, rejects efforts to explain the barriers interposed by the USSR to unfettered exchanges of persons and personal communications by reference to alleged fears of foreign military power. He notes that, over time, restrictions on contacts increased as Soviet military power grew. Originally they were imposed, he believes, to conceal from the outside world Stalin's terror against Soviet citizens. Although he fails to systematically develop this line of argument with respect to the post-Stalin period, the strong implication of his account is that it remains applicable.[17] In addition, one gathers from Medvedev's well-informed discussion that denial of exit visas to Soviet citizens serves such purposes as punishment for the holding by applicants of views objectionable to the party and state bureaucracies and concealment from the West of internal conditions and practices, disclosure of which to foreigners by independent-minded citizens might be embarrassing to the authorities. Certainly such an interpretation flows naturally from the vivid, detailed account Zhores provides of the frustrations and tribulations associated with his own persistent, indeed insistent, efforts to obtain the clearances needed if he were to accept invitations, tendered by a number of leading American and West European scientific organizations, to participate in or present papers at international conferences. These invitations were offered over a period of years, beginning in 1960.

The intricacies of Zhores Medvedev's meticulously detailed, low-key, at times grotesquely humorous account defy summarizing. One mildly shocking, though perhaps not surprising, episode deserves special mention: viz., the apparent effort by the Soviet political police to obtain the scientist's "cooperation," while on his hoped-for visit to the United States (which the authorities thought it worthwhile, after numerous rebuffs, to let him believe was still possible), in (ostensibly) obtaining information from American colleagues. Medvedev, though, saw through the ruse, interpreting the effort as in fact intended to determine whether or not he would be amenable to "cooperation" directed not against Americans, but against Alexander Solzhenitsyn. While the KGB was probing Medvedev's moral and psychological defenses, a scheme was afoot to create a surveillance network, taking account of the fact that Solzhenitsyn's first wife, the biologist Reshetovskaya, was then being considered for a post in the laboratory where Zhores was employed. During the sparring between Zhores and the police agents entrusted with the task of setting up the operation against Solzhenitsyn, one agent referred to a factor that undoubtedly played a big part in causing the authorities to reject all of his applications for foreign travel. This was his authorship of a powerful, bitingly negative study of the enormous damage done to biological and agricultural science in the USSR by the charlatan Trofim D. Lysenko during the years when Lysenko dominated these fields.[18]

In a poignant chapter on the "state frontier," the author describes the incredibly tight restrictions imposed by the KGB's border guards on the private use of even the smallest boats on Soviet seacoasts, observing that concern about alleged danger from foreign spies leads to maintenance of a costly system, employing tens of thousands of persons, which deprives millions of "the use of the sea." In this, as in numerous other areas of surveillance, he argues, restrictions have enormously increased, though the justification for them has vanished. But he predicts that the USSR will have to prepare for the day when the government will "open our frontier both ways," for "the time when an attempt to cross the frontier without the permission of the government was punished by incarceration in a prison-camp for six or seven years and was accompanied by the risk of being shot on the spot will have receded into the past."[19]

Difficult, but rewarding, is that part of the *Medvedev Papers* devoted to analysis of the workings, and, in Medvedev's opinion, the extremely harmful effects, of Soviet international postal censorship. Apart from revealing Zhores Medvedev's ingenuity in decipher-ing, by methods that doubtless owed much to his background in laboratory research, some of the secrets of the censors, this section is packed with startling information on the impact of censorship on the work of Soviet scientists. We learn, for example, that pages of *Science*, the well-known weekly publication of the American As-sociation for the Advancement of Science, that the postal censors regard as politically harmful—and, in some cases, entire issues—have been withheld from Soviet readers.[20]

Medvedev condemns the restrictive practices he exposes on a number of grounds. His criticism of these practices is couched in terms of moral norms, in terms of pragmatic considerations, and, finally, in terms of a defense of professional autonomy and other pro-fessional values.

Although Zhores Medvedev has a scientist's discipline and the logico-experimental thought habits of a highly competent labora-tory worker, the moral element appears, as is true of virtually all Soviet dissenters, to be the dominant element in his thinking. To be sure, he writes, much more so than say, Solzhenitsyn, in a con-trolled, sometimes dry style. But moral indignation keeps surfacing, along with, occasionally, the anger and hurt pride of a skilled pro-fessional distracted, obstructed, and humiliated by the machinations of unenlightened, but cunning, bureaucrats.

Medvedev's statement that the secret perusal of personal letters "by some organization" nowadays "seems so immoral, unworthy and disgraceful" that it is difficult to believe it is practiced, or his asser-tion that "the chief aim of Communism...in the works of Karl Marx, consists of 'destroying all attitudes under which a man can be humiliated, oppressed or outcast,'" reflects his deeply ethical ap-proach to freedom of expression, contact, and communication, both domestic and international, and to politics generally.[21] And moral idealism and pragmatism are blended when he writes that "the principal force capable of leading the world towards peaceful and gradual cultural, political and economic integration will be mutually advantageous, scientific technological and cultural co-operation and freedom of contact of the peoples of different countries, freedom of travel, freedom of exchange of information."[22]

In parts of his book Medvedev also stresses the pragmatic eco-nomic benefits of international scientific contacts. For example, he criticizes the waste of resources involved in buying expensive foreign scientific instruments, which could be avoided by sending Soviet scientists abroad for training and research. He condemns, at length and severely, useless duplication by Soviet scientists of work already done abroad. These and other defects and diseconomies he attributes to rigidity, overcentralization, and, above all, officially imposed restrictions on Soviet scientists both in respect to access to information originating abroad and, worst and most ruinous, in respect to personal contacts.[23]

Medvedev also takes note of a peculiar feature of Soviet intellectual life, to wit, the fact that more often than not experts who specialize in the study of foreign societies are not given the opportunity to visit the countries that they study. He quotes at length the writer Daniel Granin regarding "Australianists" whom Granin consulted in preparation for travel to Australia, none of whom had ever set foot in Australia. Granin's and Medvedev's observations on this point are corroborated in some of the most touching passages in Svetlana Allilueva's second book, written in the United States after her flight from Soviet control.[24]

As I noted earlier, Zhores Medvedev, like the anonymous compilers of the *Chronicle of Current Events*, refers to the Universal Declaration of Human Rights. The *Chronicle's* compilers, at least by implication, seem to have sought to fortify their demand for freedom of expression and information by this association. Medvedev asserts, in the section of his *Medvedev Papers* dealing with this topic, that the Declaration has "great spiritual force," and he notes that, although the USSR abstained from voting on the General Assembly resolution by which it was adopted and could not veto it, has, in any case, ignored it.[25]

OTHER APPROACHES

On this issue, Valeri Chalidze seems to take a position similar to that held by Zhores Medvedev. Chalidze's standpoint differs somewhat from Medvedev's, however, in its considerably greater emphasis on legalistic considerations. As Chalidze notes, "The Soviet Union advocates the principle of the unlimited sovereignty of states vis-a-vis the individual, and considers inadmissible any interference in questions of human rights on its own territory." Since the days when Vyshinski adamantly upheld that doctrine in 1948, during the debate on the Universal Declaration, the USSR, adds Chalidze, "has ratified many conventions on human rights, but the thesis

Vyshinski advanced has remained unchanged." And Chalidze adds that he is "unable to understand the dialectics of such an approach, when on the one hand a state makes commitments to guarantee human rights on its own territory, while on the other hand it tells those to whom the commitment was made that securing human rights is exclusively its internal affair."[26] Chalidze credits Soviet domestic legislation with a "respectful attitude" toward international obligations, but points out that—in respect, for example, to the obligation under the UN Convention against Discrimination in Education prohibiting discrimination on the basis of political convictions —domestic practice tends to nullify pledges to observe international legal norms. And, albeit in moderate language, he proceeds to what amounts to a warning—with implications similar to some of the statements of Sakharov and Solzhenitsyn on the pitfalls of "détente" —when he writes that "a state's partners in international relations should take a natural interest in, its compliance with human rights conventions, simply from the consideration that the contractual capacity of any person, including a state, must be judged from his behavior."[27]

An approach to problems of freedom of international communication and contact with foreigners somewhat different from Zhores Medvedev's blend of moralism and pragmatism or Chalidze's legalism can be found in some of the writings of Andrei Amalrik. Certainly Amalrik shared the general democratic dissenter respect for freedom of expression and rule of law, as will be evident to any careful reader of *Will the Soviet Union Survive Until 1984?* or his *Involuntary Journey to Siberia,* a fascinating account of the events that led to his exile to Siberia in 1965 and of his experiences there as a worker for about a year and a half on a collective farm.

Curiosity about sensitive topics, such as modern Western art, early on got Amalrik in trouble with the authorities. After his expulsion from Moscow University because he refused to bow to the orthodox Stalinist hypothesis according to which foreigners had played no part in the creation of the Russian state, he had his first brush with the secret police after he sought the assistance of the Danish Embassy in sending an essay, setting forth his heretical views, to a leading Danish historian. His contacts with foreign journalists and diplomats interested in "abstract art" (as modern art is often referred to in Russia) and with Soviet practitioners thereof, together with the fact that, to help support his invalid father, he did free-lance work at home rather than take a full-time job, led to his exile in 1965 on the charge of being a "parasite." One result of his absence from Moscow was his father's death. In view of all this and more—including such earlier events as the summary execution of an uncle in 1937 by Stalin's police and the years his father spent in a forced labor camp—small wonder that, as Amalrik told *New York Times* correspondent James Clarity in 1970, he felt "organic revulsion" against the Soviet system.[28]

Obviously, freedom of expression always was, to the fiercely independent Amalrik, the most precious of values. In some of his most eloquent statements, with full consciousness of the risks involved, he chided those—both Soviet citizens and foreigners—whom he regarded as derelict in fulfilling their duty to protest against what he regarded as the regime's muzzling of truth. In his open letter, sent in 1969, to the writer Anatoli Kuznetsov shortly after the latter's defection from Soviet rule while on an official visit to England, Amalrik accused Kuznetsov, in effect, of cowardice and opportunism for justifying, as a necessary compromise with superior force, his past cooperation with the KGB and the censorship. Amalrik pointed out that, in contrast to Kuznetsov, he had never collaborated with the KGB and had, as a result been exiled to Siberia. Later, of course, he was to be given a stiff sentence to a labor camp despite his poor health, and he was subsequently sentenced on trumped-up charges to another three years in camp, commuted, after a worldwide outcry, to exile. Amalrik went on to say that it was "not only the right but also the duty of every Russian who desires that Western public opinion should better understand his country...honestly to inform independent public opinion of what is happening in our country."[29] In conclusion, he congratulated Kuznetsov on "being now in a free country."[30] Amalrik then compounded his political "criminality," as far as the regime was concerned, by daring, along with two other Soviet dissenters, Vladimir Bukovski and Peter Yakir, to be interviewed by CBS correspondent William Cole for a film shown in the United States on July 28, 1970. During this interview, evidence was cited of the misuse of psychiatry as an instrument of political oppression, and of near-starvation of political prisoners in camps and prisons—disclosure of which was regarded by the authorities as criminal "anti-Soviet slander." At Amalrik's trial in November 1970, his books, the Cole interview and another he had with American television journalists, and his letter to Kuznetsov were all cited against him. It should be noted that the case against Bukovski, at his trial in January 1972, was similar to that against Amalrik, but

Bukovski, who had made available to the world a great deal of material that the regime was obviously very anxious to conceal on confinement of dissenters in prison psychiatric hospitals, received a very much severer sentence than Amalrik.

Amalrik, Bukovski, and Yakir—the latter's long service to the struggle for human rights should be remembered, despite his recantation at his well-publicized trial in August–September 1973—as well as Pavel Litvinov and others pioneered in bringing to the attention of interested and responsive groups abroad (or, as the dissenters put it, of "world public opinion") the Soviet regime's violations of human rights. According to Litvinov this practice dates to 1967 and 1968, when Amalrik and he "decided to make a regular practice of approaching Western correspondents in Moscow."[31] Thus there took shape a strategy of exposure, and, one may say, of internationalization of what had hitherto been accepted both by Soviet dissidents and the regime and by Western opinion as purely internal affairs of the Soviet Union. Since the regime's massive crackdown of 1972, the main burden of continuing this operation has fallen to Academician Sakharov: in the period from the beginning of 1973 to the present Sakharov has issued scores of appeals on behalf of victims of political persecution. This unmasking of the secretive Soviet regime, this puncturing of the myth of universal compliance with its commands, this rallying of an aroused world conscience has dealt heavy blows to the image of the Soviet Union in world opinion.

In December 1973, in a statement accepting the prize of the International League for the Rights of Man, Sakharov linked the defense of human rights in the USSR with the principles affirmed by the Universal Declaration of Human Rights, by first referring to "hundreds" of his friends "in camps, prisons and psychiatric hospitals" and then stating that in adopting the Universal Declaration the United Nations "took upon itself the defense of human rights in every country." In the same vein, he listed such "still unsolved" human rights problems as "public disclosure," "freedom of one's convictions and conscience," and the "key problem" of "assuring freedom of emigration." And he expressed the hope that awarding the prize to a Soviet citizen "demonstrates that international attention to assuring human rights" in the USSR would "increase and have a deep influence."[32]

In a message, dated April 18, 1975, to "Amnesty International, Secretary General Martin Ennals, and the international community," Sakharov protested the arrest of Andrei Tverdokhlebov, at the time secretary of Amnesty's USSR group, and other recent regime actions as constituting "a challenge to world opinion" and "a blow to legality and to those humanitarian and democratic principles which have been consistently championed" by Amnesty throughout the world and in the USSR. "Open and decisive action by the world community," he asserted, "is needed."

Sakharov also noted in this appeal that a member of Amnesty, Sergei Kovalev, had earlier been arrested. It will be recalled that Kovalev had long been active in the human rights movement, as a founder of the Action Group and otherwise, and that Tverdokhlebov had been a founding member of the Moscow Human Rights Committee.[33]

We have treated the vast subject of the approaches to the concept of human rights taken by various leading Soviet dissenters more illustratively than exhaustively. It could be argued that the foregoing remarks not only failed to cover all the data available, but did not even identify all of the categories under which the data might have been classified. Both charges could perhaps be sustained. It is probably true, for example, that an "expressive" type of protest regarding violations of human rights, characterized by and flowing from irresponsible indignation and disgust, might be identified. Lidia Chukovskaya's denunciation of Mikhail Sholokhov for his outburst, in a speech at the Twenty-third CPSU Congress, in 1966 against Sinyavski and Daniel might fall under this category—but it would also fall under our category of the demand for a measure of professional autonomy. When, in an open letter attacking Sholokhov Chukovskaya wrote, "a book...cannot be tried in any court... except the court of literature," she was, in the tone of high moral indignation characteristic of the Soviet democratic dissenters, raising the issue of professional autonomy—and also, obviously, that of freedom of expression. The same mixed demands are to be found in many of Solzhenitsyn's statements.[34] This combination had also been characteristic of much critical thinking during the Khrushchev era and for a year in the early post-Khrushchev period, especially in the pages of *Novy Mir*, where the USSR's best critics and scholars discreetly but unequivocally articulated the demand that in Soviet intellectual life more weight be accorded to professional criteria and less than had been the case in the Stalinist past to bureaucratic and ideological interests.

Aspects of two topics—emigration and the right to travel abroad for purposes other than emigration, and the closely related issue of nationality rights—which have already been somewhat tangentially treated, will now engage our attention. The resolution of—or failure to resolve—these issues, especially the second, could perhaps decisively affect the future of the USSR, as Amalrik and, less dramatically, Sakharov, Solzhenitsyn, and other leading dissenters have pointed out. It will be necessary to be somewhat selective in the discussion of these topics, especially, again, in respect to the enormous field of nationality problems.

Emigration and the Right to Travel

It is not surprising, in light of the Democratic Movement's demand for effective observance by the Soviet authorities of the Universal Declaration of Human Rights, that freedom of emigration and the right to other travel abroad are topics of deep concern to its supporters. Article 13 of the Declaration states that "everyone has the right to leave any country, including his own, and to return to his country." But, presumably since the USSR does not accept the Declaration as a legally binding document, the most "legalistic" participants in the struggle for expansion of human rights in that country, such as the exiled Valeri Chalidze, do not even refer to it in their discussions of freedom of movement.[35] It and other relevant articles of the Declaration have been referred to, however, by many Soviet protesters, especially by Jews wishing to emigrate or to secure exit visas for relatives denied them by Soviet officials.[36]

In fact—as Chalidze indicates in some detail, with reference to both law and practice—travel of any kind to foreign countries by Soviet citizens is subject to numerous, almost unbelievably arbitrary administrative and political restrictions and also depends heavily, of course, on economic considerations. Chalidze also thinks that a very powerful factor is the residue of traditional Russian reluctance to allow anyone to leave Russia. The result is that "permission to travel abroad is obtained only by those loyal citizens who, the authorities hope, will not only come back, but will come back relatively uncontaminated by foreign ideology." The situation is further complicated by cases, in recent years, of permitting emigration by some dissenters or even forcing some to leave—as in the cases of the physicist Boris Zuckerman, the poet Joseph Brodski, the writer Andrei Sinyavski, and many others—or, as in the cases of Chalidze himself or of Zhores Medvedev—of granting permission for travel abroad and then revoking their citizenship. Perhaps a special case— not mentioned by Chalidze—is the kidnapping/ejection/exiling of Alexander Solzhenitsyn.[37]

There is, of course, a close connection between the demand made by many Soviet dissenters that restrictions on foreign travel be reduced or abolished, and the issue of Jewish emigration, which in turn is an important, in fact probably by far the most important, aspect of what has been termed the Jewish "freedom movement."[38]

THE SOVIET JEWISH MOVEMENT

There is significant overlap, but also substantial differences, between the values, sentiments, interests, and goals of the Jewish movement and those of the Democratic Movement, especially among Moscow intellectuals. Fundamental is the fact that "since 60% to 70% of the democrats are Jews or married to Jews, they have social or family ties as well."[39] Another basic element of the relationship is that of mutual support, articulated on numerous occasions by leading members of the two partially overlapping groups. Thus the Moscow Human Rights Committee protested to the USSR Supreme Soviet in May 1971 regarding "'persecution of Jewish repatriates,'" arguing that the "'only aim'" of the defendants in several trials of Jews had been to protest against "unlawful refusals to give them visas for repatriation."[40] And Sakharov, in his appeal to the United States Congress, in support of the Jackson–Vanik Amendment in September 1973, linked the general human rights issue to the right of individual persons to choose the country and the political system under which they wished to live. While the reference of his appeal was, in context, primarily to Soviet Jews, it is worthy of note that he claimed the right not only for Jews. One key paragraph of his statement reads as follows:

> But as you know, there are tens of thousands of citizens in the Soviet Union—Jews, Germans, Russians, Ukrainians, Lithuanians, Armenians, Estonians, Latvians, Turks, and members of other ethnic groups—who want to leave the country and who have been seeking that right for years and for decades at the cost of endless difficulty and humiliation.[41]

An issue that was raised in connection with Jewish emigration, especially in cases of Jews who had been participants in the general

Democratic Movement until they emigrated or until, before leaving the USSR, they reoriented their activity from it to purely Jewish concerns, was that of the alleged harmful effect of emigration on the struggle to democratize the Soviet Union. The scope of this issue is, of course, very broad; its implications exceed the limits of the Jewish, or "Zionist," emigration movement. Insofar as its Jewish aspect is concerned, Schroeter reports, on the basis of information gathered mostly in the USSR, that while some democrats considered that "if the Jews were successful, many intellectuals would, by leaving the Soviet Union, weaken the Human Rights movement," nevertheless, Vladimir Bukovski and other leaders of the mainstream democrats successfully argued, at Moscow meetings in the fall of 1970, that "the democrats must fully support Jewish efforts to leave for Israel."[42]

More generally, the question as to the effect on the struggle for change in Russia of voluntary departure—as distinguished, presumably, from the forced departure of Solzhenitsyn, who, it is well known, refused to go to Stockholm in 1970 to receive his Nobel award for fear that he might not be permitted to return to his homeland—continued to fuel controversy among dissenters, at home and abroad, in 1975. According to an article in a New York Russian language daily, Igor Shafarevich, the distinguished Moscow mathematician, associate of the Human Rights Committee, friend of Solzhenitsyn, and contributor to the Maksimov–Solzhenitsyn emigrant journal *Kontinent,* had published in *Le Monde* of Paris an article "that strongly rebuked those Russian intellectuals who, like Rostropovich, voluntarily left their homeland." This was clearly aimed at, among others, the cellist Mstislav Rostropovich, Solzhenitsyn's friend and benefactor, to whom Shafarevich had also been close. Rostropovich defended his departure on the ground that only in the West could he and his wife, the singer Galina Vishnevskaya, fulfill their art, and he pointed out that they had felt constrained to leave Russia because of harassment resulting from the support and help they had given to Solzhenitsyn. Among other things, the Rostropoviches had given refuge at their summer cottage to Solzhenitsyn when the writer was denied official permission to reside in Moscow. Also, as the cellist noted in his reply to Shafarevich, he and Vishnevskaya were subjected to discrimination unique in the Soviet musical community partly because of Rostropovich's refusal—unlike, one recalls, Shostakovich—to sign any letters "previously prepared by official organs." Rostropovich referred in this connection to his refusal to abet press campaigns against "Israeli aggressors," Pasternak and

Sakharov, and "various composers, writers, artists and scientists." He also described in telling detail the measures taken by the Soviet cultural bureaucracy in retaliation against him and his wife for their nonconformity, including his exclusion from the leading Soviet opera theater and the blacklisting of Vishnevskaya by the Soviet radio and television networks.

Rostropovich was defended by Yuli Daniel, quietly living in the USSR after having served a term in a labor camp following his 1966 trial, with Andrei Sinyavski, on charges of having "slandered" the Soviet state in literary works published in the West. Daniel—unlike Rostropovich, who gently chided his old friend Shafarevich—harshly criticized the latter, particularly for having accused "the best representatives" of the Soviet literature, criticism, and music of having "voluntarily" left Russia because they "simply could not withstand pressure," and also for having asserted that persons who deprived themselves of their cultural values by emigrating would as a result be unable to contribute in the future to culture. Daniel denied that the departures from the USSR of many leading cultural figures were in any real sense voluntary. He expressed deep indignation at the implication that Sinyavski's sufferings in prison and camps were glossed over by Shafarevich. And he presented a long list of Russians, such as the Nobel Prize-winning author Ivan Bunin, who had in emigration published works now read in the homeland. (Interestingly enough, Daniel also referred in similar fashion to the philosopher Berdyaev. Of Berdyaev he wrote that, although his works were still not published, they were read in the USSR.[43]

Many leading Jewish activists, such as Roman Rutman, a friend of Larisa Bogoraz and Yuli Daniel; Bogoraz's former husband Grigori Svirski, a defender of Solzhenitsyn against press attacks; and Mikhail Zand, spoke out in support of the Democratic Movement, both before and after they emigrated to Israel.[44]

But the Jewish freedom movement differs significantly both from the general movement—or movements—for civil rights and democratization and from the dissent and resistance to Russification of many members of the Crimean Tatar, Ukrainian, and other non-Russian peoples. Unlike the "mainstream" Democratic Movement, to borrow Peter Reddaway's term, the Jewish liberationists essentially sought not to reform the Soviet system but to separate themselves from it, by emigrating to Israel or, in some cases—especially if they were not of "Zionist" persuasion—to other countries, particularly the United States. Of course the Jews were in a more fortunate position than other "nonterritorial" or "diaspora" minorities, such as the Crimean Tatars, the Germans, or even the Armenians, in that they possessed, in the state of Israel, a homeland, and also in terms of the support they received from Jewish communities in the United States and elsewhere. On the other hand, the Jews were perhaps worse off than any of the non-Russian minorities in terms of the "relative deprivation" they experienced—inflicted by a drastic change, stemming from alteration of official Soviet policy, from a relatively privileged status to one as objects of discrimination—and the long-term social trends of which that policy was, in part, a reflection (though I am not arguing that the chauvinistic policy the Kremlin chose to pursue was its only available course). As Aleksander Voronel pointed out in a perceptive 1972 analysis, Moscow's objective of lowering the representation of Jews in the Soviet intelligentsia from the 1972 pattern—in which Jews, who constituted less than one percent of the total population, made up five percent of persons with higher education and ten percent of scientific workers—down to a percentage "in line with the national composition of the population of the USSR" was "tantamount to planning the degradation of the Jewish people." He added that "whereas past restrictions hampered Jews, today's threaten the very foundations of their existence as a group," since, by threatening to deprive the Jews of the one value, education, for which they had sacrificed every other value, the new Soviet policies threatened Jews with "loss of meaning of life."

To some degree, however, other formerly "privileged" peoples, such as the Georgians and the Armenians, also experienced a deterioration in expectations as a result of increasing Russification and related trends. Voronel recognized that the plight of the Jews was not unique when he asserted that "it is precisely on this kind of search for meaning that Soviet intellectuals of all nationalities are concentrating increasingly as the rate of the development of higher education declines and social mobility slows down."[45]

The impact of deterioration in socio-economic status, both already experienced in the form of exclusion of Jews from "sensitive" posts in, for example, the military and diplomatic fields, and expected in the form of more grievous future deprivations, was not the only factor impelling Jews to seek emigration. Lack of provision of cultural facilities; the murder, during Stalin's "anti-cosmopolitan" drive, of leading Jewish intellectuals and artists, such as the famous Shakespearean actor Solomon Mikhoels; and, as perhaps the final precipitant, the "anti-Zionism," scarcely distinguishable from outright anti-Semitism, unleashed after the 1967 Arab–Israeli war all played their part. So, too, did the example set by the limited but real success of the Democratic Movement in drawing the attention of sympathetic elements of Western public opinion to restrictions imposed by the Soviet authorities on individual and group freedoms and, perhaps most important, in demonstrating that resistance was not hopelessly foolish but could achieve victories and, even in defeat, provide moral satisfaction.

In terms of relevant indicators of achievement, such as cohesiveness of organization, solidarity and mass support for its goals from the group it sought to mobilize, and, most important, response to its demands by the Soviet authorities, the Jewish emigration movement has been by far the most successful movement of dissent resistance in the history of the Soviet Union. While precise data on the scope of Jewish emigration seems to be unavailable, a total figure of about 100,000, mostly in the years 1971–1974, seems reasonably accurate.[46] However, many thousands of Soviet Jews have been refused exit visas, and probably thousands, or tens of thousands of others who wanted to leave have not applied for fear of harassment and persecution. Even the professed Leninist Roy Medvedev—who in a *samizdat* essay distributed in May 1970 argued that a return to the "Leninist nationality policy" and, more specifically, abolition of such discriminatory practices as quotas governing the admission of Jews to higher educational institutions would lead to the desirable result, in his eyes, "of accelerating assimilation, which fully corresponds to the Leninist nationality policy on this issue"—also indicated, in the same study, that two or three hundred thousand Soviet Jews wanted to emigrate.[47] Some, in fact probably the vast majority, of the leaders of the Jewish emigration movement would reject Medvedev's prescription, in accordance with Mikhail Zand's argument—which seems plausible, in view of the considerations referred to above—that assimilation on the democratic and egalitarian basis advocated by Medvedev was impossible in view of deeply rooted official and popular anti-Semitism in the USSR, and other weighty factors.[48]

If Zand's analysis is correct, Medvedev's prescription could not provide a solution to the Soviet "Jewish question," even in the long run. And in the short run, thousands of Jews would be left waiting for exit visas, or wanting to emigrate but afraid to apply. A detailed description of the tribulations and in many cases persecution that have been the lot of Jewish applicants for emigration visas would require many pages, and in any case is available in the above-cited works on Soviet Jewry (see notes 36 and 38) and in many other sources. It should be emphasized, however, that, especially in the cases of highly trained professionals, whose departure can be a serious loss to the economy, the emigrants' experiences have often been harrowing. The majority of those arrested for applying to leave, or for related activities, apparently received only fifteen-day jail sentences, but there were hundreds of such sentences.[49] It should be noted that many prominent Jewish scientists have had to wait years for visas, and of course were dismissed from their jobs immediately after declaring their intention to emigrate. In some cases—for example, that of the distinguished chemist and corresponding member of the USSR Academy of Sciences, Benjamin Levich—application for emigration was followed by reprisals against members of the applicant's family. Levich's son, Eugene, was drafted into military service, despite ill health, though he was subsequently—probably because of internal and foreign protests—released, and with his brother Alexander, given permission to emigrate in 1975. However, despite reported assurances that he would be permitted to depart in 1975, Benjamin Levich and his wife had still not been permitted to leave as of mid-February 1976. In any case, Soviet policy on emigration tightened following disavowal by the USSR on December 20, 1974, of "any understanding linking American trade concessions to freer emigration from the Soviet Union."[50]

According to one highly reliable source, as early as March 1975 visa refusals were increasing, the departure of "activist leaders" was "slow and selective," and harassment—including arrests on trumped-up charges, as in the case of Dr. Mikhail Stern, and, in one case, a threat of trial of the scientist Alexander Lunts for treason—was increasing also.[51] The further tightening of emigration controls and prosecution of some applicants throughout 1975 indicated that in the future Soviet Jews desiring to emigrate might face the Catch-22 dilemma of staying in a country where they felt unwanted and which they wanted to leave, or applying for a visa and then, after automatically being fired from their job, being prosecuted as "parasites" because they had no regular employment. Whether because of heightened anxiety over possible reprisals in the new, less favorable situation created by the disappearance of even the tacit, informal, and reluctant official acceptance of limited emigration that prevailed prior to the above-mentioned disavowal, or because of negative reports from emigrants in Israel, the United States, and elsewhere regarding the difficulties of adjusting to conditions of life abroad, or both, there was, in 1975, a sharp reduction in the number of applications by Jews for permission to emigrate.[52]

As Schroeter has observed, the future of emigration for Jews is "problematic at best" and is dependent on "many variables outside their control," including, of course, relations between the USSR and both the United States and the Arab countries.[53] Schroeter estimates that if "absolutely free" emigration were permitted, as many as two-thirds of all Soviet Jews would eventually leave, perhaps half a million by 1980.[54] Since there are probably about three million Soviet Jews, Schroeter's estimate of the long-term potential of emigration involves a very large number of people.[55]

In light of what is known about the relationship between the Soviet Jews and the Soviet regime, it seems likely that the Kremlin will either have to drastically alter its present contradictory and illogical blend of discriminatory and assimilationist policies toward Soviet Jews or ultimately face the alternatives of very large-scale emigration, on the one hand, or resort to a repression fiercer than any that it has launched since Stalin, on the other.[56]

Nationality Rights and National Resistance

There are a number of other ethnic groups, including the Crimean Tatars, the Soviet Germans, and the Meskhetians, the members of which, as Edward Allworth has noted, also "formerly enjoyed much higher standing than they do today," whose situation and response thereto, is roughly comparable to that of Soviet Jews.[57] And in terms of the long-term future prospects of the Soviet system, Moscow's success or failure in imposing upon large ethnic groups— such as the more than forty million Ukrainians (approximately three-fourths of whom reside in the Ukrainian Soviet Socialist Republic) —its goal of cultural assimilation, leading to the creation of a Russified "Soviet" people, free of "nationalism" and related "residues of the past," bulks very large indeed.[58]

The Kremlin's avowedly assimilationist, homogenizing national and cultural policy, seeking to create a "Soviet" cultural and even a "new Soviet man," is antagonistic to all national subcultures. Of course the official ideology is hostile to and contemptuous of much in the Russian tradition also. But under this policy Russians can preserve, and indeed glory in, their language—and language is the most potent instrument and symbol of national identity. Moreover, through their domination of the central integrating agency of the polity, the CPSU, Russians effectively control the political and economic life of the USSR.

Small wonder, then, that members of probably every non-Russian ethnic group have in one way or another resisted, perhaps usually only passively but in some cases openly and persistently, Moscow's centralist, Russifying policies. Among the Ukrainians, for example, there is a long tradition of resistance, manifested in intraparty conflicts in the 1920's and 1930's and in active guerrilla warfare in the early postwar years. Crushed by Stalin, Ukrainian resistance revived in the early and mid-1960's. Some concessions were made to non-Russian nationalities in the mid-1950's. But, as Bohdan Bociurkiw has noted, they stimulated "the beginnings of a new cultural renaissance in the Ukraine and some other republics"—Moscow, alarmed, resumed harsh assimilationist and centralist policies in the late 1950's and early 1960's. One response to this renewed centralizing pressure was protest, spearheaded by a group of intellectuals known as the shestydesiatnyky, or "generation of the sixties." The impact achieved by these young writers and critics has perhaps best been described by the young historian Valentyn Moroz in his essay *Amid the Snows,* written between his completion of a four-year labor camp term in 1969 and his re-arrest and conviction to fourteen more years of prison, camp, and exile in 1970. According to Moroz, "they restored *meaning* to words and concepts, and they renewed the faith of the people in the *reality* of the spiritual world. Theirs was a genuine feat: to have faith in an atmosphere of complete nihilism, and rekindle that faith in others"[59] (italics in original).

Essentially, the "faith" that Moroz had in mind was belief in the value of Ukrainian national identity, though it should be emphasized that Moroz was by no means intolerant of other cultures. His call to battle in defense of a culture that he regarded as having been badly undermined by Moscow's assimilationist policy and also by the worldwide trend toward "mass culture"—on this point, there is affinity in his views with strands in the thinking of Solzhenitsyn and Sakharov—was accompanied by evident respect for cultural diversity, combined, however, with a defense of tradition against centralist pressures. Moroz perhaps best articulated his belief in the preciousness of ethnic tradition in his "A Chronicle of Resistance," in which he praised the Hutsuls, a little-known subgroup of the Ukrainian people, for their defense of their religious tradition against administrative interference. He healed the example set by the Hutsuls for other Ukrainians, most of whom, in his opinion, lacked a sense of national self-preservation. In his essay on the Hutsuls Moroz expressed admiration for the exiled Germans in Kazakhstan and for the Armenians, Georgians, and Chechens, peoples who, he noted, had stubbornly and successfully resisted assimilation.[60]

Like most Ukrainian critics of Russification and of interference by Moscow in what they regarded as matters that, according to both the Soviet and Ukrainian constitutions, properly belonged to the jurisdiction of the Ukraine alone, Moroz "professed loyalty to Soviet constitutional and legal norms."[61] Thus, in his "A Report from the Beria Reservation," written in 1967 and smuggled out of a labor camp, Moroz cited, in justification of his statements (which the KGB, the prosecution, and the judges in his case had characterized as anti-Soviet) not only the Soviet and Ukrainian constitutions but also the Universal Declaration of Human Rights and other United Nations documents."[62]

Moroz is a strikingly brilliant writer and a fresh, original thinker. In talent, he compares well with such better known Soviet dissenters as his fellow historian Andrei Amalrik, or even with giants like Sakharov and Solzhenitsyn. But perhaps his greatest gift to the cause he espouses is the example he has set of steadfast resistance to deprivations and punishment that only a person of unsurpassed moral strength could have endured.[63]

Less endowed than Moroz with steely resolution, but enormously important for having provided Ukrainians—and the world—with valuable data and analysis on Moscow's policy in the Ukraine was the literary critic Ivan Dzyuba. Moroz himself has asserted that Dzyuba's book *Internationalism or Russification?* "opened everyone's eyes," sparking resistance to Russification, because Dzyuba became a symbol of resistance, "a god for the people."[64]

But Dzyuba, under intense public and behind-the-scenes pressure, was prone to temporize and compromise. In a 1969 statement he engaged in limited self-criticism, renouncing the "Ukrainian bourgeois nationalism" attributed to him by regime spokesmen.[65] So it is not surprising that Moroz was already reproaching Dzyuba in early 1970 for having "forgotten the thousands upon thousands of people throughout Ukraine for whom he had become a god."[66]

After the removal in May 1972 of Petro Shelest—who had headed the Ukrainian party organization since 1963 and had reportedly protected some leading dissenters against hard-line charges of "bourgeois nationalism"—and his subsequent dismissal from the CPSU Politburo, Dzyuba, a prime victim of a KGB drive aimed at eliminating dissent in the Ukraine, was forced to repudiate the views he had expressed in *Internationalism or Russification?* This was done in statements which, according to official Soviet sources, he made in November 1973—after nineteen months of interrogation—and again in the spring of 1975.[67] The value of Dzyuba's forced "recantations" to the regime, though probably considerable, was diminished by the fact that they could only be regarded as dubious under the circumstances, especially in view of the well-known fact that he was weakened by tuberculosis.

But what had Dzyuba said? Why had he been pressured to "recant"? According to Bociurkiw, his book "proved to be the most incisive analysis of the Soviet nationalities policy ever to emerge from the USSR."[68] And it is true that the wealth of telling detail and skillful, eloquent argumentation in Dzyuba's book on such topics as Moscow's economic exploitation of the Ukraine, linguistic Russification, the "sense of doom hanging over the [Ukrainian] nation, the lack of national prospects and of national growth beyond the village boundaries, the denationalizing pressure from above," and so forth, makes a powerful impression.[69]

Although Ukrainian resistance has thus far not assumed the proportions of a mass movement, to the extent that Jewish or even Crimean Tatar protest has, the number of dissenters arrested or severely harassed in the Ukraine in 1972 and 1973 alone is estimated at "as many as 250 individuals from all walks of life."[70] Clearly, Moscow considered that Ukrainian dissent might prove dangerous unless it were crushed by terror. This is evident from the very long prison and camp terms imposed on many Ukrainian dissenters—they seem substantially more severe than in the cases of leaders and activists of the Moscow Democratic Movement—and from the maniacal determination of the "psychiatrists" in the prison mental hospital to which the gifted Ukrainian mathematical biologist Leonid Plyushch was confined to either extract a recantation, by means of massive doses of drugs, of his "subversive" views, or, failing that, to kill them.[71]

The severity of recent repression in the Ukraine appears to be part of a larger pattern of fierce repression of dissent when it takes the form of criticism of official doctrine or Kremlin policy in the sensitive field of relations between non-Russians and the dominant Russian ethnic group. This extraordinary harshness is also, perhaps, a product of fear on the part of Ukrainian—and, elsewhere, of other non-Russian—police officials, prosecutors, and judges that if they do not combat "bourgeois nationalism" with impressive zeal they may be harshly penalized. Another factor, probably, is the relative ease, in localities remote from Moscow and Leningrad, of concealing from foreign news media and the diplomatic corps police operations aimed at dissenters. In Moscow, especially, dissenters have had at least some opportunity for disclosure to the international community of the regime's reprisals against their efforts to avail themselves of their constitutionally guaranteed human rights. In the provinces, the cost to the regime of suppressing dissent (in terms of danger of disclosure) is lower than in Moscow, and the cost of tolerating it is high, at least in the non-Russian republics, since the airing of criticism of the "Leninist nationality policy" constitutes a threat to one of the cornerstones of the regime's legitimacy. For, if what Moscow calls a "bourgeois nationalist" critique were fully aired, it would completely undermine the myth that the "friendship of peoples" flourishes in the Soviet Union.

While it would doubtless be correct to assign a lesser weight, in terms of direct impact on the West's image of the Soviet Union or other aspects of international politics, to Ukrainian than to Jewish protest, the former has already had international repercussions. For example, a report published in 1967 by a Canadian Communist Party delegation that had visited the Ukraine criticized "secret trials of Ukrainian writers" as involving "violations of socialist democracy and [the] denial of civil rights."[72] And the experience of John Kolasky—before his period of study at the Higher Party School of the Ukraine a deeply committed Communist—is also relevant. His sojourn in the Ukraine in 1963–65 led to his breaking with the Communist Party of Canada, and exerted influence inside the Ukraine.[73]

To round off this brief survey of links between the general struggle for human rights waged by Soviet dissenters and ethnic aspirations in the USSR, at least some mention should be made of the increasing evidence that members of more and more non-Russian nationalities are contributing to what Teresa Rakowska-Harmstone calls "the swelling tides of nationalism."[74] Thus, for example, in 1972, in Lithuania, more than 17,000 Roman Catholics signed a petition protesting against persecution of the clergy, the closing of churches, and the like, and a few weeks later, on May 18 and 19 of that year, large-scale riots, quelled only by army units brought in from outside the city, were touched off by the self-immolation of the youth Roman Kalantas.[75] Some Lithuanians—like some Jews and some Ukrainians—have also in recent years produced regular *samizdat* periodicals, presumably modeled on the Democratic Movement's *Chronicle of Current Events;* and, on a smaller scale, there have been similar activities by Latvians and Estonians.[76] In 1974, the "Estonian Democratic Movement" and the "Estonian National Front" protested in letters to United Nations Secretary-General Kurt Waldheim against arrests in Estonia and stated their intention, as reported in *Soviet Analyst,* of "continuing their struggle until the Soviet occupation of Estonia is ended and a secret referendum, under United Nations supervision, is held to determine the country's fate."[77] Even in Soviet Armenia, long considered the most contented of the constituent republics of the Soviet "federation," there have been reports in the last few years of dissent, leading to trials and sentences to labor camps."[78]

The abundant fresh evidence of recent years tends to verify the opinion expressed in 1970 by Andrei Sakharov, Roy Medvedev, and Valentine Turchin on the danger of exacerbation of nationality problems if the regime did not embark on a course of "democratization" in this field. They warned then that "in the national republics the movement for democratization, arising from below, inevitably takes on a nationalist character."[79] As we have observed, Sakharov and other leading dissenters continued with increasing urgency to sound this warning note. Of course, Andrei Amalrik had sounded the alarm even earlier.

Finally, despite the widespread persistence of traditional ethnic prejudice in the USSR, especially among the "masses," there is also much evidence that particularist traditionalism is being transcended, at least among dissenters, both Russian and non-Russian, in favor of a growing appreciation of the compatibility of universal democratic values and ethnic diversity—which bodes well for the future. If and when the present oppressive political structure is reformed or replaced, a more enlightened pattern of relations among the peoples now controlled by Moscow—whether or not they continue to be members of a single political community—may be possible.

4.

Suppression of Dissent and the Clash Regarding Soviet Foreign Relations

THE ARGUMENTS REGARDING LINKAGES between Soviet dissenters' critique of the conduct of Soviet foreign relations in the "détente" era that will now be set forth can be briefly presented; they were implicit, or were partially developed, in preceding parts of this book. In my attempt to explain why the Kremlin regards suppression of dissent at home as a necessary concomitant of "détente" abroad, I shall argue that the efforts of the Soviet leadership to associate its policies abroad with such positive and reassuring concepts as "relaxation of tensions" and "peaceful coexistence," while at the same time steadily tightening internal controls over freedom of expression, must be judged to have been instruments of a foreign policy consistent with *Stalinist* traditions, although I grant that Brezhnev's expansionism has been consistently cautious, carefully calibrated, and incremental, rather than blustering or precipitous as Stalin's or Khrushchev's sometimes was. I shall argue that:

1. Moscow's professed adherence since 1969 to a policy of "détente," or "relaxation of international tensions," has been a major instrument of a foreign policy designed to enhance the global influence of the USSR at the expense of the interests of the United States and of the "capitalist" world generally. Asserting this proposition does not necessarily amount to accusing the Kremlin of

119

deception. While, as always, Soviet policy in recent years has sought to manipulate foreign public opinion, its successes, such as they have been, probably owed at least as much to Western self-deception as to Soviet deception. CPSU policy directives and propaganda for domestic consumption, which are far more reliable indicators of the leadership's intentions than are the "confidential" assurances offered by Soviet leaders in private conversations with foreign statesmen, have only partially concealed, if indeed they have concealed at all, the continued intransigence that underlies the policies of "détente" and "peaceful coexistence"—these terms denoting a state of affairs which, as Soviet texts intended for internal consumption or for foreign Communists invariably warn, can, because of the existence of the "class struggle" which ultimately dominates political relations everywhere, apply only to "nonideological" areas such as trade. Communist parties and other ideological and political partisans are, then, free and indeed obligated to conduct a relentless political struggle against "capitalism" and "revisionism," the definition of which, at any given time, is a prerogative of the Soviet leadership. Perhaps because this doctrine seems to most "bourgeois" Westerners to be somewhat metaphysical, they find it difficult to take seriously.

While many practices associated with the conduct of Soviet foreign policy, particularly in the areas of communications and propaganda, seem peculiar and menacing in terms of the values sustaining Western democracy, this negative judgment needs some qualification. Post-Stalin foreign policy is increasingly sophisticated. It obviously draws upon fuller and more accurate information than did the policy of Stalin or even Khrushchev. Soviet policy makers tend, more than in the past, to reject a "zero-sum" approach to international conflicts. Also, they seem increasingly to at least partially exempt from a strict "class-conflict" approach such areas of international interaction as scientific exchanges, though progress in this direction has been very slow.

However, while these trends may hold promise, over the very long run, for a less stormy future in Soviet–Western relations, they are certainly as yet far from dominant. The exponents of rationality and goodwill in foreign affairs—a dissenter like Sakharov represents their point of view in its purest form—remain subordinate to party bosses who are imbued with the Leninist spirit of irreconcilable hostility to "bourgeois ideology," or who at least feel constrained to proclaim that they are—a stance that is balanced however, as the historical record (including that of the Stalin era) shows, by caution, realism, and expediency. One wonders, however, if such caution would not vanish if Moscow gained military superiority over the West.

2. The still one-sided, dominance-maximizing tendency of Soviet "détente" policy was incompatible with aspirations and values, pertaining to both domestic and foreign affairs, of the adherents of the Democratic Movement. They tended, in fact, to regard official Soviet claims regarding Kremlin foreign policy as fraudulent and dangerous to the cause of freedom throughout the world. Some of them—especially Solzhenitsyn, but also men like Maksimov, Mikhail Agurski, and others—feared that the West was being taken in by the Kremlin's talk of peace while Moscow armed more heavily than ever. They regarded it as their moral duty to expose and denounce "détente." Insofar as the Kremlin sought, despite the expansionist essence of its policies, to project an image of a new-found willingness to restructure East–West relations on lines of mutuality of interests, friendship, and cordiality, the dissenters' warnings that no fundamental change had occurred or could soon occur in Soviet attitudes or behavior, domestic or foreign, could only be regarded by the Soviet rulers as highly objectionable, as it might interpose an obstacle of perhaps substantial weight to the success of a carefully orchestrated and expensive foreign-policy operation. Hence, the Kremlin and its KGB agents felt—as indicated by their treatment of dissenters—that severe measures of repression were required in retaliation against Soviet citizens opposing such high-priority objectives.

I am not asserting that criticism of Soviet-style "détente" was a necessary condition of repression, for certainly repression has been visited upon critics for many other reasons—such as, for example, articulation of religious and/or ethnic values. But it was, apparently, a sufficient condition for severe repression; indeed, it appears that criticism of any aspect of Soviet foreign policy, or related behavior, such as persistent unauthorized association with foreign correspondents, has been regarded by the Soviet authorities as highly objectionable conduct, deserving of severe punishment.

3. It seems probable that the Soviet authorities have repressed internal dissent in the era of "détente" not only—as was argued above—because the dissenters called attention to the "fine print" of Soviet policy (which, they feared, foreigners unaccustomed to deciphering Soviet "dialectics" were bound to overlook in their gratitude over Kremlin assurances that a new era was dawning in

East–West relations) but for other reasons as well, among which the following deserves emphasis. The Politburo is aware that any substantial increase in access to information about Western life—especially about goods and services, but also, and for intellectuals, crucially, about personal freedoms and civil liberties—tends to activate latent discontent and even dissent among independent-minded Soviet citizens. The possibility of disaffection, alienation, and other negative attitudes—which Soviet ideologists characterize as "residues" or "survivals" of "capitalism" in the popular consciousness, or even as the products of CIA subversion—are still viewed with a degree of alarm in the Kremlin that casts doubt on the regime's endless assertions about the unity of government and society.

For Soviet intellectuals and professionals and for Soviet people generally—probably including many rank-and-file CPSU members as distinct from members of the ruling apparatus—"relaxation of tensions" abroad logically connotes relaxation of controls at home. They tend to welcome "détente" in principle and to regard it as the harbinger of peace and freedom and an end to struggle. More specifically, they tend to associate it with expansion of personal contacts with foreign professional colleagues, on a basis of mutuality and reciprocity. In the eyes of the still overwhelmingly dominant elements of the Soviet party and government elite, however, such an interpretation of "détente" facilitates the "penetration" of Soviet society by "bourgeois" ideas and agents. It is therefore necessary, as a prophylactic measure—or at least this is strongly indicated by tightened censorship and communication controls in recent years and by militant anti-Western propaganda—to rigorously rebuff, curtail, and indeed extirpate "subversive" foreign influences, which if not countered could bring demoralization and disintegration in their wake.

Also—and this is directly relevant to policy toward dissent and dissenters—it has obviously been considered advisable, as the strongest possible form of warning, to make examples in the courtroom of citizens who have allegedly committed "especially dangerous state crimes" because they have come under the influence of ideas emanating from abroad or, worse yet, have been bribed by foreign agents sent into the USSR.

Now unfortunately for the KGB and its Kremlin bosses, such prophylactic measures can be somewhat counterproductive. On a number of occasions in the 1960's and 1970's for example, their utilization stimulated resistance and indeed led to effective, and from the Politburo's viewpoint highly embarrassing, protest activities, such as the founding of the *Chronicle of Current Events* and Pavel Litvinov's appeals to "world public opinion." But—and this was one of several significant indications of the Soviet rulers' intolerance of dissent—the leadership displayed its willingness to pay the price of tarnishing the Soviet image abroad that was involved in crushing the Democratic Movement.

4. The persistence in the USSR of a cyclical, or vicious-circle, pattern of repression–relaxation–dissent, followed by renewed repression, reminds us of how difficult it is for "hegemonic" regimes, in their handling of dissent and opposition, to escape or refute the "self-fulfilling prophecy" formulated by Robert Dahl:

> *Since all opposition is potentially dangerous, no distinction can be made between acceptable and unacceptable opposition, between loyal and disloyal opposition...Yet if all oppositions are treated as...subject to repression, opposition that would be loyal if it were tolerated becomes disloyal because it is not tolerated. Since all opposition is likely to be disloyal, all opposition must be repressed.*[1]

It should be kept in mind, however, that repression of dissent in the contemporary USSR, while draconian by Western democratic standards, is very mild in comparison with Stalin's practices. But despite the substantial reduction after Stalin's death in the use of terror as an instrument of political control, it seems prudent to assume that little further progress in this direction is possible without significant alterations in the ethos and structure that sustain the Soviet system. No other conclusion seems possible if the past performance of the regime is any guide to the future. Thus far, periods of relative tolerance of dissent and of the voicing of moderate "within-system" reformist aspirations, which occurred in the 1920's and in the Khrushchev era, to some degree in the twilight period after the end of the war of 1941–45, and again briefly for some six months after Khrushchev's fall, have been succeeded by rededication to ideological fundamentalism, and tightened police controls.

5. The foregoing statements essentially boil down to the argument that the conduct of the Soviet "détente" policy of recent years is logically associated with domestic repression. It is difficult to escape, also, the conclusion that central features of the Soviet system, in particular its reliance for legitimacy largely (though not exclusively) upon the official creed of "Leninism" and the power monopoly of the highly centralized CPSU, strongly impel and indeed almost certainly force the Soviet authorities to create an atmosphere of hos-

tile "vigilance" toward the "bourgeois" world. Since the Soviet leadership dares not dispense with a Manichean myth system that offers perhaps the only or at least the most convincing available explanation and justification of the enormous past sufferings and continued relative deprivation experienced by the Soviet people, Moscow feels constrained to continue to disseminate the official creed with all the force, vigor, and audience saturation capabilities made possible by monopoly control over the mass media of communication.

"Marxism–Leninism" justifies past deprivations and present frustrations by providing an arsenal of arguments that plausibly blame all difficulties on the "imperialists." It also diverts the attention of the Soviet "masses" from the unequal distribution of power and wealth in the USSR to which Sakharov and other dissenters have pointed— though of course their critique has been largely prevented by the official control mechanism from reaching the Soviet public, except for the considerable extent to which Soviet citizens have been able to clandestinely learn of it by listening to foreign radio broadcasts.

In arguing that the oppressive nature of the Soviet dictatorship, and in particular the legitimizing role of Marxism–Leninism in Soviet political life, generates hostility toward the outside world, I am not necessarily asserting that this factor must cause the Soviet rulers to pursue an aggressive, let alone a reckless, policy. On the contrary, the tight control over foreign policy exercised by the experts in the uses of power who govern the USSR is probably, on balance, conducive to caution and prudence in foreign affairs. It seems sensible to assume, however, that rulers who so vigilantly restrict the freedoms of their own people could be expected, given the opportunity, to be restrictive, coercive, and punitive in their treatment of foreign peoples who might come under their control, particularly of individuals and groups whose "bourgeois" social status or ideological preference would, by "Leninist" definition, render them suspect. The regime's habit of labeling dissenters who have persisted in telling the truth as they saw it as agents of foreign intelligence services may be seen as a kind of political Geiger counter, warning of potential dangers to the non-Soviet world inherent in the "hegemonic" Soviet system.

In connection with the foregoing, it might not be unwarranted to assert that an important difference between the foreign-policy outlook of Soviet-type regimes and that appropriate to polyarchies is that the elements that shape policy in polyarchies believe, to a degree probably decisive in the long run, that extension of their system abroad, while desirable, can occur only if the majority of the politically relevant elements in a given country can be persuaded to urgently desire and work for democratization. By contrast, Leninist regimes are committed to a doctrine that regards as not only desirable but inevitable the forcible transformation of all societies not yet revolutionized by organized, militant revolutionary minorities. Recent events in Cambodia, while perhaps somewhat shocking even to the present Soviet leaders, may represent an interesting if extreme example of this political philosophy in action.

In the following sections, evidence will be presented in support of the above assertions. Unfortunately, given the present state of knowledge regarding Soviet foreign policy, particularly in regard to such fields as cultural exchanges, foreign propaganda, and international political communication generally, a full, systematic examination of the arguments I have laid out is not feasible. For one thing, the detailed quantitative analyses (of trends in the volume, settings, and outcomes of face-to-face encounters between Americans and Soviet citizens and of other, related processes) that would be needed for a full and systematic analysis of the nature of Soviet–American interaction, especially at the nongovernmental level, are obviously not available.[2]

Also, it is difficult to relate Soviet acts of repression against dissenters directly and obviously to dissenters' criticism of Soviet foreign policy, since, as has been made clear already, dissenters have usually criticized both Soviet domestic and foreign policy. How, then, does one determine, for example, what weight the Soviet authorities assigned, in deciding to bring criminal charges against Sinyavski, Amalrik, or Bukovski, to foreign-policy considerations as against domestic ones? An even more fundamental and difficult problem is posed by the question of the typicality of treatment of well-known dissenters, since we are vastly ignorant regarding absolutely basic matters such as the scope of the total universe of individuals who have been repressed and the breakdown within this universe among various categories of charges brought and sanctions imposed.

Now of course—although this is not immediately relevant—it is perhaps worth noting that the Soviet secrecy that ensures our ignorance about such matters also arouses our suspicion. But in spite of the many difficulties generated by Soviet secrecy, censorship, and reluctance to admit that there is legitimate dissent in the USSR or that criticism of foreign policy—or domestic policy either—is punished, there is a good deal of evidence to support the propositions contained in the above-listed statements, especially in respect to the Janus-like concept "peaceful coexistence" and its subordinate slogan, "relaxation of international tensions"; on these, an abundance of reliable documentation is available.[3]

Before examining some of this evidence, I should like to make a general point, which perhaps constitutes the strongest general argument in support of my overall thesis that in the Soviet system as it is presently constituted, there cannot be any significant toleration of dissent, and that this intolerance is a powerful indicator of the limited, one-sided character of "détente" as practiced by the Kremlin. This point is, quite simply, that it is in my judgment extremely difficult—indeed, I am tempted to assert, impossible—to find evidence that casts much doubt on, let along falsifies, the assertions I have made.

Examination of Evidence

"DÉTENTE" AND "COEXISTENCE"

The present Soviet policy and propaganda of "détente"—as distinguished from, for example, "Khrushchev's deténte strategy"—can be traced to the June 1969 International Conference of Communist and Workers' Parties, at which Leonid Brezhnev set forth a program —endorsed by the overwhelming majority of the eighty-odd delegations assembled—to, among other objectives, "intensify the struggle against capitalism and imperialism on a global scale," while simultaneously "conducting a 'struggle for peace.'"[4] In fact, the terms "relaxation of tension" (in Russian, razryadka napryazhennosti, or often simply razryadka) and, more especially, "peaceful coexistence" (mirnoe sosushchestovavanie), or variants such as Lenin's expression "peaceful cohabitation" (mirnoe sozhitelstvo), denote formulas almost as old as the Soviet regime. But to trace the uses of these terms and the strategies denoted by them, even in recent years, would vastly exceed the scope of this book.[5]

One clue to the Kremlin's expectations in pursuing "deténte" is, it seems to me, provided by the fact that, on the basis of authoritative official statements, "détente" appears to be considered as an instrument of or a desired result of "peaceful coexistence" and, in any case, as distinctly subordinate to the latter. Thus Brezhnev, in his already mentioned 1969 speech, after first asserting that "peaceful coexistence" did not apply to the "struggle between ideologies," pointed out that it did open possibilities for "regulation" of international problems and for achieving other objectives, including "mutually beneficial" economic, scientific/technical, and cultural relations and also "relaxation of international tension." He also argued that for the USSR "peaceful coexistence" was not merely "a temporary tactic, but an important principle of a consistent peace-loving socialist foreign policy"—thus asserting a claim about the most recent phase of "coexistence," namely, its long-term character, that many Western analysts have tended to accept as valid, though of course few informed Western experts would take at face value the other assertions contained in his statement.[6] The principle of "peaceful coexistence of states with different social systems" was reaffirmed millions of times, it seems, though with various nuances, after 1969 and especially after proclamation at the Twenty-fourth CPSU Congress in the spring of 1971 of the Soviet "peace program" for the world. This was followed, among other things, by the stridently anti-Western October 1973 World Peace Congress. During the years after 1969 there was a perceptible, if at times erratic, trend in the daily press and especially in more scholarly publications such as *SShA (USA)*, the magazine of Georgi Arbatov's USA Institute, toward expression of wary hopefulness about the actual and potential payoffs for the USSR of the policies of "relaxation" and "coexistence."

Evidence of a trend toward optimism, still tempered by mistrust, in Soviet evaluation of the events in the international arena and especially in Soviet–American relations becomes available to one who compares the speeches of Politburo members and alternate members, during, respectively, the June 1970 and June 1974 Supreme Soviet election campaigns. In the 1970 speeches, there was very little indication that the majority of those full and alternate Politburo members who addressed themselves to Soviet–American relations thought that there was any likelihood of early improvement. Brezhnev, to be sure, alluded to the possibility of improving relations, but demanded that the United States take the initiative by engaging in actions that would prove it was interested in "relaxing international tensions." And Brezhnev was more outwardly hopeful than his colleagues, several of whom, especially Mikhail Suslov and Alexander Shelepin, expressed bluntly anti-American views.

In 1974, in contrast, virtually all Politburo members agreed that the international atmosphere had greatly improved. Even the gloomy Kosygin expressed satisfaction that the U.S. and the USSR had "committed themselves to building their relations on the basis of the principles of peaceful coexistence."[7] Brezhnev expressed considerable enthusiasm about the ongoing achievements of the Soviet policy of "peaceful coexistence"; this is apparent in the published text of his long speech, in which, among other things, he perceived a strengthening of "the foundations of peace and security, [and] the waning of the threat of nuclear war." He attributed this and other desirable improvements to "the influence on the course of events of world socialism, its achievements, its power, its example."[8] However, Brezhnev, and to a much greater degree most of his colleagues, in particular Defense Minister Marshal Grechko and also Suslov and Shelepin, expressed reservations about the stability of the new state of affairs. Grechko even warned that "the most reactionary imperialist circles" were conducting "frenzied attacks" on the process of "relaxation of tensions," and that "the danger of war" remained "a grim reality of our times." He thus expressed the deep reservations of the Soviet military generally about prospects for Soviet–American peace.[9]

It is noteworthy, however, that while in 1970 only the Belorussian Kirill Mazurov and the Latvian Arvids Pelshe raised the issue of Western "ideological subversion" against the USSR, in 1974, Brezhnev and Podgorny touched on this issue briefly, and Mazurov and KGB chief Yuri Andropov adverted explicitly and sharply to this subject. Mazurov asserted that the forces of imperialism were attempting to undermine the Soviet people's faith in "Communist ideals"; he affirmed confidence, however, that this fell purpose would never be fulfilled.[10] Andropov, who in the following year was to speak out even more sharply against the West, charged that "imperialists" sought to take advantage of the developing relaxation of tensions to intervene in the internal affairs of the USSR, and that they were forced "to extol all kinds of traitors and renegades"— presumably an oblique reference to dissenters.[11] Probably all four were concerned, at least to some degree, about foreign support for dissenters and would-be emigrants.[12]

Indicative of the caution and circumspection characteristic of Soviet foreign-policy statements despite Kremlin hostility to the "capitalist" world is the fact that although a number of speakers, both in 1970 and in 1974, exuded satisfaction about "the general crisis of capitalism" and "the world revolutionary process," in 1970 only Suslov, and in 1974 Suslov together with Boris Ponomarev, Alexander Shelepin, and Peter Demichev expressed cautious optimism about prospects for revolution in the West, and appeared to advocate revolutions in "capitalist" states.[18]

Language affirming the principle of "peaceful coexistence" was included in the Declaration of Principles supposedly to govern relationships between the United States and the Soviet Union, dated May 29, 1972, and in the Joint Statement issued by Prime Minister Harold Wilson of Britain and First Secretary Brezhnev on February 17, 1975. Both of these documents promise that the respective parties will seek mutually beneficial cooperation (British–Soviet statement), mutual advantage (American–Soviet statement), and the like.

But while there is much to be said in favor of public pledges of adherence to such irreproachable objectives, it is unfortunately the case that in numerous Soviet statements intended for the politically literate Soviet public one finds explanations of the "coexistence" concept that definitely do not associate it with mutuality and cooperation. For example, as Foy Kohler pointed out in his previously mentioned testimony to the House Foreign Affairs Committee, Brezhnev at a Kremlin banquet for Fidel Castro shortly after Richard Nixon's departure from his Moscow meeting with him in 1972, reaffirmed the orthodox Soviet view that coexistence was not in any way incompatible with continued and even intensified "antagonism between the two social systems."[14] In 1974, the entry on "peaceful coexistence" in a volume of the *Large Soviet Encyclopedia* defined it as "a form of the class struggle between socialism and capitalism in the international arena"; and in February 1975 a leading Soviet ideologist credited "coexistence" with having made possible "the overthrow of the fascist regimes in Portugal and Greece" and other recent events.[15]

I believe that the evidence presented above is representative of the ambiguous, contradictory, and on occasion deceptive usage in Soviet propaganda and diplomacy of the terminology of "relaxation" and "coexistence." But of course vastly more such evidence is available in Russian sources, as any moderately attentive reader of *Pravda*, *Izvestiya*, and other Soviet newspapers or even of the scholarly journal *SShA (USA)* will be aware. While there are interesting nuances in this material, and evidences of differences of opinion regarding the wisdom, in terms of CPSU interests, of Brezhnev's "détente" policy can certainly be gleaned from it, its essential content remains "monolithic" in comparison with the sharp, variegated debate on the same subject in the United States. There seemed to be a solid consensus in Soviet discussions of "relaxation" and "coexistence" that whatever promoted the interests of "socialism" must by definition be good for the peoples of the world—and critics of the Kremlin's prescriptions were, by the same token, necessarily "professional anti-Communists," "reactionaries," and even "warmongers."

To an unsurprising yet striking degree, official Soviet doctrine about what is called "détente" in the West has continued to assume that it is the sacred duty of Communists—that is, of the Moscow-oriented variety and not including those under Peking's control or influence, who are not considered to be true Communists—to propagate the faith globally, but that any corresponding Western effort to influence political or ideological perspectives in the "socialist commonwealth" constitutes "ideological subversion." To be sure, the prospect of an adversary relationship tempered by cost-benefits calculation is less frightening, in an era of superweapons, than the nightmare vision of inevitable East–West military conflict which it appears to have displaced. But the new, qualified adversary relationship still bore a sufficient resemblance to the unlamented "cold war" pattern which it had, according to official Soviet dictum and in the opinion of many in the West, supplanted to leave in many minds a sense of perplexity and uneasiness. Continued Soviet ideological intransigence and regime-fostered xenophobia, manifested, for example, in warnings about the dangers inherent in all but prescribed—and circumscribed—contracts between Soviet citizens and foreigners, undoubtedly contributed to this puzzlement and unease.

THE SOVIET AUTHORITIES, "IDEOLOGICAL SUBVERSION," AND DISSENT

Perhaps the most potent single source of the CPSU's power and authority is its control over political socialization, communication, and public information. And "peaceful coexistence," for all its merits as an instrument for gaining goodwill abroad and lulling "bourgeois" suspicions of the USSR, is potentially dangerous to the morale and perhaps the legitimacy of the system that has relied heavily, in mobilizing political support and compliance, on fear of external enemies. Hence it is not surprising that despite "détente" no significant relaxation has occurred in control over such sensitive, potentially destabilizing activities as foreign travel, contacts between Soviet citizens and foreigners, and access to information originating abroad.

To be sure, in 1975 and 1976, some American scholars, who had previously been denied admission to the USSR, were granted visas. Surprisingly, at least one Western scholar was permitted contact with surviving relatives of the late Nikolai Bukharin, once, next to Leon Trotski, the most bitterly denounced "enemy" of the Soviet people. Minor concessions such as this were doubtless intended to demonstrate Kremlin sincerity in accepting the pledges contained in the Final Act of the Helsinki Conference on Security and Cooperation in Europe to facilitate travel "for personal and professional reasons" and to "respect human rights and fundamental freedoms, including the freedom of thought, conscience, religion or belief."[16]

It appears that Moscow interpreted Helsinki as giving the green light for expansion of exchanges of persons with the West, especially in science and technology, and for increased access by Soviet specialists to Western industrial know-how—or, as one of this writer's scientist friends put it, for "industrial espionage." But at the same time, a series of major Soviet statements and actions in the months after Helsinki furnished impressive evidence of the Soviet leadership's determination to interpret the human rights aspects of the Final Act in the narrowest and most limited fashion possible. A particularly striking example, of course, was the refusal of the Soviet authorities, announced on November 12, 1975, to permit the physicist Andrei Sakharov to travel to Oslo to receive in person the Nobel Peace Prize awarded to him in October. This action followed a series of press attacks on Sakharov even more abusive than those unleashed against him in 1973, including a statement by seventy-two members of the USSR Academy of Sciences accusing him of seeking to "undermine peace." Incidentally, while the exploitation of the names of noted Soviet scientists for such purposes inspires sadness, it is encouraging to note that the managers of this enterprise succeeded in pressuring less than a third of the Academy's membership into lending their names thereto.

The vengeful, despotic Kremlin spirit that had earlier deprived Boris Pasternak and Alexander Solzhenitsyn of the opportunity to receive in person their Nobel prizes also prevented Andrei Sakharov from traveling to Oslo for the presentation of his Nobel Peace Prize on December 10, 1975. His wife, still in Western Europe after treatment for an eye ailment—long delayed because of slowness in granting her the necessary exit visa—read the scientist's acceptance statement. Permission to make the round trip was, however, a major concession.

The dominant theme of the low-key but forceful message was the indispensability of success in the struggle for human rights everywhere if there were to be peace, "true détente," and "genuine disarmament." Sakharov characterized the struggle for a general political amnesty, for which he appealed, as "the struggle for the future of mankind." He asserted that men must act on behalf of political and civil rights and against illegal and arbitrary actions if they are to keep their self-respect. He praised the Nobel Committee for its intellectual courage in awarding the Peace Prize to one whose ideas did "not coincide with the concepts of the leadership of a big and powerful state."

Perhaps the heart of his address was to found in the following words:

> But what made me particularly happy was to see that the committee's decision stressed the link between defense of peace and defense of human rights, emphasizing that the defense of human rights guarantees a solid ground for genuine long-term international cooperation. Not only did you thus explain the meaning of my activity, but you also granted it powerful support.[17]

As far as those Soviet citizens to whom the authorities—by a process that remains shrouded in mystery—granted the coveted opportunity to go abroad (for study, research, sports competition, or artistic performance) were concerned, their mission continued to be the promotion of Soviet state interest. In addition to holding their own as professionals, thus generating prestige for Soviet "socialist" culture, Soviet exchangees must take care not to be seduced by a "bourgeois" civilization which their rulers obviously still credit with a dangerous attractiveness for some Soviet intellectuals. And Soviet participants in the area of cultural diplomacy, especially in fields in which the USSR lags behind "capitalist" countries, are also expected, while doing their best to generate good will and radiate influence, to import foreign know-how. Perhaps such expectations are, to a degree, common to all participants in international cultural transactions, or at least to their governments, but the tendency to demand much and offer little in return seems to be inordinately strong in the Soviet case.

Naturally, the functions performed, and the audiences to which messages are directed, vary with the categories, occupational and professional, to which members of Soviet "delegations" sent to perform abroad belong. Thus athletes project, to mass audiences, an aura of physical health, vitality, and power; ballet companies and symphony orchestras engage in high artistic culture, probably appealing in the main to middle-class audiences; while technical specialists, engineers, and scientists are expected to demonstrate Soviet achievements in their fields. But in every case, though probably with lower priority in science and technology than in sports and the arts, the representatives of Soviet "socialism," especially in their performances for and contacts with "bourgeois" publics, are assigned the role of demonstrating the achievements and advantages of the Soviet way of life.

The main function of scientists, engineers, and members of other technical professions involved in exchanges is to acquire information and skills needed by the Soviet economy and its military–industrial complex. This is indicated, among other things, by the fact that scientists and engineers constitute, as they have for years, the overwhelming majority of members of the contingents in academic and educational exchanges sent to the United States since regular exchanges began in 1958 under an official U.S.–USSR agreement. In contrast, a large majority of the Americans who have studied in the USSR since regular exchanges began have been specialists in the humanities and the social sciences.

It is also important to keep in mind the fact that, while tens of thousands of Americans and West Europeans journey to Russia every year, tourism for Soviet citizens, at least in the United States, is on such an infinitesimal scale that, relatively speaking, it hardly exists at all.

The effort of the Soviet regime to turn cultural, scientific, and other exchanges to political advantage is of course not confined to the uses made of Soviet citizens for this purpose. Everything possible is also done to "use" foreign participants as well, beginning with the economic benefits to the Soviet treasury of much-needed "hard" foreign currencies and proceeding through all of the range of propaganda, information-acquisition, and other potential payoffs involved. At the same time, through guided-tour techniques, restrictions on foreigners' access to "sensitive" information, and the myriad other well-known Soviet devices for "damage control" in this field, which were developed over the centuries by tsarist Russian rulers and have been perfected by their Communist successors, the threat of "subversion" of Soviet citizens by foreign visitors is contained.

It is obvious that if—as I think is the case—I have grasped the essence of Soviet "exchanges" policy, this is a policy which, to say the least, is asymmetrical in motivation and execution. Fortunately, its richly asymmetrical intentions are not fully matched by the capabilities at the disposal of the planners in Moscow. Many, perhaps the majority, of the Soviet intellectuals, professionals, and performers who are regarded, in effect, by the party and government bureaucrats who administer Soviet exchange programs as instruments and agents, resent being so treated. A few exceptionally independent ones, such as Zhores Medvedev or Victor Nekrasov, have had the courage to express the indignation generated by humiliating selection procedures, which often give priority, in the choice of exchange participants, to conformist mediocrities over talented but annoyingly independent men and women and, even after they have been finely screened, often subject those finally sent abroad to vigilant surveillance—by party "nannies" and KGB "goons" who, in various guises, accompany Soviet delegations; by requiring frequent reports to Soviet embassies from Soviet citizens abroad, etc. And, it should be kept in mind, Soviet exchangees, at least in the United States, are seldom accompanied by spouses or children; this may well be one safeguard against danger of defection.

It might be a serious exaggeration to conclude from the evidence offered in Zhores Medvedev's book, referred to earlier, or from our knowledge of the elaborate surveillance techniques applied to Soviet visitors, that most Soviet applicants for or participants in exchanges are disaffected or alienated from the Soviet system. On the basis of data gathered from American veterans of Soviet–American exchanges and from conversations with responsible American government officials, I would judge that most Soviet citizens who come into contact with foreigners are passive conformists, loyal to their country, who identify with "socialism" but are often critical of much in Soviet domestic and foreign policy, in particular insofar as it affects the professional values and interests of their occupational group. Moreover, they often display, to foreigners who gain their confidence—and this is surprisingly easy, at least for highly qualified Western professional colleagues—clear evidence of political apathy, and even of downright disgust with CPSU propaganda. As one highly competent American scientist, whose judgment I respect deeply and who has had years of successful and rewarding experience in collaborating with Soviet colleagues, said to me recently, there is an "utter contrast" between Soviet "public opinion" as it is represented in the Soviet press and the "real opinions" of his Soviet friends and colleagues. According to this source, the "reality" he knows is that perceived by working scientists who try to make the best of a bad situation. Much that this American scientist reports about the opinions of his Soviet colleagues tallies with statements made by some Soviet dissenters, such as Zhores Medvedev or Alexander Solzhenitsyn, about the plight of Soviet scientists and other members of the intelligentsia, and how they cope with their problems. My source reported that his friends, by listening to foreign radio broadcasts and otherwise escaping dependence on official news sources, were able to piece together a surprisingly accurate picture of the flow of world events. Such "working scientists" apparently coalesce into small groups of mutually trusting colleagues who more or less freely, but guardedly, exchange and pool information and even exchange opinions. When repression becomes severe, however—and in this connection he cited the situation in Czechoslovakia after the Soviet invasion—the authorities attempt to drive wedges among the members of such groups. Much of this, incidentally, reminds one of accounts of their experiences in Russia by such former Soviet citizens as, for example, Lev Navrozov.

Also of great interest in the account by the American scientist to whom I refer was his statement that men like Sakharov and Solzhenitsyn were "symptoms" of the "reality" he perceived but not the reality itself. By this he meant that the scientists he knew would, among other things, "obey orders" when asked to make statements, for public dissemination, in support of the party position on this or that issue, even when they did not believe in the veracity of those statements.

The foregoing illustrates what are undoubtedly widespread attitudes among members of the Soviet intelligentsia. Such attitudes arouse uneasiness in the ranks of party leaders and cadres. To put matters plainly, the party leadership does not trust its own rank and file, and it apparently feels particularly uneasy about the state of mind of Soviet intellectuals, especially if they are not CPSU members and hence are not subject to party discipline, and in particular about their potential susceptibility to "bourgeois" influence. At least that seems to be the conclusion which it is logical to draw on the basis of the warnings constantly issued by party and police spokesmen about the alleged subversive activities inside the USSR on the part of foreign intelligence services and former Soviet citizens abroad.

It is instructive to examine, for example, the book entitled *The Secret Front* by Semen Kuzmich Tsvigun, since December 1967 First Deputy Minister of State Security and, judging by the scant biographical information available, a long-time political associate of Brezhnev.[18] Tsvigun's book presumably was written to foster suspicion on the part of Soviet citizens of foreign visitors to the Soviet Union and to instill fear of the disastrous consequences that could befall Soviet citizens who established unauthorized relationships with foreigners, as well as to alert Soviet citizens who might be sent on foreign missions to the dangers lurking in the "capitalist" environment. It may also be regarded as propaganda justification for increased Soviet espionage and counterespionage activity, and for harassment or prosecution of Soviet citizens whom the Soviet authorities chose to categorize as dupes, or willing accomplices, of "imperialism." Certainly any Soviet reader who took its contents at face value would be forcefully reminded of the fragility of "détente" as perceived by the KGB, and would presumably act in accordance with the warning conveyed by the reminder.

Tsvigun's overall thesis—fully consistent with the post-1969 Kremlin line on "détente" that was analyzed earlier—was that Soviet power and policy had put the "imperialists" on the defensive, forcing them to accept "a relaxation of international tension." Since the "imperialists" were no longer strong enough to resort to all-out military attack on Soviet Russia, they were increasingly turning to a strategy of political and ideological subversion.[19]

Tsvigun painted a lurid picture of the activities of American centers for research on the USSR and Eastern Europe, especially those associated with Columbia and Harvard universities, and, of course, of American intelligence agencies and agencies producing radio programs broadcast to the USSR. To all of these academic and governmental agencies Tsvigun attributed the intention of subverting and disintegrating the Soviet system.[20] Tsvigun also accused Western journalists in the USSR of engaging in subversive and near-subversive activities. One of his targets was the well-known former American correspondent in Moscow, Anatole Shub.[21]

Tsvigun asserts that all of the subversive efforts of the foreign enemies of the Soviet Union are doomed to failure because of the lack of any social basis for counterrevolution inside the USSR, but he warns that foreign intelligence services have in some cases been successful in recruiting for their fell purposes "renegades," "traitors," and "dissenters."[22] He accused foreign governments, along with the emigrant organization NTS (Natsionalno-trudovoi soyuz; in English, National-Labor Alliance), Radio Free Europe, and Radio Liberty, of using diplomats, scholars, scientists, businessmen, tourists, and students—especially members of religious groups—for the purpose of establishing links with Soviet citizens morally weak enough or naive enough to become their tools.[23]

At the end of his nearly four hundred pages of dire warnings about the dangers posed by "bourgeois" ideological espionage and sabotage, Tsvigun did, be it noted, strike one faintly positive note. Having thoroughly terrified his readers, he told them that, while vigilance must be intensified, "this must not be done in such a way as to generate an atmosphere of suspicion and mistrust.[24]

In concluding our discussion of Tsvigun's tale of horrors, it is worth pointing out that whatever doubt there might have been in anyone's mind as to its authoritativeness and conformity to contemporary Soviet doctrine on international affairs should be laid to rest by noting its full congruence with the line taken by Tsvigun's superior, Yuri Andropov, in his very important 1975 speech, referred to near the beginning of Chapter 1.

Although outbursts such as Tsvigun's seem almost ludicrous—so shrill is their language, so slender and unconvincing the evidence they present in support of their charges against the "imperialists" —they must nevertheless be taken seriously. They reflect the Soviet rulers' deep determination to do everything in their power to exclude dissonant information from their vast realm. It is highly probable that the frightening, minatory message they convey is convincing to many Soviet citizens. It is apparent that most citizens heed it. Also, the linkage that the Andropovs and Tsviguns seek to establish between "kowtowing to the West" and criminal subversion fits well into a pattern of prosecution of dissenters (provided they are not simply declared insane) wherein one finds KGB, prosecutor, judge, and if selective publicity is deemed expedient, the media asserting in unison the identity of propagation of "bourgeois" ideas, dissent, and criminal "anti-Soviet agitation."[25]

One purpose of Soviet propaganda on the dangers of subversive "bourgeois" influence is probably to instill the belief and arouse the fear, that nonconformist behavior, such as the authorship or dissemination of *samizdat* materials, is a result of Soviet citizens having been seduced by foreign agents, or by having read or heard exogenous communications. Why else would a KGB general have written in 1969 that "lately all kinds of literature with harmful contents have been circulating in manuscript form. Advice on this activity comes from abroad. This so-called *samizdat* is composed at the direct instigation of Western intelligence and is actively supported by it."[26]

In light of what has already been said about official attitudes toward the dangers involved in contacts between Soviet citizens and "subversive" foreigners, it is not surprising to find that dissenters are often portrayed (as were Ginzburg and Galanskov for example) as victims or agents—or both—of foreigners, who have supposedly led them, by gifts of subversive literature and money, to stray from the path of Communist virtue.[27] Of course, those who are judged to have succumbed to foreign wiles are also often depicted as weak and venal characters.

Heavy play was made by the prosecution in the Sinyavski-Daniel case of the fact that the works of the accused were sent abroad for publication—though this is not, under Soviet law, in itself a crime. In the course of playing up the sensation produced by publication of their works in the West, the prosecution insinuated that the pair had expected to reap handsome profits in return for "slandering" the Soviet way of life.[28]

In a slightly different vein, the indictments of Vladimir Bukovski at his 1967 and 1972 trials charged, respectively, that he had been in touch with "representatives of the NTS" and that he had been interviewed by a CBS television correspondent and, furthermore, had at Valeri Chalidze's residence met the Belgian Hugo Sebreghts and there given Sebreghts a copy of the *Chronicle of Current Events.* (In fact, Sebreghts was not present at this second trial, having been expelled from the Soviet Union, and Bukovski denied the accusation.)[29]

The evidence available on the relationship between criticism of Soviet foreign policy by dissenters and sanctions instituted against them, including that afforded by face-to-face and other communications with foreigners involved in this protest–repression pattern is somewhat inconclusive. However, on the basis of the available evidence it seems clear that any Soviet citizen who engages in such criticism runs a high risk of suffering more or less severe deprivation, especially if he coordinates his activity with others, expresses his views in language the authorities regard as contumacious, or persists in protesting after being warned by the KGB. The probability of relatively severe sanctions, such as arrest and prosecution or commitment to a mental institution, apparently varies inversely with the international reputation, status, and prestige of the particular dissenter. This latter hypothesis presents us with something of a paradox, for a high-status, internationally prestigious dissenter presumably can damage Moscow's image abroad more than one of humbler rank; hence the regime must, logically, wish to punish him more severely than his lower-status fellows. Nevertheless, the relatively high cost, both at home and abroad, of severely punishing outstanding and well-known scientists, for example, seems to act as a significant countervailing factor.

The foregoing reflections are based, in part, on the fact that of the fifteen original founding members of the Action Group for the Defense of Human Rights who signed that group's series of appeals to the United Nations Commission on Human Rights, fourteen had by mid-1973 either been sentenced to labor camps, committed to special psychiatric hospitals, or subjected to severe harassment. Perhaps the most horrifying punishment inflicted on any of the fifteen, incidentally, was the subjection, for years, of the brilliant, idealistic young mathematician Leonid Plyushch to misapplication of drugs, in what has been described as an effort "to find a chemical means of annihilating independent thought and unsanctioned ideas."[30]

It should be noted that some of the original members of the Action Group who for a rather long period had escaped arrest were in the end subjected to that punishment. Take, for example, the historian Peter Yakir and the biologist Sergei Kovalev. The latter, who joined the Soviet chapter of Amnesty International when it was established in September 1974, was arrested in December of that year and taken to Lithuania, apparently in keeping with the charge that he was involved in distributing the *samizdat Chronicle of the Lithuanian Catholic Church*. However, as Andrei Sakharov suggested in a statement protesting the arrest, the real basis for Kovalev's punishment was "revenge for courage and honesty"—and very likely his earlier participation in the Action Group and his helping to found the Amnesty International chapter contributed to the regime's decision to arrest him. It is worth recalling, that, as has been mentioned earlier, beginning in the spring of 1975 and culminating in the winter of 1975–76, there was a campaign of harassments and arrests directed against the eleven persons who founded the USSR Amnesty International Group, including Andrei Tverdokhlebov, who in early 1976 was awaiting trial, Valentine Turchin, Vladimir Albrekht, and others.[31]

Returning to the fate of the Action Group's members and more precisely to that of its nonmember supporters, objectivity requires noting that, to my knowledge, most of the fifty-odd signatories of appeals to the United Nations disseminated by the Action Group but signed on an individual basis, rather than in the capacity of membership therein, had, at least as of early 1976, not suffered repression that could clearly be connected with those appeals (some had been harassed, dismissed from their jobs, etc., apparently for other actions). A notable exception, however, was a group of Kharkov engineers, all eight of whom were arrested, tried, and sentenced to camps or otherwise severely penalized.[32]

It is perhaps even more difficult to precisely document the correlation between repression of dissenters and direct personal communication with foreigners, such as the unauthorized interviews given by some of them to foreign correspondents. However, the general pattern, which can include such stages as vigilant surveillance, attempted intimidation, and in some cases, judicial repression—such as befell Amalrik, Bukovski, and Yakir after their 1970 interview with CBS newsman William Cole—is similar.

The case against Amalrik at his trial in November 1970 was based —judging from the indictment against him and the prosecution's statements—partly on his having given "slanderous" interviews to foreign correspondents, including, obviously, Cole of CBS and James Clarity of the *New York Times*, though neither was mentioned by name.[33] A sign of the regime's determination to conceal persecution of dissenters from Western opinion may be gleaned from the fact that the trial of Amalrik and his co-defendant Lev Ubozhko was not held in Moscow, where Amalrik had made his "subversive" statements, but in faraway Sverdlovsk to which no foreign journalists were permitted access.

Relevant also is the justification of police surveillance and investigation preceding Amalrik's exile to Siberia for "parasitism" in 1965, as well as the charge against him at his trial in that year, by reference to his contacts with foreigners.[34]

I have already mentioned the part played by acquaintance with foreigners in the harassment and prosecution of Vladimir Bukovski, leading to the extremely severe sentence imposed on him in January 1972. Yakir, for his part, had for years associated freely with foreign newsmen. For years, also, prior to his 1972 arrest, the apparently illegally long period during which the KGB interrogated him and his codefendant Victor Krasin in Moscow prisons, and the pair's still mysterious "recantation," which was followed by a very light sentence, in September 1973, Yakir was subjected to harassment and attempted intimidation.[35] The most relevant aspect of the Yakir-Krasin prosecution is the effort made by the managers of this first "show trial" since the Stalin era to use it to support the contention that Soviet dissenters were puppets of foreign reactionaries, and that indeed the Democratic Movement and other manifestations of dissent in the USSR were in reality concoctions of anti-Soviet Western newspaper editors and subversive emigrant groups. Thus, according to reports by the Soviet news agency TASS (Telegraphic Agency of the Soviet Union), Yakir reportedly testified at his trial that the "program" of the Democratic Movement had been worked out abroad by the NTS and smuggled into the USSR.[36]

When such world figures as Sakharov and Solzhenitsyn granted interviews and in other ways brought their views to the attention of foreign audiences, the subsequent official response was much more restrained than in the three cases noted above. Still, the meanness of denying an entry visa to the member of the Swedish Academy of Sciences who was to have presented the Nobel Prize to Solzhenitsyn, on the very day after the novelist had held a conference with Western correspondents in April 1973, is startling. And although it is impossible to prove that the December 1974 letter warning Sakharov to stop his "antinational activity" and other tactics in the KGB's war of nerves against the physicist were reprisals for his continued efforts to inform world opinion about the intensification of Soviet political repression in the 1970's, the presumption is strong, for Sakharov's struggle to alleviate the sufferings of political prisoners, widely reported in the West, consumed virtually all of the scientist's energies after 1972.

The KGB's intensification of pressure against Sakharov in late 1974, which included thinly disguised death threats against him and members of his family, appears to have been part of a larger effort to silence a number of prominent civil rights activists who, despite ominous threats and the repression or emigration of most of their fellows, had continued to make their views known to the outside world, often with the help of Western newspeople or through other Western channels. Peter Reddaway has reported, for example, that in May 1974 the biologist Sergei Kovalev and the linguist Tatyana Khodorovich, together with a third person, "openly handed copies" of the *Chronicle of Current Events* (revived after its suppression by the police in 1972) to Western journalists, "together with a statement that they regarded it as a legal publication."[37]

Mention should also be made of the series of science seminars held by Soviet Jewish savants who had been dismissed from their jobs after applying for emigration. The series was inaugurated by a plan to bring together Soviet Jewish scientists and Western scientists in Moscow, in connection with the scheduled commemoration of the 250th anniversary of the USSR Academy of Sciences in July of 1974. The authorities prevented this gathering by canceling the commemoration and jailing its would-be participants, but they were released after the departure of then-president Nixon, then in the USSR to confer with Brezhnev. (The fact that invitations to the conference were issued to a number of Western correspondents may have spurred the Kremlin's decision to squelch it.) Subsequently, however, private seminars were held more or less regularly by Jewish scientists, despite press criticism of the participants' alleged connections with "reactionary Zionists" abroad, as well as severer forms of harassment in some cases.[38]

There have, of course, been many cases of police harassment of foreign journalists who have made contact with dissenters including expulsion or subsequent refusal to grant entry visas. (For example, Anatole Shub, Anthony Astrachan's predecessor as *Washington Post* correspondent, and David Bonavia, *London Times* correspondent, were expelled from the USSR, apparently because of their contacts with dissenters and their full and candid reporting of the regime's repression of dissent.[39])

Along with similar practices directed against foreign scholars, they add up to a pattern of continued interference with what in most of the other "developed" nations of the world are regarded as normal patterns of international communication.

For some time in 1970 and 1971, in connection with the efforts of some foreign correspondents to establish and maintain contact with Soviet Jewish and civil rights activists, several correspondents, including *Washington Post* correspondent Anthony Astrachan, were roughed up, and in some cases, beaten, by KGB thugs. These episodes represented extreme manifestations of Soviet efforts to intimidate the foreign press that can have the effect of inhibiting a journalist—or, for that matter, a diplomat or businessman on long-term assignment. As one very trustworthy American journalist has observed, such methods can render a foreigner "wary of conversations and contacts with Soviet citizens lest he get them into trouble."[40] While "détente" brought with it some lessening of crudity in implementing this policy—especially after 1971, when the CPSU's "peace program" went into full gear—there is no reason to amend *Christian Science Monitor* correspondent Charlotte Saikowski's 1971 description of the Soviet system of controls on journalists, including as she described it, "travel restrictions, surveillance, a segregated life in special foreigners' compounds and an official policy of secrecy, which makes this one of the hardest countries in which to gather news."

Although the relationship between the Soviet authorities and the foreign journalists who attempt to pursue their craft in accordance with Western professional standards is exceptionally tense, scholars, businessmen, and even tourists in the USSR have on occasion been subjected to a wide range of restrictions and even to harassment and provocations, with overtones of blackmail. Summary expulsion, arrest, brief detention, or even, in a few cases, criminal prosecution on trumped-up charges (as happened to me in 1963), may be the outcome. A few of these episodes are featured in the Western press; the majority, except for the most dramatic, are quietly endured by the victims. So far as I have been able to ascertain, the likelihood of such harassments of Western exchange scholars and other foreigners is significantly associated with the interest the latter take in establishing close contacts with non-conformist Soviet citizens— although other factors, including, apparently, the ability to speak Russian fluently and the ability to make friends easily with Soviet citizens, seem in some cases to arouse Soviet official suspicion. So also does a reputation for inquisitiveness and for taking a sharply critical attitude toward the regime.

Of a piece with the attitudes and policies described above is the apparent assumption on the part of the Soviet authorities that mere possession of Western periodicals and books written by "bourgeois" foreign authors—and also those by socialists not in favor with Moscow, or by Soviet writers living abroad—constitutes evidence of subversive, hence punishable, thinking. The writer Victor Nekrasov reported early in 1974 on a thorough KGB search of his apartment, lasting several days; among materials confiscated were some issues of English- and French-language magazines, a copy of George Orwell's *Animal Farm,* and even an Italian translation of Solzhenitsyn's *One Day in the Life of Ivan Denisovich*—though not the Russian edition.[41]

When KGB operatives searched the apartment of the physicist and civil rights activist Andrei Tverdokhlebov during the night of November 27–28, 1974, they seized, among other items, an English-language brochure published abroad—because, Tverdokhlebov reported, "it had a map of Lithuania printed on its cover"—and copies of letters to United States Senators Henry Jackson and Edward Kennedy.[42] As was earlier noted, Tverdokhlebov was arrested a few months later.

But of all the known cases in which the Soviet regime has deemed subversive a Soviet citizen's connection with the intellectual life of the non-Soviet world, perhaps the most peculiar was the arrest in 1974 of the writer Vladimir Maramzin and the historian Michael Kheifets for jointly editing a collection of the works of the distinguished poet Joseph Brodski, now residing in America. Maramzin's release, after protests by a number of Western writers and champions of civil rights, including the Nobel Peace Prize laureate René Cassin, occurred under mysterious circumstances which are pertinent to this discussion. For by disseminating reports of Maramzin's alleged expression of regret for "the harm he had done his country," the Soviet authorities were indirectly indicating their concern about the damage done to the USSR's image abroad by their repression of intellectuals—in this case involving an apparently totally unpolitical individual who had been engaged in purely literary activity. However, Kheifets, who had written a preface for the edition of Brodski's poems which the authorities chose to categorize as subversive, was sentenced to four years in a strict-regime camp, plus two years of exile.[43]

We have not discussed some important elements of the elaborate system of defenses constructed by Stalin against "penetration" of the USSR by dangerous "alien" ideas, which his heirs seek to maintain intact, though sometimes in a form modified to reflect changing conditions in East–West relations—as with the area of copyright legislation, for example. Regarding copyright, serious treatment of which would require a complex and lengthy analysis, it can be said that it may be regarded as a positive development to the extent that the USSR's adherence, finally, to the Universal Copyright Convention accords to foreign authors whose works are published in the Soviet Union a degree of protection against previous arbitrary, confiscatory practices. But by creating in 1973 a powerful new all-Union Copyright Agency with very broad legal and administrative powers for control of authors' rights to disseminate their works abroad, the new legislation may have given the Soviet authorities potentially powerful new weapons for prosecuting or otherwise intimidating Soviet authors who bypass the new agency by publishing abroad without its permission, or who might contemplate such action. However, as Peter B. Maggs has noted, evaluation of the potential effects of the new legislation "must be highly tentative," in view of the difficulty of knowing how the Soviet authorities will attempt to apply it to particular cases, and with what resolution and skill Soviet writers who wish to publish in the United States, for example, defend their interests and the principles of freedom.[44]

I believe that the evidence I have presented above supports the assertions set forth at the beginning of this chapter. Anyone who takes the trouble to consult the relevant sources will be able to find a wealth of additional similar evidence, some of it perhaps more impressive than that which I have cited. Pondering the record of repression revealed by the events and processes described above, one gains increased understanding both of the behavior of the Soviet authorities and of the dissenting responses which that behavior generates. On one side of this unequal contest is a regime with enormous organizational and physical power at its disposal, but which seems to be desperately anxious not only to compel dissenters to bow to its power, but to confirm its authority to act in the name of a "scientifically" derived morality. Certainly at least in part because its pretensions far exceed its capacity to satisfy the material, cultural, and moral aspirations of many Soviet citizens the regime is inordinately sensitive to criticism, especially that which threatens to undermine Soviet prestige abroad. This sensitivity may to some extent be a product of the mingled inferiority/superiority complex toward the West inherited from the pre-revolutionary past, intensified by the experience of "socialist construction" under difficult conditions and by chauvinistic indoctrination.

But perhaps the most important source of the practices I have described lies in the simple fact that the occurrence of "crime," especially if it is "ideological" in nature, is enormously embarrassing in a polity the leaders of which claim to have created a "developed socialist society." The resulting anger and embarrassment help to explain—though in no wise to justify—the doctrine developed by the notorious psychiatrist Professor Daniel Lunts, according to which "any unlawful act, precisely and simply by virtue of its being unlaw-

ful, calls for psychiatric analysis," because under socialism no social basis for crime exists.[45] In practice, this attitude toward dissent
can lead to what can only be described as monstrous evil.

Perhaps the most appropriate response to repression on the part
of a dissenter was given by Andrei Amalrik after sentence had been
passed on him at his 1970 trial. Amalrik dismissed official talk of
an "ideological struggle," asserting that the Soviet authorities, sens-
ing their own "ideological helplessness," were capable of opposing
ideas only by means of "the criminal code, prisons, camps, and psychiatric hospitals." Turning to official allegations that some of his
statements were "directed against my people and my country," he
declared that his country's main task was to throw off "the burden
of a grievous past," and that his accusers were motivated not by
love of country but only by love of privilege. His trial, he concluded,
was intended "to intimidate the many, and many will be intimidated."[46]

SPECULATING ABOUT THE FUTURE

What is the significance, for American understanding of Soviet
foreign policy and particularly its policy toward the United States,
of the conflict analyzed in this book between the Soviet regime
and Soviet dissenters regarding "deténte" and related matters? As
I interpret it, the record examined in these pages should help to
alert us to the threats to American national interests and to democratic values throughout the world posed by a Soviet foreign policy
which professes dedication to the "relaxation of international tensions" while in fact working unremittingly, albeit cautiously and
deliberately, to weaken the United States and its allies and to expand Soviet influence throughout the world. While I would agree
with those who say that the Soviet leaders still retain some faith
in the prediction that "capitalism" is doomed, in any case, to collapse, it is clear that they consider it desirable to expedite the process. The analyses of Soviet foreign-policy strategy offered by Amalrik, Solzhenitsyn, Sakharov, and other dissenters, and awareness
of the regime's reprisals against these candid critics, shed light on
the value system and operating principles of the Soviet regime,
making clear the priority accorded to the pursuit of power, as
against concern for—in terms of the language developed by Harold
D. Lasswell and Abraham Kaplan—other values, such as "en-

lightenment."[47] I would argue that only to the extent that the domestic and foreign policies of the USSR are reshaped along the lines advocated by the Soviet democrats will it be possible to make substantial progress toward converting the partially regulated rivalry that now passes for East–West "détente" into a less tense, more reciprocally beneficial relationship.

Probably no one has more perceptively diagnosed the unsatisfactory state of Soviet–Western relations, or come closer to prescribing remedies, which if conscientiously applied might effect salutary change, than did Andrei Sakharov in a statement he made at the end of 1973. Bluntly denying that he was "an opponent of 'détente,' trade, or disarmament," as the official Soviet media had charged, Sakharov observed:

> But I consider it my duty to point out all the hidden dangers of a false détente, a collusive détente, or a capitulation détente, and to call for the use of the entire arsenal of means, of all efforts, to achieve real convergence, accompanied by democratization, demilitarization and social progress.[48]

The appropriateness of this warning has, I believe, been confirmed by the course of Soviet policy since its utterance. Since I have already dealt at some length with the Soviet concept of "peaceful coexistence," and other related matters, I shall limit myself here to some evidence of what appear to have been significant developments in Soviet foreign-policy perspectives and strategy since the end of 1973.

About a week before Sakharov made his above-quoted statement, a theoretical article in *Pravda* hailed the success of Brezhnev's "scientific," "Leninist" foreign policy. It quoted from the statement by the CPSU General Secretary at the celebration a year earlier of the fiftieth anniversary of the establishment of the USSR, in which he attributed the party's achievements—in this case with special reference to nationality policy—to the fact that "the party has always decisively fought each and every deviation" from Leninism. A typical expression of the ideological orthodoxy that has been reaffirmed since the slogan of "relaxation of international tensions" became the order of the day, the article was replete with confident assertions regarding the increasing force of "the process of relaxation of tensions," which, it asserted, proceeded from the "fact that the basic revolutionary forces of the modern world" were ineluctably growing. Interestingly enough, the article cited, besides two of Brezhnev's speeches, the 1969 conference of Communist parties that I have referred to earlier. And it castigated Western "imperialists" and "cosmopolitans" as well as "Maoist renegades"—the latter for allegedly joining up with the former in opposing "national liberation" and "anti-imperialist" movements.[49]

Perhaps the most arresting argument made in another long "theoretical" piece, published in *Pravda* a month after the above article, was that "peace" promoted revolution more effectively than "war"—I use quotation marks because neither of these key terms was defined. The article made it clear, however, that peace, and peaceful coexistence, under contemporary conditions—"when the comparison between the socialist and the bourgeois ways of life" was "especially timely"—implied no abatement of "the class struggle between socialism and capitalism in all its forms." It added that as the result of generations of effort by the Soviet people, the "imperialist powers" were today forced to accept coexistence.[50]

In August 1974 the CPSU Central Committee launched a vast new political indoctrination drive with a resolution on the "selection and training of ideological cadres in the party organization of Belorussia." Both the resolution—published, though not in full, in the central press for August 31, 1974—and numerous follow-up items appeared to have the purpose of intensifying and broadening propaganda and socialization designed to keep alive the theme of the conflict between the "two worlds" of "socialism" and "capitalism."[51]

In September 1974 an unsigned article appeared in *Pravda*, devoted in part to hammering home the demands for more efficient and zealous indoctrination contained in the August resolution, but focusing on the related topic of the beginning of a new year in the party's vast network of "political enlightenment" schools. It referred to "the constant duel of two systems, of various classes, of progressive and reactionary forces," characteristic of the contemporary international situation. It also disclosed that in the most elementary stage of the political education program, the initial item to be studied would be Brezhnev's speech during the most recent Supreme Soviet "election."[52]

In contrast to the grim tone of the above-mentioned statements, veteran Soviet "peace partisan" Nikolai Tikhonov struck a relatively positive note at the October 1974 "Soviet Conference of Partisans of Peace," judging by *Izvestiya's* coverage of his keynote address. To be sure, he made standard propaganda attacks on Israel and on "opponents of détente," but he also devoted considerable attention to "problems of humanity as a whole" such as environmental and health questions, the resolution of which, he stated, required "the common efforts of all peoples." But, said Tikhonov, the members of his organization, "as realists," gave first priority to "the problem of disarmament."[53]

A harsher tone characterized press reporting of the "All-Army Conference of Ideological Workers," which in January 1975 brought together the leaders of the political information and indoctrination network of the Soviet armed forces. As was to be expected, press reporting of the conference stressed the party's traditional attention to "increasing the military might of the motherland," to defense of the "great achievements of socialism," and to maintaining "vigilance." The extensive report of the speech by Boris Ponomarev, alternate member of the Politburo and one of the party's leading specialists on the international Communist movement, had him expressing satisfaction with the increased "international authority" of the USSR while emphasizing two points, namely, "relaxation of tensions" and "crisis phenomena in the economy of capitalism and their influence on social/political development and international relations." Regarding the first point, Ponomarev stressed, in line with many other Soviet statements of recent years, the desirability of making relaxation of tensions "irreversible." On the second, he asserted, among other things, that there was at hand "a new sharpening of the general crisis of capitalism," but, at least as his speech was reported in *Izvestiya*, he refrained from drawing any conclusions from this assertion with respect to Soviet–Western relations.

Regarding the "Communist movement," Ponomarev reportedly hailed "coordination" among the ruling parties of Eastern Europe and the USSR, along with the "constantly increasing role in international development played by the Communist movement in the nonsocialist part of the world." He maintained that the "deep political changes" that had occurred in recent years in Europe, and on other continents, were "inseparable from the purposeful activities of the Communist parties."[54]

In February, Politburo member and Chairman of the USSR Supreme Soviet Presidium Nikolai Podgorny published a long article in *Izvestiya*, half of it devoted to Soviet victory in World War II, the other half to the weaknesses, evils, and failures of "capitalism" and the contrasting merits of Soviet and East European "socialism." Podgorny criticized those in the West who, he said, were trying to introduce into relations with the Soviet Union a "mercantile spirit" (torgasheski dukh) and make the Soviet Union pay for "détente" by imposing requirements with respect to emigration and other areas strictly within "the competence of any sovereign state." Podgorny rhetorically asked why, if the USSR would not compromise its principles even in its earliest, weakest days, it should do so now that it had become a superpower. Podgorny's critical remarks were undoubtedly directed primarily against the American Congress for its refusal to grant the Soviet Union trade terms satisfactory to the latter, especially in the matter of providing credits at low interest rates. But they could also have reflected, in part, irritation over Western insistence, at the Geneva negotiations, on widening "human contacts" between people on the two sides of the East–West boundary line.[55]

Let us briefly consider another important indicator of Politburo perspectives on international (and domestic) politics: namely, the slogans issued annually by the CPSU Central Committee in advance of the May Day and October Revolution (celebrated on November 7) political holidays. Beginning with the 1974 May Day slogans, these contained a new appeal—urging the "peoples of the world" to "unmask the intrigues of the forces of aggression, revanchism and reaction—the enemies of the peace and security." In this connection, the comment offered by a seasoned analyst of Soviet policy shortly after the new element appeared in the slogans still deserves attention. Christian Duevel suggested that "at least two major factors were involved": to wit, "the uncertainties caused by the U.S. domestic situation as a result of the Watergate affair, the question of the next presidency, etc., and the apparent ascendancy of that Soviet school of thought which sees the present great domestic difficulties ...experienced by most of the leading Western countries as foreboding social unrest which could ultimately lead to the emergence of more authoritarian ... regimes, as was the case in a comparable situation in some European countries during the interwar period."[56]

Official Moscow in 1974 and 1975 could derive satisfaction from mounting evidence that the "contradictions" Lenin had regarded as the chronic and ultimately fatal ills of capitalism were ascendant as at no time since the 1930's. In more concrete terms, as Alec Nove pointed out in a balanced analysis, the West had "more or less conceded" the first three of the four main aims of Soviet policy for the past two decades—nuclear parity, recognition of the status quo in Europe, and recognition of East Germany—and the fourth, credits from the West, was being seriously discussed."[57] Nove argued, and the Soviet denunciation of the trade agreement under negotiation with the United States in January 1975 seemed to support his contention, that while the Kremlin desired to substantially expand trade with the United States, its need was not desperate enough to induce it to change any of its basic domestic policies, such as censorship or the repression of dissent.

It is possible that a combination of irritation in Moscow over failure to obtain all the economic/technical benefits originally envisaged from expanded trade with America, and the desire to take advantage of developing opportunities in such areas as Portugal, the Middle East, and Southeast Asia (in the latter, however, the desire to checkmate China was probably dominant), was gradually imparting to Soviet policy toward the West a more demanding tone. Of this there was evidence, albeit not very conclusive, in the first half of 1975. It was worrisome that even in regard to the status of West Berlin, an issue apparently settled by the four-power agreement of 1971, the West German Foreign Ministry felt it necessary to state at the end of May 1975 that "routine" and "normal" West German activities in West Berlin were being sharply criticized in the Soviet and East German press.[58]

Soviet foreign policy in the period of the West's troubles and of increasing opportunities for the expansion of Soviet influence could perhaps be described as one of cautious aggrandizement of Soviet power. The guiding principle appeared to be maximum expansion with minimum fanfare, so as to avoid alarming or excessively antagonizing the West and thus reduce the risks of effective Western resistance, such as had been generated by Stalin's and Khrushchev's tactics. But there were still problems, and also potential dangers, in the situation, and awareness of them doubtless contributed to the edginess that surfaced from time to time in Soviet commentary on international politics.

Could this undercurrent of anxiety be traced to the increasing imminence of new problems of political succession, in view of the dubious state of Leonid Brezhnev's health and the high average age level of the leadership? Such presuccession moves as the precipitous removal of Shelepin from the Politburo and even from leadership of the Soviet trade unions in April 1975, after the unfriendly reception accorded him in Britain had provided a pretext, must have generated, and reflected, uneasiness.[59]

One problem that was probably on the minds of the Soviet decision makers arose, I assume, from the likelihood that any significant shift in the power balance among the superpowers—such as might occur even in Europe, especially in its unstable Southern tier, or in the oil-rich Middle East—might trigger a return to American–Soviet confrontation. Also, while negotiations on Soviet–American arms control had been institutionalized—a development that compared favorably with the situation a few years earlier—the arms race remained a potentially mortal threat to civilized life on the planet. And of course there was the spectre of Sino–Soviet relations, posing more of a long-term than an immediate threat to Soviet security, but, according to many qualified observers, constituting a greater source of concern to both of the Communist giants than their relations with the United States.

On balance, the Soviet leaders appeared to have good grounds for satisfaction with the results of "détente." One of the Kremlin's achievements, of particular relevance to this book, was its apparent success in quarantining Soviet society from penetration by unsettling "bourgeois" concepts of freedom while reaping many benefits from what it called a relaxation of tensions. On this subject, first-hand reports by two seasoned observers of the Soviet and East European scene made sobering reading for those in the West who a few years earlier had hope that East–West "détente" would be accompanied by some degree of "liberalization" inside the Soviet bloc. Hedrick Smith, fresh—if that is the appropriate word—from a three-year stint as *New York Times* Moscow bureau chief, wrote:

> It is apparent now, however, that the Soviet leadership–with increasing self-confidence and pragmatism–has found a formula for achieving the foreign policy and economic dividends of accommodation with the West without paying the price of relaxing controls at home.[60]

Five months later, Henry Kamm reported from Budapest that:

> While Eastern European officials and people with an official reason to consort with outsiders are more relaxed in their relations nowadays, those outside the privileged circle feel more isolated than ever.[61]

Smith's long, fact-crammed report, full of cogent observations and comments, was especially pertinent. Thus, in regard to the substantial expansion of U.S.-Soviet medical, scientific, and other exchanges of persons, Smith noted that "even American officials feel that the first two years of work under scientific exchange agreements have been devoted...to procedure...rather than...research," while Soviet working scientists complained about the persistence of the traditional Soviet practice, well known to students of Soviet exchange policy, of giving preference, in selecting Soviet exchangees, to administrators over "real practicing scientists." He referred also to such restrictions on communication as orders by security officers— often, I might note, described by American and Soviet participants as "cops" or "nursemaids," if not in earthier language—prohibiting Soviet scientists to divulge information about unpublished research to foreigners. He also referred to apparently "politically" motivated denials of visas to a number of senior American specialists on Soviet affairs, a subject I have alluded to earlier.

Even more pertinent to the central concerns of this book were Smith's negative findings on the plight and prospects of Soviet dissenters. The Kremlin, he reported, had "managed to check dissent," though "outcries in the West" had "brought some help to individuals." Reporting on the process and results of repression of dissent—including the death in a labor camp of the Buddhist leader Bidiya Dandarov, which I have not previously mentioned—Smith concluded on a faintly hopeful note. There were those, he said, who "still" believed that "expanded trade and other contracts over the decades" would "bring reforms, first in the economy and later in scientific, cultural and other intellectual realms, and perhaps ultimately in politics"—even, he added, in the words of one Soviet citizen who, according to Smith, considered himself an optimist, "in a generation or two."[62]

Such wistfulness and the lonely despair Smith found among other Soviet intellectuals apparently resulted from a shrinkage in the number of active protesters and a change in the dissenter population, from a "loose coalition of freethinkers" to a handful of prestigious individuals engaged in "an intermittent debate on the nature of détente and the future of Soviet society."

And if the Kremlin had reasons for satisfaction with the world situation and with its diplomatic and power position at the beginning of 1975, its masters must have been positively jubilant seven months later, after what former Under Secretary of State George W. Ball termed the West's "capitulation" at the Helsinki Conference on Security and Co-operation in Europe. Terming the conference "a triumph for Brezhnev and a defeat for the West," Mr. Ball noted, among other things, that the West was "solemnly agreeing never to challenge the Soviet system in Eastern Europe just when a Kremlin-directed Communist Party in Lisbon" was "blatantly trying to add

Portugal to that Soviet system," and when the Soviets were "cracking down with renewed vigor on dissenters."[63]

It is not surprising, in view of the hazards perceived by George Ball and many other authoritative interpreters of international political trends, that both Sakharov and Solzhenitsyn again warned, in statements discussed elsewhere in this book, that "détente," as it was developing in the summer of 1975, was worsening the West's position vis-a-vis that of Moscow.

PROSPECTS FOR DEMOCRATIC DISSENT

Alexander Volpin for years before his enforced emigration from the USSR in 1972, one of the most creative thinkers among those Soviet dissidents who championed a "legalist" and "constitutionalist" approach, has indicated, in an interview with Irina Kirk, his certainty that if the Soviet authorities continue to refuse to recognize the legal rights of Soviet citizens, "new dissidents will constantly be appearing"—despite the emigration of activists like himself.[64] On the basis of a great deal of evidence—much of which has been examined in this book—and of what seems to me to be valid inferences from this evidence, I believe that Volpin is right. I forecast that, barring resort by the Soviet authorities to terror of something like Stalin-era scope and intensity, dissent, including demands for the democratization of Soviet political life, will persist indefinitely, though for some time on a smaller scale than in the 1960's. Such a regression seems unlikely, since it would not only do incalculable damage to an increasingly complex and hence fragile economy, but might mortally threaten the personal security of many members of a political elite whose behavior in recent years indicates that it gives highest priority to maintaining stability. There are other reasons, including concern about the Soviet image abroad, which, I believe, reinforce the efforts of these factors. But perhaps enough has been said to indicate that in my opinion a return to full-scale arbitrary terror is rather unlikely, and that dissent both because repression will be insufficient to fully suppress it and because it is generated by conflicts inherent in the Soviet system as it is presently constituted, will survive—if, as seems likely, the conditions that gave rise to it in the past persist into the future.

I shall contend that the record to date of the development of dissent, and especially the steadfastness and depth of moral commitment displayed by many dissenters, points to a momentum of protest that is likely to endure. For one thing, dissent is sustained by indignation aroused by past repression and reprisals against those who protest against it, the result being a vicious circle of protest—repression—renewed protest—further repression.

I shall offer an explanation of post-Stalin and especially post-Khrushchev dissent in terms of three sets of factors. The first, it appears, reflected possibly unique elements, such as the personality of Nikita S. Khrushchev. The second, which might be categorized as cyclical, stemmed largely from post-Stalin succession problems. The third consisted of fundamental, or "systemic," factors. I use the term "systemic" to refer to conflicts and apparent incompatibilities between the interests and values of the present (and of recent) Soviet leaders and those of elements of Soviet society—mainly but not exclusively drawn from the scientific—technical and literary sectors of the "creative intelligentsia"—whose struggle, in some cases involving open public protest, for the democratization of Soviet society culture, and politics not only has roots in the immediate post-Stalin years but also can be traced back to the 1920's and even to the pre-Bolshevik attitudes of the Russian intelligentsia as the "conscience of society."[65]

Associated with my discussion of the probability of the persistence of democratic dissent is the assumption that it will remain a force with potential—impossible, unfortunately, to measure—not only for the rationalization and liberalization of domestic politics in the USSR but also for promoting similar ends in Soviet foreign policy. Central themes in the thinking of leading Soviet dissenters, especially but by no means only Andrei Sakharov, such as criticism of the parochialism of the ideologically tinged ("messianic") Soviet approach to foreign affairs and the deep concern displayed by them for the problems of mankind as a whole (poverty, the environment, and "mass culture," to mention a few), lend support to such an assumption.

Of course, I do not necessarily assume that the democratizing impulse is indestructible. Whether or not dissent—which I do unqualifiedly assume will persist—will be rational and constructive will depend on many factors, the most important of which perhaps will be the capacity of the Soviet political leadership to adapt policies, practices, and structures of governance to emerging conditions in an era of unprecedentedly rapid and complex scientific technological development. But the stance taken by other members of the international community, particularly the United States and the West (including Japan) in general, will obviously be of crucial importance. If the Soviet political leadership proves in the future to be as unresponsive to well-intentioned proposals for reform as it has been to date, it is conceivable that dissent will become less moderate, rational, and democratic in spirit and will take on accents of militancy and even fanaticism, which thus far have been notably minor notes in the total body of *samizdat* sociopolitical expression. In this connection, it is not irrelevant to point out that both Sakharov and Solzhenitsyn, whose attitude toward the Soviet authorities when they began to articulate their opinions on matters of public concern was that of respectful petitioners, became hostile critics after, and only after, they encountered official indifference and harassment and, of course, perceived with anguish and guilt the persecution of other democratic dissenters. And if such an emotionally mature, intellectually sophisticated, and morally sound person as Sakharov felt constrained to abandon the role of a "within-system" critic, it is all the more likely that less balanced and less privileged persons— especially, as Amalrik and Solzhenitsyn both have warned, dissident members of minority groups, whose grievances are compounded by bitterness engendered by affronts to their ethnic dignity—will abandon ideals of democracy and legality in favor of very radical objectives, militant ideologies, and conspiratorial methods of struggle.[66]

Let us now turn to a discussion of the prospects for the persistence of democratic dissent, beginning with the evidence of its persistence to date, in the face of increased repression, since 1971. After 1971 repression was intensified, but at least on the part of some individuals, resistance became stronger than ever. The authorities apparently decided late in 1971 that despite the tarnishing of the Soviet image abroad that might result from the imposition of increasingly harsh sanctions against dissenters, such a cost would be less than that of even the limited toleration prevailing until then. But they did not, it seems—and perhaps felt that they could not, if they were to have any success in projecting an aura of "détente"— pursue a sufficiently ruthless policy to completely stamp out resistance or—what was worse, from their point of view—completely conceal what they were doing from the outside world.[67] The protests against cruel and inhuman treatment of dissenters such as Bukovski and Plyushch—articulated and brought to world attention not only by Sakharov but also by the linguist Tatyana Khodorovich, the physicist Andrei Tverdokhlebov, the computer scientist Gregory Podyapolski, the world-renowned algebraist Igor Shafarevich, the botanist Sergei Kovalev, and many less-known individuals—of course continued for years even after the massive 1972-73 KGB sweep had signaled the Politburo's intention to eradicate public protest. Indeed, surprisingly enough, there is solid evidence of an increase in *samizdat* production and distribution during the third quarter of 1973, when, as Albert Boiter, director of the highly respected Radio Liberty Archive of *Samizdat (Arkhiv samizdata)* in Munich, has pointed out, the Soviet government "chose to deliver what was obviously planned to be the final blow...to...dissent." Boiter also reported that the Archive, during that period, registered fifty-six *samizdat* documents, comprising more than eight hundred manuscript pages. During this time of troubles, he remarked, *samizdat* "showed remarkable powers of tactical adaptability and its messages found an unprecedented Western echo and response."[68]

It is perhaps even more remarkable that the total number of *samizdat* documents as well as the total number of pages registered during the year 1974 exceeded the 1973 figures by 57 percent. (In 1974, 445 new documents, comprising 5,500 pages, were registered; the corresponding 1973 figures were, respectively, less than three hundred, and 3,485.) Some idea of the continued vitality of dissent in 1974 can be gained by a glance at a few of the varied items that were circulated in the fourth quarter of that year. These included "thoughtful essays on a number of social, literary or historical themes," by Gregory Pomerants and other writers; accounts of the KGB searches to which Andrei Tverdokhlebov and Vladimir Maramzin were subjected; protests against Soviet nationality policy by Armenian, Georgian, Ethnic German, Lithuanian, and Crimean Tatar sources; "an anguished announcement," from Latvia, of KGB confiscation of the "self-built printing press of the dissident Baptist movement"—on which 30,000 Bibles and other church literature had been printed in the three and a half years of its clandestine operation—much material protesting political trials; and the first issue of a new *samizdat* journal, *Zemlya (The Land)*. Despite the arrest of its editor, Vladimir Osipov, a second issue, edited by Vyacheslav Rodionov, had appeared as of January 1975.[69]

It will be recalled that the hectic third quarter of 1973 was marked by the Yakir-Krasin trial, featuring the two defendants' "recantations," intended to demonstrate that no real dissent existed in the USSR. Following the trial, the massive press campaign, mentioned earlier, directed against Sakharov and Solzhenitsyn, was mounted. The apparent failure of these operations—indicated by continued distribution of *samizdat* while and after they took place and by Sakharov's success in gaining access to Western communications channels for the purpose of rebutting the official charge that he was opposed to "détente" and other accusations—tends to confirm Boiter's judgment that "in many respects" the regime's antidissident propaganda had "suffered a severe setback."[70]

It does appear that the Kremlin's psychological warriors were initially overly optimistic about the impact that these operations, especially the Yakir–Krasin affair, might have on world opinion. One factor that may have led to their miscalculation may have been overeagerness to exploit an achievement conspicuous by its rarity in the post-Stalin era—success in extracting guilty pleas from two prominent dissidents and their willingness to make statements in support of official antidissident propaganda. To be sure, as was noted earlier, the KGB could also boast of having obtained from the tubercular Dzyuba an (somewhat ambiguous) admission of error along with a promise to rewrite his celebrated book, *Internationalism or Russification*. By so yielding, Yakir, Krasin, and Dzyuba—and a few other Ukrainians who also confessed—doubtless weakened the will of some other dissenters to go on fighting against heavy odds, although it is impossible to know how much damage they inflicted and to what extent Solzhenitsyn's and Roy Medvedev's severe condemnation of Yakir and Krasin, or Moroz's harsh criticism of Dzyuba, was justified.

In any case, there is a stark contrast between the behavior of the very few dissenters accused of anti-Soviet agitation or other "especially dangerous state crimes" who have compromised their principles, and the steadfastness displayed by many. The deep commitment underlying the behavior of men and women like Larisa Bogoraz, Amalrik, Bukovski, Plyushch, Gluzman, Moroz, Grigorenko, and many others not only refutes KGB charges that the dissidents are moral weaklings or Western hirelings. It also, it seems to me, indicates that precedents have been set, by dissenters and authorities alike, the consequences of which will plague the regime far into the future unless the conditions that led these freethinking personalities to protest are corrected. Surely no one runs the risks faced by these people unless he has deep faith in the justice—and probably the ultimate victory—of his cause. In pondering the conflict between the Democratic Movement and the Kremlin, one can scarcely fail to perceive parallels with the corresponding struggle of nineteenth- and twentieth-century rebels against tsarism—though of course there are also striking contrasts, particularly between the utopian goals and violent means of antitsarist revolutionaries and the contemporary democrats' preference for legalism and gradualism. But what is strikingly common to both groups is their depth of moral commitment, and that similarity prompts one to believe that contemporary dissent will survive. For it derives part of its inspiration from the nineteenth-century liberation struggle and, what is perhaps more important, reflects the values and aspirations of people who consider, as their predecessors did and for similar reasons, that they have a moral obligation to publicly and vigorously defend principles proclaimed but not practiced by the established authorities and to criticize the latter for dereliction of duty.

Nikita Khrushchev's revelations, and his condemnation, of some of Stalin's monstrous acts—especially of the wrongs Stalin did to many loyal party, state, and military chiefs—together with his promises of justice and freedom for all Soviet citizens (within a Marxist–Leninist framework, of course) generated hopes which must be taken into account in attempting to explain the transformation of dissenters in the years after Khrushchev's ouster—at least in the case of such major figures as Sakharov—from loyal petitioners to militant polemicists. To the extent, which was considerable, that Khrushchev's assault on past practices included withering criticism of appalling inefficiency in such fields as agriculture and other technical and administrative domains, it was encouraging not only to moral idealists, but also to wide circles of the scientific and technical intelligentsia. Now the scope of Khrushchev's tolerance for freedom of expression—except for himself—should not be exaggerated. While he was alive and in power, he often, in word and deed, provided striking indications of the limits of that tolerance—though of course they far exceeded those set by his more conservative successors. For our purposes it will suffice perhaps to refer briefly to a passage contained in the second volume of his posthumously published memoirs. Commenting on the "thaw" (which took its name, of course, from the title of a novel by Ilya Ehrenburg)—or, as Khrushchev also called it, "the new leniency"—in party policy toward literature and the arts after Stalin's death, Khrushchev remarked:

> *We in the leadership were consciously in favor of the thaw, myself included, but without naming Ehrenburg, we felt we had to*

criticize his position. We were scared—really scared. We were afraid the thaw might unleash a flood, which we wouldn't be able to control and which could drown us. How could it drown us? It could have overflowed the banks of the Soviet riverbed and formed a tidal wave which would have washed away all the barriers and retaining walls of our society.[71]

In light of this admission, it is understandable that the "leniency" granted independent thinkers during the Khrushchev period was so insufficient, in the opinion of some of the boldest Soviet intellectuals (especially young people such as Vladimir Bukovski), that in the late 1950's and early 1960's, while Khrushchev was still in power, they protested sufficiently vigorously—for example, in some cases, by organizing street demonstrations—that they soon found themselves in forced labor camps or mental institutions. In the eyes of the most critical dissenters, moderate reformists were like the poet Evgeni Evtushenko—then still regarded in the West as an angry young man, Soviet style, and seen by Khrushchev, probably, as a useful, if sometimes impudent and presumptuous articulator of the "de-Stalinization" campaign that he, in his usual zig-zag fashion, was conducting—were compromising hypocrites.[72]

But if some impatient rebels angrily rejected the limited liberalization made possible by Khrushchev, men like Andrei Sakharov, Alexander Tvardovski, and Alexander Solzhenitsyn found it possible, within channels and behind the scenes, so to speak, to lobby for a moderate reformist line. Tvardovski, as editor of *Novy Mir*, persuaded Khrushchev to approve publication of Solzhenitsyn's novella *One Day in the Life of Ivan Denisovich*, and he even urged an apparently sympathetic Khrushchev to abolish censorship of *belles lettres*. Khrushchev approved publication of *One Day*, which aroused fear and anger among "dogmatists" in the Soviet bureaucracy, as part of his successful effort to end mass terror. Solzhenitsyn, although he—like other dissenters—deplored Khrushchev's lack of the skills and resolution required for the maximum possible effectiveness of the liberalization campaign he conducted, credits him with human qualities and even with unconscious "Christian" traits, unique among Communist leaders.[73] Solzhenitsyn goes on to report that despite the foreboding that he, not to mention Tvardovski, experienced when Khrushchev was deposed, he also felt a sense of release from the "debt of honor" and "gratitude" he had owed Khrushchev, as a result of which he had not enjoyed "real freedom of action." It is interesting, however, that Solzhenitsyn also says that he looked forward in those days to "better times" in the future, even including full freedom to publish, though he resolved to pursue a very cautious strategy, avoiding any action that might serve as a pretext to the now victorious "conservatives" to institute repression against him.[74]

Whatever may have been Khrushchev's motives in qualifiedly supporting Tvardovski's struggle for freedom of artistic expression, a considerable measure of freedom was forthcoming while he remained in power, and it vanished soon after his fall. Perhaps an even greater contrast between the Khrushchev and post-Khrushchev periods lies in the fact that while the quasi-charismatic Khrushchev —Solzhenitsyn suggests that he was a tsar who did not understand his own powers, or how to use them—relied on persuasion to control the USSR's cultural life, his more bureaucratic successors resorted to a neo-Stalinist mix of administrative and coercive methods.[75]

Khrushchev had fostered, or at least tolerated, the posing by writers of the fundamental questions about the meaning of life, morals, culture, and politics traditionally central to the concerns of the Russian intelligentsia. His pragmatic, efficiency-oriented, politically conservative successors terminated this colloquy, and when some intellectuals refused to be silenced, they resorted to selective terror. Among the policies of Khrushchev's successors that alienated intellectuals who valued freedom more than privilege were the ending of de-Stalinization and the revenge taken by the party command and its literary control apparatus on Tvardovski and *Novy Mir*, culminating in Tvardovski's forced resignation as *Novy Mir's* editor early in 1970, for having had the temerity to publish works casting doubt on the legitimacy of Stalin's policies. Many motives were involved in the frustrating disillusionment, despair, embitterment, and exasperation that led to the burgeoning of *samizdat* and other manifestations of protest in the post-Khrushchev period, but it seems clear that one of the prime factors was the new leadership's regressive course.[76]

To the extent that post-Stalin dissent was a product of Khrushchev's permissiveness or of other personality traits of his—and much in the behavior of his successors indicates that this was what they believed, or wanted the world to think they believed—this conclusion, which I would regard as superficial, would not warrant our regarding this period of dissent as a unique, unrepeatable episode. For, after all, it is obvious that not only did Khrushchev's personality play a part in the shaping of events after Stalin's death, but so also did the complex, peculiar, and repeatable though by no means uniform process of selection of new leadership for the hegemonic Soviet polity. There may in the future be a "succession crisis" so acute as to create conditions for the articulation of dissent even more favorable than those present after Stalin's death. However, Hodnett seems on firm ground so far as present trends can be extrapolated, in asserting that "systemic instability generated by nonresolution of the succession issue is not inevitable"—and also in adding that to say this "does not mean that it cannot occur."[77] Hodnett's stress on the regime's stability was provisionally confirmed by the placid course of the CPSU's Twenty-fifth Congress in February and March 1976.

Yet, previous changes of leadership, and other episodes that served to facilitate relatively free expression, such as obtained during and for a brief period after World War II, would presumably not have been associated, as they in fact were, with the (partial and temporary) airing of unorthodox sentiments and opinions had there not existed an accumulation of grievances and of latent dissent, needing only modestly favorable conditions to surface. Hence it is appropriate to proceed to a consideration of more fundamental and durable, or "systemic," issues and problems, to the challenge of which individuals who can to some degree be regarded as representative spokesmen of the liberal elements of the Soviet intelligentsia responded with demands and proposals for "democratization," a term I am using here to refer to the point of view of democratic dissenters. It will be recalled that in the introduction to the reform program that they addressed to the Politburo in 1970, Sakharov, Turchin, and Roy Medvedev asserted that there were grounds for believing that their "theses" were shared by a "significant portion" of the Soviet intelligentsia and "the advanced portion of the working class." They added, in the introduction, that "this outlook finds reflection in the views of the student and working youth and in numerous discussions in small circles," and in a later section they asserted that "most of the intelligentsia and youth realize the necessity of democratization." Particularly significant was their warning that continued suppression of the intelligentsia's "legitimate and natural" desire for "freedom of information and creativity" would widen the already existing gap between the "party–state structure" and the intelligentsia, "which cannot be called anything but suicidal."[78]

The message that the authors of this remarkable document addressed to the Soviet political leadership was, it seems to me, in essence, as follows: if you create the conditions necessary for "fruitful cooperation"—this expression occurred in the text—between a "democratized" political structure and the most enlightened and skilled sectors of the fastest growing stratum of society, there are good prospects of a bright future for the USSR. But if, instead of carrying further, indeed much further, the Khrushchev precedent (Khrushchev, however, was not mentioned) of according to the intelligentsia opportunities for at least participating in the identification, definition, and clarification of issues of concern to the political community—which would require, for example, free access to all pertinent information, and freedom of inquiry and expression in science, scholarship, and literature—if instead, you, the leaders, persist in the reactionary course of jailing dissenters and the like, the results will include economic stagnation. Furthermore, if a "sometimes too ambitious foreign policy on all continents" is not abandoned, there will perhaps be "catastrophic consequences."[79]

There is in fact some limited consonance between Soviet policy since 1970 and the reform proposals contained in what Churchward termed the "Reform Charter of the Intelligentsia."[80] Indeed, an optimist might take a measure of satisfaction from the parallelism between the three's advice and the regime's current policies in respect, for example, to the organization of production combines or firms, which may have somewhat fostered managerial efficiency, the cessation of the jamming of some foreign broadcasts, Soviet accession to the international copyright system, improvement in the training of leaders in management techniques, and expansion of the functions of the Soviets—and indeed Roy Medvedev expressed measured gratification over some of these developments. But the general course of Kremlin policy in recent years has been one of flat rejection of the more fundamental and sensitive proposals contained in this document (and in other programmatic documents), such as those for amnesty for political prisoners (accompanied by public control of places of detention and psychiatric hospitals), public disclosure of popular attitudes on domestic and foreign policy issues, provision of means by which groups of citizens could set up new press organs, and introduction of a measure of competitiveness in Party and government elections.[81]

In light of the regime's unresponsiveness to these and other reform proposals and its hostility toward their authors, even the fairly limited claim made by Sakharov, Turchin, and Medvedev regarding the representativeness of their views is of great interest to anyone pondering the future of dissent. So too, of course, is their prediction that dire consequences would ensue if their advice were not heeded. It should be noted, however, that the future troubles the three foresaw if the regime failed to heed their counsel did not include revolution or anything of the kind, nor did they, even by implication, advocate any sort of political opposition, organized or not. In a word, the document, like virtually all dissent literature known to Western scholars, was far from "counter-revolutionary" in content or tone.

Why then was there no response to it—with the result that its authors permitted its *samizdat* circulation? And why did the authorities order, or authorize—their usual secrecy obscures the details of decision making and implementation—increased harassment for Sakharov, and deprivation of regular employment for Turchin and Medvedev (in the case of the latter, a year or so after his expulsion from the CPSU)? It should also be recalled that Sakharov, after world dissemination of his 1968 "memorandum," had been barred from classified research and demoted in rank in the Academy of Sciences. Presumably, the immediate motives were retaliation for violation of the traditional ban on unsolicited inputs into the policy-making process, and for bringing to the world, and—via foreign radio broadcasts—to the attention of the Soviet public, information embarrassing to Moscow. More fundamentally, the hostility indicated by socioeconomic sanctions against the three men was a manifestation of the post-Khrushchev leadership's generally conservative policies. In particular, it is apparent from the general course of Soviet policy in recent years, especially in the pivotal area of economic policy, that although the Politburo and men like Sakharov agreed on the cardinality of the goal of rapid development, they disagreed sharply on the means by which it could and should be achieved. Briefly, to a Sakharov, rapid economic development was both impossible and undesirable without "democratization," whereas to the Soviet "establishment" it was impossible and undesirable without centralized political controls, severe discipline at all levels, and ideological mobilization. The differences of orientation were also great in the foreign policy area, as has been indicated previously. Here the regime rejected what it regarded as Sakharov's woolly-minded and disorienting advocacy of "convergence"—meaning, among other things, acceptance of "ideological coexistence"—while he and also Roy Medvedev, who agreed with him on this point, rejected the "messianism" of Soviet foreign policy.

What can be said about the three's unsubstantiated but confident claims of support in Soviet society for their sentiments and proposals? The question raises important issues, for if the regime were really on a collision course with the skilled and creative elements of Soviet society, on the quality of whose efforts the future of the Soviet system so largely depends, the Soviet future might indeed be grim. Not incompatible with the analyses and forecasts of Sakharov and Roy Medvedev, and also those of Amalrik and Solzhenitsyn, would be a Stalinesque regime, maintained by coercion but lacking the dynamism derived from Stalin's titanic will and from the simpleminded developmentalism more appropriate to an earlier, cruder age. Forebodings of such an ugly, crippled future may have led some dissenters to consider it their duty to appeal, for a reversal of the course of Kremlin policy, to men whose previous behavior offered precious little basis for believing that they would listen. It is also possible that their sense of urgency impelled some dissenters to exaggerate the degree of support they enjoyed in Soviet society as a means of increasing their leverage on the political leadership; or—and this seems more likely—they may have unconsciously projected their own intensity of conviction onto their peers. These remarks reflect my belief that although Sakharov, Turchin, and Medvedev were not incorrect in asserting in 1970 that their sentiments and goals were at that time widely shared, they probably overestimated the breadth, the intensity, and perhaps most of all the steadfastness of the support they enjoyed even among dissidents— not to mention within the intelligentsia as a whole. In this connection, a statement Sakharov made to Olle Stenholm in 1973 is pertinent, and poignant. In answer to the Swedish correspondent's question regarding what might be done, in view of Sakharov's skepticism at that time, "to improve the system of the Soviet Union," the physicist replied, "Well, there is a need to create ideals even when you can't see any route by which to achieve them, because if there are no ideals then there can be no hope...."[82]

Earlier, I cited statements by Solzhenitsyn and other sources pertinent to the question of the attitude of dissidents generally toward "democratization." Unfortunately, this evidence is highly inconclusive.[83] One obvious and important reason for caution in estimating the extent and quality of support for the tendencies articulated by Sakharov and like-minded people is the considerable, though as I have made clear, incomplete, success to date of the regime's efforts to suppress them. Repression and intimidation have undoubtedly played a key role in this process—fear is certainly still one of the most potent instruments of social control in Soviet Russia. But it appears to be the case that the positive controls and incentives that are also major instruments of Soviet rule have generated considerable support for the Soviet system not only among the "masses" but also in the ranks of the intelligentsia. This support is somewhat passive and fluid; it cannot be, and is not, taken for granted by the authorities. This is indicated by their continued commitment to the "Leninist" theory and practice of large-scale, institutionalized, and intensive political mobilization—in the conduct of which increasing use is made of relevant techniques of applied social science, such as opinion surveys.[84]

Of special relevance here is the series of measures undertaken since 1967 to combat political apathy and ideological indifference among scientists and other members of the intelligentsia.[85] These have included public pressure in the form of press campaigns, reindoctrination efforts, and, perhaps most important, the granting, by the Twenty-first CPSU Congress in April 1971, to primary party organizations of the right—apparently for the first time—to oversee the activities of scientific research institutions.

According to Churchward, whose findings are based not only on careful analysis of published sources but also on perceptive on-the-scene observation, "most Soviet intellectuals seem to accept the socialist system and are prepared to work within the Communist political system, to observe its rules and to respect its restraints."[86]

Although he does not explicitly link what he regards as the basically supportive attitude of most Soviet skilled personnel—especially the 10 percent holding official posts—toward the sociopolitical system to the question of dissent, Churchward does seem to believe that the "intellectual culture" of the intelligentsia inhibits "alienation." "The basic ethical attitude of the Soviet intellectual," he observes, "is that of the highly trained specialist," one who as long as "he can continue to work as an intellectual...and to receive better than average income and facilities...will continue to work without open rebellion." But Churchward also reports that "during the 1960's the number of 'alienated intellectuals' was certainly increasing," and some were "reasserting the traditional role of the intelligentsia as 'the conscience of humanity.'"[87] And he found that "those under thirty-five in 1970" were likely to be "more critical and independent in their thinking than their parents."[88] He notes that in some cases of expulsion of dissidents from the party, the action was carried out by district party committees rather than by the primary organization to which the dissidents belonged—this was true, for example, though Churchward does not mention names, in Roy Medvedev's case in 1969—which, he observes, "suggests a considerable amount of support for dissidents among peer groups."[89] Churchward also pointed out that it was becoming more difficult than formerly for graduates of secondary schools to gain admission to higher (in his language, tertiary) educational institutions, owing mainly to "the slower rate of expansion of tertiary education [as] compared with secondary."[90] I would surmise that in the short run this trend fosters political apathy and conformism among Soviet youngsters, anxious to minimize the risks of failing to achieve the training that is the main key to economic preferment aod social status. In the long run, however, it would seem that the decline in social mobility resulting from increasing difficulty in getting a college education might be an important source of "relative deprivation" and perhaps of social protest.

Churchward's findings on the social situation and political attitudes of the Soviet intelligentsia tally on the whole with those of other Western scholars.[91] They are also perhaps not incompatible with the views of dissenters such as Sakharov and Roy Medvedev—especially with those expressed by the latter in his book on "socialist democracy." The outlook seems to boil down to something like the following. The intelligentsia will continue to grow, but probably more slowly than in the past, both absolutely and in proportion to other social strata. It will remain relatively privileged culturally and economically and—through its superior access to CPSU membership—politically. But taken as a vast and heterogeneous social stratum, numbering many millions and composed of dozens of occupational subgroups, all of them controlled by the CPSU—which constantly drains off some of the ablest and most ambitious of their members for work in party and government leadership posts—the intelligentsia is politically powerless, and it seems highly probable that its group powerlessness will long persist. And if even the best-trained and most skilled stratum of society seems unlikely soon to possess the perspectives and coherence required to effect a democratic transformation of the Soviet system, it would appear even more unlikely that the Soviet workers or the collective farm peasantry will in any foreseeable future develop the desire or the capability to move in that direction. (Although according to the official myth the workers are the leading class of Soviet society, in fact, of course, in terms of access to higher education, membership in the CPSU, and other indices of social power they rank far lower than the intelligentsia. And at the bottom of the scale, in terms of disposition of the socioeconomic and political resources now available in Soviet society, are the peasants, especially those belonging to the least developed ethnic groups.)

Much less is known, both to Western observers and to Soviet dissenters, about the political attitudes of the workers and peasants than about those of the intelligentsia. Clearly, however, these classes seem less likely than the intelligentsia to produce individuals who will be capable of articulating views challenging the presently dominant political structure and culture. Of course it is possible that citizens drawn from various sectors of society might someday form a reformist coalition led or inspired by dissenters. On this possibility, as on most questions, there are widely conflicting opinions among dissenters. Perhaps the most pessimistic view is Amalrik's well-known opinion that the political potential even of the Soviet intelligentsia is low, and that that of the "Russian people" as a whole is nil, except in a negative sense. Amalrik has asserted that the "ideas of self-government, of equality before the law and of personal freedom—the responsibility that goes with these—are almost completely incomprehensible to the vast majority of the population."[92] On the basis of my own experience and study I must say I believe Amalrik is right on this point.

Alexander Solzhenitsyn's views on this question seem to be similar, as we indicated earlier, to those of Amalrik. Much more optimistic, of course, were Sakharov, Roy Medvedev, and Turchin, at least up to 1970. And more recently the former Soviet journalist Vadim Belotserkovsky, who clearly regards Sakharov as the representative man of the Democratic Movement, has written that although "the conscious mind of the worker or engineer may still be clouded by the poisonous smoke of Soviet propaganda," nevertheless for such persons "freedom is associated with order and not with anarchy: with an order based on democracy and self-government." Belotserkovsky believes that Amalrik's negative views apply mainly to the Soviet "lumpenproletariat" of "petty service and trade employees" and also to "a large part of the humanistic intelligentsia," but not to the "scientific intelligentsia." He even expresses the view that the "broad and ever growing layer of engineers and technicians contributes to the intellectualization of the body of factory workers and transforms it into an independent force which, hopefully, will become a base for democracy in the future."[93] The fact that a few workers, such as Anatoli Marchenko and Ivan Yakhimovich, have already played important roles in the Democratic Movement tends to support Belotserkovsky's position. I would guess that his balanced view is nearer the truth than either Amalrik's pessimism or the optimism expressed by Sakharov, Turchin, and Roy Medvedev. If a peaceful transformation of the Soviet political order ever occurs, it will presumably be a joint product of pressures from below and creative, wisely adaptive reform from above.

In attempting to assess prospects for reform it is necessary to take into account not only open dissent but also critical views that have been articulated in articles and books passed by Soviet censors during periods of relative liberalism—for example in the 1960's in such journals as *Novy Mir*. The articulations of the interests of some groups, such as the military and military scientists, may have increased in scope and effect since Khrushchev's ouster. But generally, in recent years all lobbying has been more controlled and confined than was the case under Khrushchev, channeled especially into "recommendations for policy changes and improvements in policy implementation"—especially, I would emphasize, the latter, and particularly but not solely in the sphere of economic administration.[94]

Time will tell how satisfactory merely implementational and, as I have labeled it elsewhere, "sectoral" articulation will be to the increasingly sophisticated young professionals who soon will be assuming command of Soviet scientific, scholarly, and educational life.[95]

However, not only the reluctant resort by men like Sakharov, the Medvedev brothers, Solzhenitsyn, and others to the weapon of *samizdat*, but also and perhaps especially the character of much of the "legitimate" discussion of socioeconomic and political issues in Soviet periodicals, especially *Novy Mir*, through the late 1960's, led me to believe that demands and programs for structural and major policy changes will again, sooner or later, be vigorously articulated. In *Novy Mir*, while Tvardovski was still its editor, and in other periodicals too, as well as in several remarkable books (especially V. P. Shkredov's *Economy and Law* [*Ekonomika i Pravo*], favorably reviewed in *Novy Mir* in 1967), "astonishingly numerous taboos, central to the functioning or to the beliefs of the system, were exposed or proposed to be scrapped." Moshe Lewin may be correct in believing that the "inroads" made by the abstract and circumspect but intellectually bold thinking he described "[seem] irreversible, at least in the intellectual life of the politically aware groups."[96] Lewin argues—and he supports his argument by a mass of pertinent evidence—that in the Khrushchev and early post-Khrushchev years innovative thinking, more Marxist than Leninist in spirit, flourished. This fresh thinking, which was sometimes partly couched in the previously forbidden terminology of "group interests" and "civil society," was cautiously critical, at least by implication, of central features of traditional Soviet socioeconomic policy—such as despotically centralized administration and planning, both industrial and agricultural—and of the sacred dogma of the primacy of production over consumption. It reflected a "craving for more autonomy for producers and social groups and the thirst for enough independence to do their jobs adequately...as well as for a say in formulating what the 'general interest' should be."[97] And, Lewin asserts, it "pointed in the direction of a version of democratic socialism."[98] It should be noted that Lewin, like Churchward, displays an awareness of the reactionary impulses that gripped Soviet policy after Khrushchev's ouster, noting, for example, that vigorous criticism of the inferior status of the peasantry was ended after the Twenty-third CPSU Congress.[99] And he observes that "for the moment, the dialogue between the spokesmen of the intelligentsia and the current leadership is a *dialogue des sourds*."[100] But in the absence of "bold political initiatives" and "methods for conscious, rational change," Lewin asserts—and I find his judgment persuasive—"more conflict and even considerable tremors can be expected to haunt Soviet political life in the coming years."[101]

In fact, one can hardly help asking whether, if the CPSU proves incapable of developing more imaginative, responsive, and relevant programs than those reflected in the clichés dominant in most late Brezhnev-era political discourse—which must seem hopelessly obsolete to intelligent, politically literate citizens—the "monolithic" ruling party will not come to be widely regarded as the rearguard, rather than the vanguard, of Soviet society. It is even arguable that in the modern scientific age the party no longer has any major functions to perform. At any rate, such basic, indeed immense tasks —successful performance of which constituted a major source of the party's claim to political legitimacy, international power status and the industrialization of Soviet society—may be regarded as already fulfilled and completed, and ready to be handed over to new national or even international institutions. Relevant in this connection is Lewin's statement that:

> *All the reformers, Shkredov included, are aware that a new stage*
> *has been reached, in which the social system and the Soviet state*
> *no longer face external dangers (the borders being more secure*
> *than at any previous time in the history of Russia); there are no*
> *more internal class enemies eager to overthrow the Soviet system*
> *and to enhance the previous order; there are no excuses therefore*
> *for delaying the indispensable rethinking and reorganization of*
> *the system; there are no longer any reasons for procrastination in*
> *rendering to economic and social factors the autonomy they need*
> *and without which the system gets jammed.*[102]

Perhaps it is now also pertinent to recall the opinion voiced in 1926 by a young party member named Ossovski, who correctly, in my opinion—an opinion obviously shared by some Soviet citizens— pointed to the illogicality of one-party rule as it was then taking shape in Soviet Russia. Ossovski argued that the party could not be both united and unique. If it exercised power uniquely, it would become an arena of struggle among representatives of conflicting interests. In order to be united, it would have to permit a number of parties, representing various interests, to compete for power.[103]

It would be difficult to imagine anything more salutary for world peace and welfare than the "democratization" of the USSR. Realism, however, counsels assignment of a much higher probability to the persistence, for many years, of the status quo in Soviet Russia than to a democratic transformation. What seems most probable is a streamlined, somewhat technocratized version of the present system; yet even a relatively efficient and affluent techno-bureaucratic Communism may prove incapable of indefinitely staving off demands for responsible freedom of choice in matters ideological and political. Nevertheless, growing Soviet research and development capabilities in all fields of science and technology, with the alluring career opportunities they generate for talented and ambitious young people, will probably continue for some years to engender support for the Soviet system and contribute substantially to its international influence. Meanwhile, steadily increasing allocations to research and development, together with the continued success of the efforts inaugurated in the 1960's to reduce the rigidities which have long obstructed the practical application of scientific research in the USSR, could significantly affect the balance of military power between the USSR and the United States.[104] In any case, whatever the "score" may be at any given moment in the scientific/technological, economic, military, or propaganda/diplomatic "race" between the two superpowers, it is obvious that the USSR will for the foreseeable future remain formidable and difficult to cope with.

CONCLUSIONS AND RECOMMENDATIONS

It seems to me that the more one learns about the aspirations and the fate of Soviet dissenters in the context of the Soviet rulers' internal and foreign policy in recent years, the more one is likely to become convinced that "democratization" of Soviet political life is a necessary, though not a sufficient, condition for transforming an aloof, circumscribed, and perhaps temporary relationship of American–Soviet coexistence into a safer, more cooperative, and more stable pattern. It is hardly necessary to argue that a democratic transformation of Russia would be immensely beneficial. It would contribute to reducing mutual mistrust and would facilitate the diversion of vast human and material resources from wasteful arms competition to cooperative, confidence-building efforts to fashion international policies and procedures and ultimately international institutions capable, one hopes, of dealing effectively with problems that increasingly defy solution within the still dominant, but increasingly malfunctioning, semi-anarchic, compartmentalized world system of sovereign nation states. Many other desirable consequences might ensue, including perhaps the strengthening of now incipient functional international subcommunities of scientists and experts whose members might exert a positive influence on policy making in both "East" and "West." Furthermore, discussion of political issues on both "sides" could become much more rational than it is within the present context of concern over whether or not a proposed policy or program threatens national security, or might give aid and comfort to the ideological adversary.

I hope that men inspired by the ideas of Sakharov will one day govern Russia. But until that day comes—and no one can be certain if or when or how it will—the odds are that we shall have to contend for far longer than we might wish with well-trained, tough-minded, and strong-willed bureaucratic politicians representative of an elite that is determined to maintain the present pattern of centralized rule in the USSR and is confident that, in the era of the "general crisis of capitalism," the realm of Soviet-style "socialism" is destined for further gradual—or perhaps even rapid—expansion at the expense, above all, of American power. Those who warn us that the very survival of the non-Soviet (or, to be more precise, the Western world's) international order, as it was constructed in the early post–World War II years, is at stake, are by no means mere panic mongers. Indeed, one can—as in effect Solzhenitsyn has—make a reasonably persuasive case for the proposition that we have in recent years been witnessing an advanced stage in the USSR's successful drive toward ascendancy in world politics. In view of the achievements of Soviet foreign policy since the 1968 invasion of Czechoslovakia, Solzhenitsyn's argument should, at least, not be ignored. At any rate, it seems only prudent for us to recognize that foreign policy consists largely in the choice of the least unsatisfactory option from among a series of never fully satisfactory courses of action.

In the era of superweapons and in the context of the actual and potential world power balance, the highest priority of American policy must be the urgent problems of security, arms control, and peacekeeping. Yet, while the interests of the USSR and the U.S. in these areas overlap, they are not identical. When the problem of arms control, for example, is viewed in the context of its relationship to other issues, such as trade and human rights—especially freedom of expression and access to information—conflicts between Soviet and American interests and values become clear. Both the security of the United States and its allies and the continued vitality of the civic political culture that we cherish require conditions, such as freedom of information and political competition, which the Soviet elite regards as incompatible with its political purposes. However, the USSR needs as much Western scientific knowledge and technology as it can obtain, especially if it can be gotten cheaply, partly because the burdens and distractions imposed by the centralized Soviet bureaucracy on creativity and its application so grievously constrict productivity. We can be sure that if the West allows Moscow to get what it needs, or thinks it needs from the West cheaply and easily—by, for example, making available advanced computer and energy technology on easy credit terms, without demanding in return concessions in respect to Western interests—Moscow will exploit such opportunities ruthlessly. But the symmetrics of Soviet–Western relations contain a potential for bargaining, if the West can muster sufficient will, clarity of purpose, and organizational cohesiveness. While we cannot expect the Soviet rulers to institute reforms, or to make concessions of any kind that would undermine their power, there may be room for some trade-offs between, for example, Soviet trade, technological, and general economic needs—perhaps

including concern over the standard of living of the Soviet people—
and Western concerns about reduction of secrecy and enhancement
of human rights in the USSR and Eastern Europe. Obviously, success
in such endeavors will be excruciatingly difficult to achieve, as the
course of negotiations at the 1975 Conference on Co-operation and
Security in Europe indicated, but on the outcome of efforts in this
direction depends, in large part, the quality of "détente." And of
course whatever can be achieved in government negotiations to
encourage enlightened reformist currents of Soviet and Eastern
European elite opinion—perhaps including, as moderate dissenters
such as Roy Medvedev have suggested, some members of the political elite—would indirectly foster democratic evolution.

In connection with the foregoing, some problems of communication and contact between the Western and the Soviet publics should
be mentioned. Of special importance is radio broadcasting, for
example of *samizdat* material, from which listeners in Communist-
ruled countries can acquire authentic information otherwise unavailable. But exhibitions, which enable visitors to ask searching
questions and receive candid and informed answers on every im-
aginable aspect of American life, are also extremely important.
Everything possible should be done to maintain such activities, and
also to expand scientific, educational, artistic, and other exchanges,
but only on a basis of overall reciprocity and equivalency. At present,
the exchange relationship between the two countries is marred by
such asymmetries as Soviet prohibition of the opening by foreign
nations of facilities where Soviet readers who so desire can read or
purchase foreign books, newspapers, and magazines—an opportunity
available, of course, to the Soviets in the West, where Soviet diplomats can publicly disseminate the Kremlin line with comparative
ease. There is, for example, no Soviet equivalent to publication of
Soviet propaganda documents on the Op-Ed page of the *New York
Times*—which, incidentally, I approve of if they do not appear frequently. And there is in this field a special danger: that of mis-
perceiving Soviet institutions and practices as being more similar
to their Western equivalents than they really are. For example, it
is difficult for Westerners to imagine the political uses to which
psychiatry is put in the USSR. For one thing, "success" in Soviet
Russia is measured so much more in terms of power, status, and
material advantages than it is in the "capitalist" West that dissent
or other behavior that risks the loss of these benefits seems evidence
of insanity, and hence of need for psychiatric treatment. Since the

Soviet state controls the distribution of all values and Soviet psychiatrists are state officials, they can hardly be expected to share the values of their Western colleagues. Hence "exchange" in this area is not likely to yield satisfactory results from the Western point of view, unless extraordinary sophistication and alertness is displayed on the non-Soviet side. There is, in any case, something morally repulsive about hobnobbing with "psychiatrists" who do not speak out against the abuse of their science for the persecution of such men as Leonid Plyushch or Peter Grigorenko.

To achieve reciprocity in any area of relations with the USSR requires sophisticated, patient, and above all determined bargaining. But hard bargaining in the area of cultural relations should of course be directed only at the Soviet bureaucrats who select Soviet exchange participants: they unfortunately influence to some degree the selection of American exchanges, and they determine the conditions governing exchanges—such as the traditional prohibition on spouses accompanying Soviet exchanges abroad. It should not penalize the Soviet participants themselves, provided they are genuine working scientists, scholars, or artists, for among these groups are found many of the West's best friends in the USSR. In this connection, it is heartening that in recent years some American participants in American–Soviet exchanges, in particular natural scientists, have reported that the younger Soviet scientists with whom they have come in contact are much less fearful of visiting foreign colleagues in the latters' hotel rooms and otherwise interacting with visitors than are older Soviet specialists, who have been unable to fully shake off the pall of past fears. This trend augurs well for the future, though it seems certain that the Soviet authorities will take protective measures against whatever systemically dysfunctional consequences they perceive to be inherent in it—though in so doing they may inflict harm on the Soviet economy by cramping the creativity of Soviet scientists.[105]

It is also highly desirable that bona fide Soviet scientists and scholars, once admitted to the United States as professionals and as guests, never be subjected to petty, tit-for-tat bureaucratic restrictions, such as have, reportedly, sometimes been applied.[106]

Governments—and, as a rule, only governments, in particular that of the United States—can provide the indirect but indispensable support and encouragement to reformist elements in the USSR envisaged above. However, except in very special circumstances, the executive branch of the government of the United States had best refrain from open and direct intervention on behalf of Soviet dissenters, lest such action hinder achievement of other American policy objectives, and perhaps also harm rather than help its intended beneficiaries. I should say, however, that I consider it most unfortunate that President Gerald Ford refused to receive Alexander Solzhenitsyn in June 1975. The President's action, apparently motivated by fear of irritating Moscow by associating himself or his office, particularly on the eve of the Helsinki conference, with perhaps the most eloquent modern spokesman for freedom of the word, was lamentable. It made one wonder what image of America was being conveyed to a world in which democracy was everywhere on the defensive, while both rightist and leftist authoritarianism were riding high.

It is desirable, of course, that both superpowers refrain from "interference" in the internal affairs of the other. Realism requires recognition, however, that it is far easier for the USSR to covertly violate this principle than it is for the United States. The secrecy with which the Soviet system operates—especially the KGB and the Kremlin—under cover of the traditional convention that the CPSU and a host of other Soviet "voluntary" organizations and their foreign affiliates are independent of the Soviet government, enables Moscow to conceal or disguise its military–political operations abroad far more easily and successfully than can the United States, for example. This much seems obvious in view of the discomfiture of the American government due to recent revelations about CIA cloak and dagger activities, though whether or not America should totally refrain from "dirty tricks" is a question beyond our ken.

As far as American help to Soviet dissenters is concerned, a major risk of overt action by the executive branch of our governments is that it might lend credence in the USSR—and among anti-Western elements elsewhere—to the official Soviet line that dissenters and critics are really camouflaged enemy agents. While such charges certainly must be partly discounted as demagogic, they may be believed by many members of the CPSU apparatus and the KGB, and more likely, by the propaganda-saturated Soviet "masses." One doubts, however, if they are taken seriously by sophisticated Soviet citizens. They are, of course, compatible with the extreme suspiciousness and mistrust which have traditionally been salient traits of the dominant Russian political culture. Inept overt actions or statements by the American government could tend to confirm the Kremlin legend that all dissent is conspiracy, ultimately instigated by "class enemies" abroad. In this connection, it is well to remember that traditionally there has perhaps been no people more fiercely resentful of even the appearance of efforts by foreign powers to meddle in their internal affairs than the Russians. Perhaps partly with this tradition in mind, the Soviet authorities have in recent years conducted veritable saturation campaigns of patriotic propaganda, with strong chauvinistic and xenophobic overtones. It seems likely that many Soviet citizens, perhaps a majority, still accept the regime's picture of "egghead" and "dropout" dissidents as hirelings of foreign intelligence services seeking to "penetrate" their country so as to betray its interests and undermine its security.

However, on the level of the "private sector," or perhaps one should term it the society-to-society level, American and Western opinion in general has played a very important part and will in the future have a significant, perhaps at times decisive, role to play in support of the struggle for human rights in the USSR. Much can be done in furtherance of humanity and decency and ultimately of democratic change by, for example, vigorously protesting and publicizing illegal persecution of Soviet citizens demanding the rights guaranteed them by the Soviet Constitution, by the spontaneous voluntary action of individuals and groups, and by supporting such respected organizations as Amnesty International, the International League for the Rights of Man, and those groups and associations specifically concerned with emigration by Jewish and other ethnic minorities and with other aspects of minority ethnic and religious rights and freedoms. One can only applaud the sponsorship by the AFL–CIO of Alexander Solzhenitsyn's public appearances in the United States in June and July of 1975.

Also, all who are concerned with the study of Communist systems and with world affairs generally should, I believe, do much more than in the past to incorporate into their thinking the information and, I do not hesitate to add, the insights that can be derived from acquaintance with the thinking of not a few Soviet dissenters. Not only can study of dissident literature tell us much about what Peter Reddaway has called the "continuing high dramas" of the dissenters' struggle, "in the name of values we claim to hold," but such literature also reveals, as Reddaway adds, "more than most other sources about the ways in which the Soviet Union is evolving."[107] With Reddaway's statements, and with the similar opinions of Karel van het Reve on this subject, I am in full agreement.[108]

One of the best statements on the significance of Soviet democratic dissent, for the West and for the USSR, is the "press statement of Pavel Litvinov," which Litvinov made upon his arrival in New

York on March 22, 1974. By virtue of Litvinov's distinguished contribution to the struggle for freedom in Russia, his sacrifices in that cause, and the statement's sincerity and grace, his remarks deserve attention. In them he pointed out—and nothing more needs to be said—that the freedom that Soviet citizens "can attain only through suffering is taken for granted in the West, like the air that one breathes." As a result, many of the struggles of Russians seeking "elementary personal liberties," such as freedom of information, are "incomprehensible" to Westerners. Litvinov concluded with the following appeal:

> I want all of you to understand that we have survived because the West exists and in it a Western press. I ask of you: write more about us, think about us and remember that we suffer for ideals we share with you—ideals of freedom and civil rights. Europe's noble traditions suffer in us, in Soviet Russia.[109]

Precisely how in individual cases to respond to Litvinov's appeal is a matter of conscience and of judgment about what action is appropriate in the light of circumstances. Detailed prescriptions would therefore be inappropriate. It is fitting, however, to mention one example of principled and apparently successful nongovernmental foreign support for democratic dissent in the USSR. I have in mind the two messages sent by Philip Handler, president of the American National Academy of Sciences, to Mstislav Keldysh, president of the Soviet Academy of Sciences, in early September 1973, immediately after the foreboding official press and radio campaign to which Andrei Sakharov was at that time being subjected. Peter Dornan notes that in volume and duration this campaign "exceeded the anti-Pasternak campaign of 1958 and recalled the Stalinist press of the mid-1930's and 1940's."[110] Both of Dr. Handler's cablegrams warned of the damaging effects on American–Russian scientific exchanges that could follow detention of Sakharov, or other measures against him. The second noted that if such measures were taken "it would be extremely difficult to imagine successful fulfillment of American pledges of binational scientific cooperation, the implementation of which is entirely dependent upon the voluntary effort and good will of our individual scientists and scientific institutions."[111]

As Dornan points out, it is not clear why the anti-Sakharov operation was stopped, or what weight to assign to Dr. Handler's forthright messages. Also, as has been pointed out earlier, Sakharov and his family were later to be subjected to a veritable war of nerves by regime agents. However, the noted scientist and his wife were at least spared arrest; and this "leniency" may have been a product of Kremlin concern over the consequences suggested in Dr. Handler's communications. Significantly, Sakharov himself attributed vital significance to the support he received from "world public opinion," including Dr. Handler's telegrams.[112]

An indication that Dr. Handler was correct in 1973 in stressing the dependence of American–Soviet scientific cooperation on the personal evaluation by American scientists of Moscow's treatment of their Soviet colleagues, was a 1975 report that "many American scientists" were "less than enthusiastic" about exchanges with Russia, because they were "increasingly put off by persecution of Soviet colleagues, especially of Jewish scientists wishing to emigrate."[113]

There are countless ways in which private American individuals and groups can, with no detriment to "détente"—on the contrary, to the benefit of a meaningful East–West relationship, going beyond mere government-to-government ties—support the goals sought, in various ways, by Soviet democrats. One that I shall mention in conclusion is the allocation of all possible resources of moral support, friendship, and money to helping the Soviet democrats who form part of the "third emigration" in Western Europe and the Western hemisphere. This involves, among other things, assistance in coping with problems of transition of life in a society so much more loosely structured than that of the USSR that it may sometimes seem chaotic. Only if the veterans of the struggle for freedom in Russia are enabled to achieve positions in Western society for which their skills qualify them can they fulfill the vocation that the best among them have chosen of helping to sustain the vision, hopes, and courage of their friends and associates in the homeland, and of encouraging future efforts to realize democratic aspirations. The effort I have in mind will, on the American side, require tact, patience, and the capacity to work with people who, though they have much in common with proponents of polyarchy in the West, nevertheless come out of a cultural and ideological background strikingly different from ours. For one thing, the intensity of their convictions, and the vehemence with which they express them, will often be startling to Americans. No less perplexing, perhaps, to those who do not take pains to inform themselves about the diversity of dissent and the striking individuality of some refugees from a rigid, unresponsive collectivism will be the widely varied, often clashing, prescriptions offered by emigrant democrats for basic changes in their homeland, or in the world as a whole. But it seems entirely appropriate that in a society that was created by immigrants a wholehearted effort be made to help this new wave of immigrants to help themselves—and to help us.

Postscript

Soviet policies in the months after I finished writing this book reflected, it seems, intensified commitment by the CPSU leadership both to domestic repression and to external expansionism. Brezhnev and other leading members of the Politburo demanded firm discipline and unity of action and will in the CPSU and in the international Communist movement. The Soviet leaders also called for a sharpening of the ideological struggle against "imperialism" and they warned the peoples of the Soviet bloc against the dangers of Western subversive influence. In the meantime, the USSR conducted a victorious proxy war in Southern Africa, an action scarcely compatible with its continued lip service to the cause of "détente." However, the Soviet leaders continued to carefully calculate not only the possible benefits but also the costs of power plays abroad and of suppression of criticism at home.

The young physicist Andrei Tverdokhlebov, secretary of the Moscow branch of Amnesty International, was sentenced in mid-April to a term of exile on charges of slandering the Soviet state. The case against him was ostensibly based on his challenge to the official statement that Leonid Plyushch was mentally ill. Perhaps a more important, though undisclosed factor in the proceedings against Tverdokhlebov was the authorities' anger resulting from Amnesty's publication in London of three new, hitherto unpublished issues of the *Chronicle of Current Events*, which the KGB had considered crushed after November 1972. The mildness of his sentence—by Soviet standards—was reportedly attributed by his friends to the interest displayed in his case in the West.

According to Western news reports from Moscow, intense police pressure to force Andrei and Gyuzel Amalrik to emigrate finally achieved its purpose. Expulsion from their homeland would be yet another harsh experience for the Amalriks. But to the extent that emigration represented a lesser evil for the frail Amalrik than the fate that might have befallen him, credit is due to Western historians, especially in politically crucial France, whose efforts on their colleague's behalf may have stayed the Kremlin's hand.

Soviet ruling circles were obviously angered by the continuing stream of revelations and criticism contained in the writings of former Soviet citizens now in exile. They were perhaps particularly irked by what Max Lerner in the *New York Post*, April 12, called Alexander Solzhenitsyn's one man campaign to awaken the West to the dangers of its own weakness in the face of Soviet expansionism. The Kremlin reacted with vilification in Soviet mass media. According to some reports it even went so far as to send secret police agents to France with instructions to silence emigrant intellectuals by intimidation.

In light of all this, it is not suprising—though still shocking—that Andrei Sakharov and his wife were subjected to perhaps the fiercest harassment they had ever experienced because of their continued efforts to publicize repression of civil rights activists, among them the Crimean Tatar leader Dzhemilev. The roughing up of the Sakharovs by police during Dzhemilev's trial in Omsk, Siberia indicated not only savage hostility on the part of the regime toward the Nobel laureate but also contempt for his Western admirers and well-wishers.

Barring a reversal of the reactionary tendencies signaled by such events, prospects for fulfillment of the human rights provisions of the Final Act of the Helsinki Conference on Security and Cooperation in Europe and of "relaxation of international tensions" seemed increasingly dubious. Soviet propaganda and policy in the spring of 1976 stressed the irreconcilability of the principles of Soviet-style "socialism" and of all alternative ideologies. The Soviet authorities appeared to be more and more determined to deny Soviet citizens access to information about Western-style democracy or other competing beliefs while also concealing from the outside world evidence that the consensus claimed by the Kremlin was not monolithic. It was logical for the regime to consider advocacy of civil rights and of "democratization"—and of foreign support for Soviet adherents of such values—as subversive. But in such a situation how peaceful could coexistence be and how much could tensions be relaxed?

Notes

Chapter 1

1. Carl A. Linden, "Dissidence and Détente: Djilas to Solzhenitsyn" *Georgia Political Science Association Journal,* vol. III, no. 1 (Spring 1975), pp. 105–13, at pp. 108–109.

2. For a discussion of political opposition to the Soviet system, couched in terms of efforts to alter its basic structure, top leadership, sets of "programs or policies," and individual policies, see Erik Hoffmann, "Political Opposition in the Soviet Union," in Barbara N. McLennan, ed., *Political Opposition and Dissent* (New York, 1972), pp. 329–79. Hoffmann's categories are essentially those used by H. Gordon Skilling in his article "Background to the Study of Opposition in Communist East Europe," in *Government and Opposition,* vol. III, no. 3 (Summer 1968), pp. 297–301ff. Although Skilling and Hoffmann refer to "opposition" rather than "dissent," for our purposes here the terms are interchangeable. I have slightly altered Skilling's language in the above summary.

3. Robert A. Dahl. ed., *Regimes and Opposition* (New Haven, 1973), pp. 2–3.

4. See Robert A. Dahl, *Polyarchy* (New Haven and London, 1971), chap. 1, "Democratization and Public Opposition," especially p. 14.

5. On the Soviet tendency to regard both dissent and opposition as subversive, see Leonard Schapiro, "Putting the Lid on Leninism," *Government and Opposition,* vol. II, no. 2 (January–April 1967), pp. 181–204.

6. Ibid., p. 202.

7. See, for Roy Medvedev's interpretation, his *Kniga o sotsialisticheskoi demokratii (A Book on Socialist Democracy)* (Amsterdam and Paris, 1972), pp. 71–74. An English translation of a somewhat revised, updated edition of this book was published in New York in 1975 under the title *On Socialist Democracy* and was perceptively reviewed by Stephen F. Cohen in the *New York Times Book Review* for July 13, 1975.

8. See, for example, V. Bolshakov's article, "Podryvnaya strategiya voiny nervov" ("The Subversive Strategy of the War of Nerves"), in *Pravda*, January 13, 1972, which divided Soviet dissenters, or inakomyslya-shchie, into two categories: ideologically unstable individuals and those who wanted to restore capitalism and thus were, in effect, counterrevolutionaries.

9. Yuri V. Andropov "Nerushimoe edinstvo partii i naroda" ("Unbreakable Unity of Party and People"), *Izvestiya*, June 10, 1975, p. 2.

10. See, for example, the account of the case of Alexander Ginzburg and Yuri Galanskov in Peter Reddaway, *Uncensored Russia* (New York, 1972), pp. 72–94, and additional accounts therein, and that in the *samizdat Chronicle of Current Events*, on the first eleven issues of which Reddaway's book is based. The importance of this issue is probably greater than it appears, for the Soviet authorities, reluctant to provide targets for foreign critics, tend to play it down.

11. Text in *Pravda*, October 6, 1968.

12. See, for example, Kh. Sabirov's article "Kuda natselenny otravlennye strelki" ("Whither Are the Poisoned Arrows Aimed?"), in *Sovetskaya Rossiya (Soviet Russia)*, May 29, 1969.

13. Unsigned report on a conference of Soviet and East European social scientists, entitled "Internatsionalny kharakter Leninskikh printsipov partiinogo stroitelstva" ("International Character of Leninist Principles of Party Building"), in *Partiinaya zhizn*, no. 16 (August 1973), p. 58.

14. Franklin Griffiths, "A Tendency Analysis of Soviet Policy-making," pp. 335–78 in Skilling and Griffiths, eds., *Interest Groups in Soviet Politics* (Princeton, N.J., 1971), at p. 358.

15. Ibid., p. 367.

16. Ibid., p. 372.

17. Ibid., p. 374.

18. Ibid., pp. 375–77.

19. On the Red Square seven, see Natalia Gorbanevskaya, *Red Square at Noon,* with an introduction by Harrison E. Salisbury (New York 1972). On freedom of expression in the United States during the Vietnam War, see Thomas I. Emerson, *The System of Freedom of Expression* (Vintage ed., New York, 1971), chap. IV.

20. L. G. Churchward, *The Soviet Intelligentsia* (London and Boston, 1973), p. 138.

21. Reddaway, *Uncensored Russia,* p. 23. As Reddaway makes clear in ibid., p. 24, he used the term "mainstream" to refer to dissenters who, despite certain differences of perspective, shared a "respect for law" and "mutual tolerance and lack of dogmatism," and who dared to publicly express their opinions by, for example, signing protest petitions.

22. Ibid., p. 23.

23. See Reddaway, *Uncensored Russia,* p. 205, for the above estimate.

24. Churchward, *Soviet Intelligentsia,* pp. 37 (noting a decline in social mobility and increasing difficulty for secondary school graduates in obtaining higher education), 84, 101, 133, 135–45.

25. See his "Progress, Coexistence, and Intellectual Freedom" in *Sakharov Speaks,* ed. with a foreword by Harrison E. Salisbury (New York, 1974), p. 83.

26. Ibid., p. 167.

27. See, for example, relevant documents in Leo Labedz, ed., *Solzhenitsyn* (London, 1970), pp. 1–171; Zhores A. Medvedev, *Ten Years After Ivan Denisovich* (London, 1973), pp. 1–110.

28. Albert Weeks, *Andrei Sakharov and the Soviet Dissidents* (Monarch Notes, New York, 1975), p. 68. Weeks, referring to a 1972 statement by Sakharov, asserts, "Clearly, Soviet intervention in Czechoslovakia had radicalized Sakharov."

29. Ted Robert Gurr, *Why Men Rebel* (Princeton, 1970), p. 113. With regard to the impulses that eventually led to Sakharov's break with the Soviet regime, which apparently had their roots in the scientist's disillusionment with Khrushchev's policies in the field of nuclear weapons testing, see Peter Dornan, "Andrei Sakharov: The Conscience of a Liberal Scientist," in Rudolf L. Tökés, ed., *Dissent in the USSR: Politics, Ideology and People* (Baltimore, Md., 1975), pp. 354–417, esp. pp. 360–62.

30. See Yuri Glazov, "Chto takoe demokraticheskoe dvizhenie v SSSR?" ("What is the Democratic Movement in the USSR?"), *Novy Zhurnal (New Journal),* no. 109 (1972), pp. 216–39.

31. Yuri Glazov, *Tesnye Vrata (Narrow Gates)* (Paris, 1973), provides an account of the protest petition campaign—Glazov calls it in Russian the "epistolarnaya kampaniya," or epistolary campaign—of 1968, and of what he describes as the mood of fright among most of its participants once the authorities had instituted serious, large-scale retaliatory measures; see especially pp. 206–30. According to Glazov, the collapse of the liberal intelligentsia's resistance to the regime's tightening of control over freedom of expression, signaled by the trial of the writers Yuli Daniel and Andrei Sinyavski in 1966 for publishing "slanderous" works of fiction abroad and by subsequent political trials, began before the invasion of Czechoslovakia, but the invasion further intimidated most of those who had protested or were still predisposed to do so. For a brief version in English of Glazov's analysis, see his article "Background to Dissent," in *Survey* (London, Winter 1973), pp. 75–91.

32. Andrei A. Amalrik, *Will the Soviet Union Survive Until 1984?* Preface by Henry Kamm, and commentary by Sidney Monas (New York, 1970), p. 13. For a brief account of the operations of the "prison psychiatric hospitals," see my chapter in Tökés, *Dissent in the USSR,* pp. 86–87.

33. On the thought and demands of this group—derived largely from the writings of the philosopher of religion Nicholas Berdyaev—see John Dunlop, ed., *Vserossiiki sotsial-khristyanski soyuz osvobozhdeniya naroda (The All-Russian Social-Christian Union for the Liberation of the People)* (Paris, 1975).

34. Amalrik, *Will the Soviet Union Survive Until 1984?* pp. 11–12.

35. See Medvedev, chap. 4, esp. pp. 76–82, 92–95.

36. Ibid., pp. 83–89.

37. This characterization of variance over time in the attitudes of dissenters is based on conversations with Soviet emigrants now in the United States, on what is known about Sakharov's striking change of mood after 1968, on which I shall have more to say later, and on Glazov's above-cited article in *Survey.*

38. Reddaway, *Uncensored Russia,* pp. 430–31; Roy Medvedev, *Kniga o sotsialistcheskoi demokratii,* pp. 104–10.

39. On some of the more extreme manifestations of Russian nationalist sentiment, see Rudolf L. Tökés, "Dissent: The Politics for Change in the USSR," in Tökés and Henry W. Morton, eds., *Soviet Politics and Society in the 1970's* (New York, 1974), pp. 3–59, at p. 28, citing Dmitri Pospelovski, "The Resurgence of Russian Nationalism in Samiz-

dat," in *Survey,* vol. XIX, no. 86 (Winter 1973), pp. 51–74; and Reddaway, *Uncensored Russia,* pp. 431–33, on the commitment of the "chauvinist" A. Fetisov and three of his associates to a mental institution in 1968.

40. For an exhaustive treatment of the Soviet nationality problem, including much pertinent data on ethnic discontent and dissent, see Zev Katz et al., eds., *Handbook of Major Soviet Nationalities* (New York 1975).

41. See Brzezinski's foreward to Vyacheslav Chornovil, ed., *The Chornovil Papers* (Toronto 1968). Abraham Brumberg has expressed a similar opinion in his article "Dissent in the USSR: Prospects and Perspectives," in Norton Dodge, ed., *After The Moscow Summit,* proceedings of a symposium sponsored by the Washington Chapter of the American Association for Sino–Soviet Studies, the George Washington University, May 4–5, 1973 (Mechanicsville, Md., n.d. [actually 1974]), pp. 53–58. Brumberg refers at p. 55 to the "explosive" potential of national discontent. An excellent survey of developments in recent years in the field of ethnic relations in the USSR is Teresa Rakowska-Harmstone, "Ethnic Politics in the USSR," *Problems of Communism,* May–June 1974, pp. 1–22. According to Rakowska-Harmstone (p. 1), "it can be argued that an increasingly assertive ethnic nationalism among the non-Russian minorities of the USSR has emerged as a major conflict area in Soviet domestic politics."

42. See, for example, Frederick C. Barghoorn, "Soviet Dissenters on Soviet Nationality Policy," in Wendell Bell and Walter E. Freeman, eds., *Ethnicity and National-Building* (Beverly Hills, London, 1974), pp. 117–33, especially pp. 119, 124; also Michael Brown, ed., *Ferment in the Ukraine* (London, 1971), *passim,* and Ann Sheehy, *The Crimean Tatars and Volga Germans: Soviet Treatment of Two National Minorities,* prepared for the Minority Rights Group (London, 1971).

43. Brumberg, "Dissent in the USSR," p. 55.

44. See Pavel Litvinov, comp., *The Demonstration in Pushkin Square,* trans. Manya Harari (Boston, 1969), especially pp. 74, 116–27, on Bukovski's spirited defense—conducted by himself—at his 1967 trial for allegedly slandering the Soviet system; on the similar but far more severe treatment of Bukovski—and his continued defiance—in 1971, see "The Case of Vladimir Bukovski," in *Survey* (London), no. 18, Spring 1972, pp. 123–60. The text of Amalrik's scornful rejection of what he regarded as the unfounded and illegal charges against him is available in several sources, including *A Chronicle of Current Events,* no. 17 (London, 1971), pp. 37–38.

45. Labedz, *Solzhenitsyn*, p. 43.

46. Andrei Sakharov, Roy Medvedev, V. F. Turchin, *Po voprosu imeyush-chemu bolshoe znachenie (Concerning a Problem of Great Signifi-cance)* (Torino, n.d.), p. 13.

47. Litvinov, *The Demonstration in Pushkin Square*, p. 15.

48. See Alexander Solzhenitsyn, "Na vozvrate dykhaniya i soznaniya" ("Breath and Consciousness Restored"), in Solzhenitsyn et al., *Iz-pod glyb (Out from Under the Avalanche)* (Paris, 1974), pp. 7–28, at p. 23. The quotation is from the postscript to a 1969 analysis in which Solzhenitsyn, though he found good things to say about Sakharov's well-known 1968 memorandum, criticized it for what Solzhenitsyn regarded as an excessively favorable attitude toward technical prog-ress, the "Western" conception of freedom, and other values. In the postscript and in a brief introduction, Solzhenitsyn expressed satisfac-tion that, in his opinion, Sakharov's thinking had become much more similar to his own, but once again criticized parliamentary democracy and, with regard to the problem of freedom, argued—as did other con-tributors to this symposium, especially the mathematician Igor Shafar-evich—that the most important freedom was "inner" and "spiritual" freedom. An English translation of this collection was published under the title *From Under the Rubble* in Boston in 1975.

49. Gayle Durham Hollander, "Political Communication and Dissent in the Soviet Union," in Tökés, *Dissent in the USSR*, pp. 233–75, at p. 270. The above quotations only faintly suggest the richness of Gayle Hollander's perceptive formulation.

50. Dahl, *Polyarchy*, pp. 2–3; quotation on p. 2.

51. By far the richest, most accessible source of information on the nature, content, scope, and impact of *samizdat* is Peter Reddaway's *Uncen-sored Russia*, which provides an excellent translation of the first eleven issues of the *Chronicle of Current Events* and valuable commentary; see also Tökés. "Dissent: The Politics for Change," pp. 51–52, footnote 45, and Gerd R. von Doemming, "A Guide to Proposals for Systemic Change in the USSR offered by Soviet Citizens," Reference Handbook 82, Research Dept., Radio Liberty (Munich, August 1971). Once it is completed, the *Arkhiv Samizdata*, compiled by the Radio Liberty Re-search Dept., will, of course, provide Russian-language texts of an enormous range of *samizdat* periodical and nonperiodical documents, including some that were originally published in languages other than Russian. The widest ranging exploration to date of *samizdat* and other relevant materials on Soviet dissent is in the earlier cited work of Rudolf L. Tökés. *Dissent in the USSR;* see, example, Tökés's introduction and such of the chapters, perhaps especially those by Professors Jancar and Kline, as deal with relatively unknown aspects of this multifaceted topic.

52. The foregoing is based, in part, on pp. 87–95 of my chapter in Tökés, *Dissent in the USSR.*

Chapter 2

1. Cornelia Gerstenmaier, *Die Stimme der Stummen* (3d ed., enlarged, Stuttgart, 1972), p. 62. English translation, *The Voices of the Silent* (New York, 1972).

2. Ibid., pp. 61–62; 196; 375. Gerstenmaier apparently obtained some of her data, including a figure of 4,300 students expelled from higher educational institutions in Leningrad alone in 1956–57, from Gunther Hillmann, ed., *Selbstkritik der Kommunismus* (Munich, 1967), pp. 208–15. Both authors base their statements on published Soviet sources.

3. Abraham Rothberg, *The Heirs of Stalin* (Ithaca, N.Y., 1972), pp. 337–40. The prosecution of Pimenov and Vail in 1970 is described in *A Chronicle of Current Events* (Amnesty International Publications, London), no. 16 (October 1970), pp. 6–10.

4. V. Nikitin, "Chekhoslovatskaya tragediya: otkliki, uroki, vyvody" ("The Czechoslovak Tragedy: Responses, Lessons, Conclusions), *Arkhiv Samizdata (Samizdat Archive)*, Munich, vol. 9, no. 676. Reprinted from *Posev* (Frankfurt, Germany), no. 8, August 1971.

5. Quotation in Andrei A. Amalrik, *Will the Soviet Union Survive Until 1984?* (New York, 1971), p. 7; biographical data on Galanskov in Abraham Brumberg, ed., *In Quest of Justice* (New York, 1970), pp. 466–67.

6. Pavel Litvinov, comp., *The Trial of the Four,* ed. Peter Reddaway, with a foreward by Leonard Schapiro (London, 1972), p. 101.

7. *New York Times*, November 9, 1972; communication by emigrant Soviet mathematician Alexander Esenin-Volpin to *Novoe Russkoe Slovo* (New York), November 11, 1972.

8. Natalya Gorbanevskaya, *Red Square at Noon* (New York, 1972); Peter Reddaway, *Uncensored Russia* (New York, 1972) pp. 95–111, *passim.* It should be noted that the well-known Red Square Demon-

stration "helped to stimulate many less-publicized demonstrations"—
at least fourteen in Leningrad alone, apparently. See Howard L.
Biddulph, "Strategies of the Soviet Intellectual Opposition," in Tökés,
Dissent in the USSR, p. 113.

9. Text, and list of signers, in Reddaway, *Uncensored Russia*, pp. 86–88.

10. *Sakharov Speaks*, ed. with a foreward by Harrison E. Salisbury (New
York, 1974), p. 32. Articles by Sakharov, Kurchatov, the distinguished
Soviet geneticist Nokolai Dubinin, and fifteen other leading Soviet
physical and biological scientists are contained in *What Russian Sci-
entists Say About Fallout*, ed. with an introd., by James F. Crow
(New York, 1962).

11. For text of the memorandum in English see *Sakharov Speaks*, pp.
55–114.

12. Ibid., p. 58.

13. Ibid., p. 109.

14. Ibid., p. 50. See also Dornan, "Andrei Sakharov," in Tökés, ed., *Dissent in the USSR: Politics, Ideology, and People*, pp. 393–94, on
Chakovski's attack as the opening gun in the anti-Sakharov campaign
that was to mushroom later.

15. *Sakharov Speaks*, p. 33.

16. Nikita S. Khrushchev, *Khrushchev Remembers: The Last Testament*
(Boston, 1974), p. 68. Khrushchev's account corroborates that of
Sakharov on several points.

17. "Sovjetische Wissenschaftler Fordern Demokratisierung," *Frankfurter
Allgemeine Zeitung*, December 18, 1968.

18. Alexander I. Solzhenitsyn, *The Nobel Lecture on Literature*, trans.
Thomas P. Whitney (New York, 1972), pp. 13, 17, 19, 28, 30, 36.

19. S. Zorin and N. Alekseev [pseud.], "Vremya ne zhdet" (Leningrad,
1969); anonymous, "Programma demokratischeskogo dvizheniya
Sovetskogo soyuza" (Amsterdam, 1970). For analysis of five major
programmatic dissent documents, including the above, see Frederick
C. Barghoorn, "The General Pattern of Soviet Dissent," in Peter J.
Potichnyj, ed., *Papers and Proceedings of the McMaster Conference
on Dissent in the Soviet Union* (Hamilton, Ont., Winter 1972), pp.
3–35; see also Barghoorn, "Factional, Sectoral and Subversive Opposition in Soviet Politics," in Robert A. Dahl, ed., *Regimes and Oppositions* (New Haven, 1973), pp. 27–88, at pp. 38–39, 43, 68.

20. Amalrik, *Will the Soviet Union Survive Until 1984?* especially pp.
41–67.

21. On the rift between Sakharov and the Medvedev brothers, see Dornan, "Andrei Sakharov," especially pp. 354, 363, 411.

22. Reddaway, *Uncensored Russia*, p. 150.

23. Valeri Chalidze, *To Defend These Rights* (New York, 1974), p. 53.

24. Reddaway, *Uncensored Russia*, p. 150.

25. For the early stages of persecution of the Action Group see Reddaway, *Uncensored Russia*, pp. 154–170.

26. Ibid., p. 153.

27. *Novoe Russkoe Slovo*, December 31, 1974.

28. See Peter Reddaway, "The Relentless KGB," *New York Review of Books*, February 5, 1976, p. 18.

29. Reddaway, *Uncensored Russia*, p.150.

30. *Sakharov Speaks*, p. 218. The statement quoted was signed by Sakharov, Shafarevich, and Podyapolski. It appealed to foreign opinion, particularly "psychiatric agencies and organizations," on behalf, especially, of Vladimir Bukovski and the psychiatrist Semen Gluzman, calling both men victims of "judicial revenge" for having combated the political misuse of psychiatry in the USSR, Bukovski by disclosure to world opinion of data on a number of cases of such abuse in the USSR, Gluzman by writing a report refuting the KGB's contention that Peter Grigorenko was insane. Test of Sakharov–Shafarevich–Podyapolski statement on pp. 218–21.

31. See *Arkhiv Samizdata*, no. 608, in which Chalidze recorded a KGB search on the night of March 29, 1971. Thousands of pages of documents dealing with legal problems of human rights, as well as texts of United Nations conventions and declarations and the archives of the HRC, were seized on the pretext of confiscation of "anti-Soviet materials." As Chalidze noted, if the KGB regarded such materials as anti-Soviet, it would be difficult to judge what it considered to be Soviet! See Also Chalidze, *To Defend These Rights*, pp. 209–46. On Volpin's fears, referred to above, concerning Chalidze's safety, see Alexander Sergeevich Esenin-Volpin, *On the Moscow Human Rights Committee* (New York, International League for the Rights of Man, 1972), p. 2. It should be noted that on pp. 179–85 of *To Defend These Rights* there is reprinted a 1971 document entitled "The Legal Status of the Moscow Human Rights Committee."

32. See Reddaway, "The Relentless KGB " *New York Review of Books*, February 5, 1976, p. 18. It should be noted that Reddaway in the above cited item expresses the opinion that prosecution of Kovalev

was motivated partly by the authorities' anger at his connection with Amnesty International. As Reddaway points out, the Soviet branch of Amnesty did not attempt to plead the cause of Soviet victims of political persecution, confining its activities to cases in Chile, Yugoslavia, and Sri Lanka. However, one must assume that both its Western connections and its violation of traditional Soviet hostility to any organized expression of political or philosophical opinion incompatible with the regime's stance rendered it liable to suppression. But, as Reddaway emphasized, the KGB's anti-Amnesty campaign raised questions about how seriously Moscow was taking its obligations under the Helsinki agreements on international freedom of communication.

33. See *Human Rights in U.S.S.R.*, the journal of the Brussels-based International Committee for the Defense of Human Rights in the U.S.S.R., no. 7–8, 1974, p. 18.

34. Quotation in Alfred Erich Senn, "An Intracontinental Forum?" *Problems of Communism*, May–June, 1975, pp. 46–47, at p. 47.

35. Litvinov, *Trial of the Four*, introd. p. 10.

36. Amalrik, *Will the Soviet Union Survive?*, 1970, p. xxiii.

37. Pavel Litvinov, comp. *The Demonstration in Pushkin Square*, with an introd. by Karel van het Reve (Boston, 1969), p. 125.

38. Ibid., p. 117.

39. *Sakharov Speaks*, pp. 98, 119–20.

40. Ibid., pp. 79–81.

41. Ibid., p. 95.

42. Ibid., pp. 67–68.

43. The language used in *Sakharov Speaks* differs slightly from mine. On the USSR's record in respect to ratification of international conventions such as the above-mentioned Declaration, see Chalidze, *To Defend These Rights*, chap. 2.

44. *Sakharov Speaks*, p. 131.

45. Ibid., p. 132.

46. Ibid., p. 130.

47. Ibid., p. 132.

48. For the entire list of recommended reform measures, which, asserted the authors, "could be carried out in the course of four or five years," see ibid., pp. 127–29.

49. For a brief interpretive summary, see Frederick C. Barghoorn, "Medvedev's Democratic Leninism," in *Slavic Review*, vol. 32, no. 3

(September 1973), pp. 590–95; see also Stephen F. Cohen's review of the English translation in the *New York Times Book Review* of July 13, 1975.

50. *Kniga o sotsialisticheskoi demokratii*, pp. 329–37; quotations on p. 330.

51. Reddaway, *Uncensored Russia*, p. 421.

52. Quoted in Foy D. Kohler et al., *Soviet Strategy for the Seventies* (Center for Advanced International Studies, University of Miami, 1973), p. 84. This study and the Center's companion volume, by Leon Gouré et al., entitled *Convergence of Communism and Capitalism: the Soviet View*, also published in 1973, contains much pertinent information on Moscow's foreign policy perspectives in the 1960's and early 1970's.

53. Litvinov, *Trial of the Four*, p. 9.

54. Ibid., pp. 9–10.

55. Text in *Grani* (Frankfurt, West Germany), no. 52 (1962), pp. 151–54. There is a French text in Michel Slavinsky, ed., *La Presse clandestine en U.S.S.R.* (Paris, 1970), pp. 35–38.

56. Text in *Grani*, no. 64 (1967), pp. 167–75.

57. Ibid., pp. 169–70.

58. Ibid., pp. 172–75.

59. Galanskov's attack came in a letter, the text of which is in *Grani*, no. 67 (1968), which attacked Sholokhov for statements belittling Sinyavski and Daniel, which Sholokhov made as a delegate to the Twenty-third CPSU Congress in 1966.

60. One indication of the intimidating effect of Czechoslovakia was the decline in attention paid to events there after the invasion, in the elite *samizdat* journal *Political Diary*—in which, moreover, the invasion itself was not discussed. See especially pp. 311–434. It should be kept in mind that this journal did not reach the West in its entirety.

61. Gorbanevskaya, *Red Square at Noon*, pp. 283–84.

62. At least this seems to have been true in the case of the former Soviet sociologist I. G. Zemtsov, who left the USSR for Israel in 1973. See his testimony in "Conversation With an Emigrant," Radio Liberty Research 269/7S, June 27, 1975.

63. *Sakharov Speaks*, pp. 144–45.

64. Ibid., p. 145.

65. Ibid., p. 157.

66. Ibid., p. 140.

67. Ibid., p. 78.

68. Ibid., p. 107.

69. Ibid., p. 108.

70. Ibid., p. 133.

71. Ibid., p. 144.

72. Ibid., p. 174.

73. Ibid., p. 157.

74. Ibid., p. 171.

75. Ibid., p. 181.

76. Ibid., p. 184.

77. Ibid., p. 204.

78. Ibid., pp. 203–204.

79. Ibid., p. 205.

80. Ibid., p. 209.

81. Ibid., p. 214.

82. Amalrik, *Will the Soviet Union Survive?*, p. 55.

83. Ibid., p. 57.

84. Ibid., p. 58.

85. James F. Clarity, "A Freed Writer Defying Moscow," *New York Times*, July 23, 1975. Clarity also reported that Amalrik had been refused a passport, necessary to apply for a visa, in turn necessary for him to proceed abroad, in response to academic invitations from Holland and the United States. Instead, the authorities had, Amalrik said, urged him to apply to go to Israel—which he declined to do—and were also pressuring him to denounce his "anti-Soviet" book, *Will the USSR Survive Until 1984?*.

86. For text, and information on Amalrik's personal situation in the fall of 1975, see "Andrei Amalrik on Detente," *New York Times*, October 22, 1975.

87. See "U.S. Interests and Priorities in Relations with the Soviet," *New York Times*, October 31, 1975.

88. Labedz, *Solzhenitsyn*, p. 84.

89. *Nobel Lecture*, p. 27. See John B. Dunlop, Richard Haugh, and Alexis Klimoff, eds., *Aleksandr Solzhenitsyn: Critical Essays and Documentary Materials* (Belmont, Mass., 1973), p. 479, for information on the composition of the Nobel Lecture. This collection con-

tains a translation thereof that differs somewhat from the one by Thomas B. Whitney. The latter, however, is better known and more accessible, and is the one cited herein.

90. Ibid., p. 28.

91. Ibid., pp. 29–30.

92. Ibid., pp. 31–38.

93. "An Interview with Alexander Solzhenitsyn," *Survey*, vol. 19, no. 4 (Fall 1973), pp. 163–77, at pp. 175–76.

94. Cited here from Alexander I. Solzhenitsyn, "Peace and Violence," *New York Times*, September 15, 1973, p. 31.

95. For the full Russian text of Solzhenitsyn's interview with Cronkite, used here, see *Russkaya Mysl* (Paris), no. 3007, July 11, 1974, pp. 6–7, 10.

96. An English translation was published in the *Sunday Times* (London) of March 3, 1974. The Russian text is available in *Pismo vozhdyam Sovetskogo Soyuza* (Paris: YMCA Press, 1974). Citation herein will be from the Russian text, but the English text has also been perused.

97. *Pismo vozhdyam*, p. 11.

98. Ibid., p. 12.

99. Ibid., pp. 13–14.

100. Ibid., p. 28.

101. Ibid., p. 31.

102. Ibid., p. 39.

103. Ibid., p. 45.

104. Ibid., p. 46.

105. Ibid., pp. 37–38, 48–49.

106. Andrei Sakharov, *O pisme Aleksandra Solzhenitsyna Vozhdyam Sovetskogo Soyuza* (New York: Chronicle Press, 1974). An English translation, by Guy Daniels was published in the June 13, 1974, issue of *The New York Review of Books*. References here will be to the Russian original.

107. *O pisme*, pp. 8–9.

108. Ibid., pp. 4–5, 9.

109. Ibid., pp. 6–7, 10.

110. Ibid., pp. 7–8; quotation at p. 10.

111. Ibid., pp. 10–12.

112. Ibid., p. 10.

113. Ibid., p. 12.

114. Ibid., p. 13.

115. Ibid., p. 8.

116. Ibid., p. 14.

117. I refer herein to the Russian text of *O strane i mire*, distributed by Khronika Press, New York, in August 1975. The English subtitle carried by that printing is "My Country and the World," but I prefer the more literal translation above. Late in 1975 Alfred Knopf published an English version, translated by Guy Daniels, entitled *My Country and the World*.

118. *O strane i mire*, p. 6.

119. On Sakharov's concern over the fate of his colleagues Sergei Kovalev, Andrei Tverdokhlebov, and others, see ibid., p. 30, and especially the footnote to p. 67.

120. *O strane i mire*, pp. 34, 35.

121. Ibid., p. 39.

122. Ibid., pp. 44–45.

123. Ibid., pp. 45, 48, and 73.

124. Ibid., p. 47.

125. Ibid., p. 45.

126. Ibid., pp. 22, 46.

127. Ibid., pp. 46–52.

128. Ibid., pp. 53–56; quotation at p. 56.

129. Ibid., p. 57.

130. Ibid., p. 58.

131. Ibid., pp. 59–64; quotations at pp. 62, 64.

132. Ibid., p. 65.

133. Ibid., p. 66.

134. Ibid., pp. 67–68.

135. Ibid., p. 69.

136. Ibid., p. 71.

137. See, respectively, points 1 and 5, at pp. 71–72 and 74.

138. Ibid., p. 76.

139. The analysis that follows is based on Roy Medvedev, "Problema demokratizatsii i problema razryadki ("The Problem of Democrati-

zation and the Problem of Relaxation of Tensions"), *Materialy Samizdata*, Radio Liberty, November 16, 1973; Roy Medvedev, "On Solzhenitsyn's *Gulag Archipelago*," *Index*, Summer 1974, vol. 3, no. 2, pp. 65–74; Roy Medvedev, "Chto nas zhdet vperedi? O pisme A. I. Solzhenitsyna" ("What Awaits Us in the Future? About A. I. Solzhenitsyn's Letter"), *Materialy Samizdata*, Radio Liberty, October 18, 1974. These documents were dated by Roy Medvedev October 1973, January 21, 1971, and May 1–20, 1974, respectively.

140. Roy Medvedev, "Problema demokratizatsii," p. 3, 7–9.

141. Ibid., p. 10.

142. Ibid., pp. 4–5.

143. Ibid., p. 3–4; quotation at p. 3.

144. Ibid., p. 11.

145. Ibid., pp. 11–12; quotation at p. 12.

146. Ibid., p. 14.

147. Ibid., p. 15.

148. Ibid., pp. 15–16.

149. Ibid., p. 20.

150. Ibid., pp. 20–21; quotation at p. 20.

151. Roy Medvedev, "Chto nas zhdet vperedi?", p. 1.

152. Ibid., pp. 3–5, 14–17.

153. Ibid., p. 9.

154. Ibid., p. 18.

155. Ibid., pp. 18–19.

156. Ibid., p. 6.

157. Ibid., pp. 13–14.

158. Ibid., pp. 9–10; quotation at p. 10.

159. Ibid., p. 3.

160. Ibid., p. 7.

161. Ibid., pp. 7–8; quotation at p. 7.

162. Ibid., p. 9.

163. Ibid., p. 18.

164. See the third of five sections of "Press-konferentsiya A. I. Solzhenitsyna," *Novoe Russkoe Slove*, January 24, 1975. It is worth noting that this remark was preceded by harshly negative sarcastic comments, in a similar vein, on Medvedev's best-known book, *Let History Judge*.

165. See Roy Medvedev, "Vtoroi tom knigi A. I. Solzhenitsyna 'Arkhipelag Gulag'" ("The Second Volume of A. I. Solzhenitsyn's *The Gulag Archipelago*," *Arkhiv Samizdata*, no. 1998. Medvedev takes exception here to Solzhenitsyn's view that labor camps under Lenin were comparable to those built by Stalin, and to much else, especially what he regards as Solzhenitsyn's inhumane attitude toward Communists tortured and executed during Stalin's terror in 1937. He praises the work, however, for truthfully revealing Stalin's crimes. See also Hedrick Smith, "Russian Praises A 'Gulag' Sequel," *New York Times*, October 6, 1974; James F. Clarity, "A Dissident Joins Sholokhov Dispute," ibid., February 8, 1975.

166. For the Murarka–Stephens interview with the Sakharovs, see the *London Observer*, June 8, 1975, p. 19; the Turchin–Roy Medvedev interview is in ibid., June 15, 1975, pp. 23–25.

167. See James F. Clarity, "A Freed Dissident Says Soviet Doctors Sought to Break His Political Beliefs," *New York Times*, February 4, 1976.

168. Text in *A Chronicle of Human Rights in the USSR*, nos. 5–6, November–December 1973 (New York, 1974), p. 8.

169. Ibid., pp. 8–9.

170. Ibid., p. 10.

171. Ibid., p. 9.

172. See Vadim Belotserkovsky, in "Soviet Dissenters: Solzhenitsyn, Sakharov, Medvedev," *Partisan Review* (vol. XLII, no. 1), pp. 35–68; for a brief, balanced evaluation of the first stage of the trialogue —which, however, like Belotserkovsky's, does not deal with Roy's May 1974 essay—see Rudolf L. Tökés, "Solzhenitsyn, Sakharov, Medvedev: The Dissidents' Detente Debate," *New Leader*, March 4, 1974, pp. 11–13.

173. See, for example, the above-cited article by Belotserkovsky and Jeri Laber, "The Real Solzhenitsyn," *Commentary* (vol. 50, no. 5, May 1974), pp. 32–35. Laber, at p. 35, calls Solzhenitsyn "an authentic reactionary."

174. This was the position taken by Boris Shragin in his "Escapes From Freedom," a review of the contributions of Solzhenitsyn, Shafarevich, and others to *From Under the Rubble*, in the *New York Review of Books* for June 26, 1975. Shragin, in conclusion, says of Solzhenitsyn and his friends that even if their search for a future is an error, "it is an error that bears the mark of tragedy." However, Pavel Lit-

vinov, in "The Human Rights Movement in the USSR," in *Index on Censorship,* Spring 1975, although he referred to "the debate that is presently in progress" over Solzhenitsyn's *Letter to Soviet Leaders,* preferred to stress "the things that unite the members of the movement," such as "compassion towards the oppressed man... towards the minority oppressed by the majority." See p. 15.

175. See, for example, the lead editorial in the *Wall Street Journal,* July 23, 1975, entitled "Jerry, Don't Go," asserting, among other things, that Solzhenitsyn was "totally right" about the pending conference and urging Mr. Ford to change his mind about going to Helsinki. The editorial also suggested that the drop in the President's rating between a recent Gallup poll and a later Harris poll might have been due to his refusal to meet with Solzhenitsyn.

176. "European 'Security,'" *New York Times,* July 21, 1975. The editorial observed that Brezhnev had "maneuvered all the major leaders of the Western world one by one into the commitment to sign the C.S.C.E. declaration at a euphoric 35-nation" conference.

177. For the original Russian text of Solzhenitsyn's statement about the Helsinki conference, see *Novoe Russkoe Slovo,* July 22, 1975.

178. "Kissinger Sees Peril in Solzhenitsyn's Views," *New York Times,* July 17, 1975.

179. My translation, from text in *Novoe Russkoe Slovo,* July 8, 1975.

180. "No Time to Say Hello, Goodbye," *New Republic,* July 26, 1975, p. 6.

181. Malcolm W. Browne, "Digging Out the News in Soviet Bloc Has Not Been Made Easy By Detente," *New York Times,* October 20, 1975.

182. G. Arbatov, "Manevry protivnikov razryadki" ("Maneuvers of the Opponents of Detente"), *Izvestiya,* September 4, 1975, pp. 3–4. A brief summary, innocuously entitled "Reciprocity after Helsinki," was published in the *New York Times* of October 8, 1975.

183. See, for example, Konstantin Zarodov, "Leninskaya strategiya i taktika revolyutsionnoi borby," ("Leninist Strategy and Tactics of Revolutionary Struggle"), *Pravda,* August 6, 1975. This article, calling for the "hegemony of the proletariat" in the revolutionary struggle—apparently with Portugal and perhaps other West European countries in mind—appeared, in the opinion of some observers, to reflect top-level Soviet foreign-policy debates and even, in view of Brezhnev's meeting with Zarodov on September 17, a shift in

Kremlin policy toward heightened militancy. The "Zarodov affair" is discussed in detail in Radio Liberty Research reports 399/75 and 420/75, dated, respectively, September 23 and October 3, 1975. Pertinent also is Flora Lewis, "French Communists Take a More Militant Position," *New York Times,* November 13, 1975, which attributed their new militancy in part to "an increasingly hard ideological tone that has been coming from Moscow."

It should be added that the French Communist Party significantly altered its propaganda line in mid-November 1975, apparently in an effort to counter the growth in influence of their main competitors on the left in France, the French Socialists. The French Communist leadership, in a joint statement with the Italian Communists, pledged to guarantee "freedom of thought and expression" and other democratic norms. On this joint declaration, see Alvin Shuster, "French and Italian Reds Concur on Aims," in the *New York Times,* November 18, 1975. Apparently one way the French Communists thought they could demonstrate their new devotion to "democracy" was by joining the Socialists in calling for the release of the Soviet mathematician Leonid Plyushch from detention in a "psychiatric" hospital, as James F. Clarity pointed out in his story on Plyushch's press conference in Paris on February 3, 1976. See Clarity, "A Freed Dissident Says Soviet Doctors Sought to Break IIis Political Beliefs," *New York Times,* February 21, 1976. And the French delegation at the CPSU Twenty-fifth Congress a few weeks later—whether or not for tactical reasons time will tell—repudiated the traditional Soviet doctrine of the "dictatorships of the proletariat, which the Italians had already earlier abandoned.

Chapter 3

1. Valeri Chalidze, *To Defend These Rights* (New York 1974), *passim,* especially chapter 1–4.

2. Ibid., p. 68.

3. Ibid., p. 69; Chalidze cites in footnote 6, p. 320, a 1969 Soviet work attacking alleged "imperialist ideological sabotage."

4. See E. P. Prokhorov, "Leninskaya kontseptsiya svobody pechati" ("The Leninist Conception of Freedom of the Press"), in *Voprosy*

teorii i praktiki massovykh sredstv propagandy, Vypusk 4 (Problems in the Theory and Practice of Mass Propaganda Media, Installment 4) (Moscow, 1971), pp. 5–40.

5. Ibid., pp. 8–10; quotations at pp. 8, 10.

6. Ibid., pp. 11, 12.

7. Ibid., p. 30.

8. Ibid., pp. 30–31; quotation at p. 31.

9. Ibid., p. 33.

10. The discussion above is based in part on Frederick C. Barghoorn, "The General Pattern of Soviet Dissent," in Peter J. Potichnyj, ed., *Papers and Proceedings of the McMaster Conference on Dissent in the Soviet Union* (Hamilton, Ont., 1972), pp. 3–35, especially pp. 19–21.

11. Peter Reddaway, *Uncensored Russia* (New York, 1972), pp. 24–25, reports on the practice of the first twelve issues of *Chronicle*. The first five carried the legend "Human Rights Year in the Soviet Union," reflecting, Reddaway notes, the "link" between the origin of *Chronicle* and the designation by the United Nations of 1968 as International Human Rights Year. The *Chronicle* changed its legend in its sixth issue to "Human Rights Year in the Soviet Union Continues," and in no. 12, in 1970, to "The Movement in Defense of Human Rights in the Soviet Union Continues," a formulation that persisted until the suspension of *Chronicle* after the appearance of its twenty-seventh issue in November 1972—and also in the continuation of *Chronicle*, under the new title *A Chronicle of Human Rights in the USSR*, published by Chronicle Press in New York beginning in the spring of 1973, as well as in issues 28–33 of *Chronicle of Current Events*, originating inside the USSR in defiance of KGB warnings of severe reprisals if further issues were disseminated, and printed in New York as *A Chronicle of Human Rights*, the latter edited by Chalidze, Peter Reddaway, Pavel Litvinov, and Edward Klein. The text of Article 19 appeared in all issues of both journals.

12. The English-language version of these two works, combined in one volume, is *The Medvedev Papers* (London 1971), with introduction by the British physicist John Ziman; on Zhores's committal and the successful struggle for his release, see Zhores and Roy Medvedev, *A Question of Madness* (New York, 1971).

13. *Medvedev Papers*, pp. 178–81; quotation in note 1, at pp. 180, 181.

14. Ibid., pp. 181–82.

15. See Harold D. Lasswell, *World Politics and Personal Insecurity* (New York, 1935), chapter VIII, for the term "primary contact" (migration, travel, etc.) and for a seminal discussion of its varied effects. In chapter IX of the same study Lasswell deals with effects of "secondary contact" (news channels, etc.).

16. *Medvedev Papers*, pp. 182–91; quotation at p. 191. On pp. 200–204, Zhores Medvedev describes the functions performed in this process by the KGB and by appropriate party agencies. That the practices described by Medvedev were still in force in 1975 was indicated by Loren Graham's report in the *New York Times* ("Other Scientific Exchanges Are Not So Smooth," July 20, 1975) that American scientists involved in exchanges with Russia, in some cases, objected to their inability "to form research teams in what they consider the normal manner, by inviting to come to work with them on the subjects they wish those particular Soviet scholars whose published research they know and admire. Instead, the Americans must wait to see whom the Soviet Government sends them...." It should be noted that in this balanced appraisal of the results to date of American–Soviet scientific cooperation, in space and elsewhere, Graham observed that there had been mutually beneficial results in some fields, and he concluded on a note of mingled hope and skepticism by asserting that, in the judgment of American scientists and science administrators, "the most difficult, but the most promising, period of negotiations between the two countries" was "still to come."

17. *Medvedev Papers*, pp. 190ff.

18. Most of the first 112 pages of the *Medvedev Papers*, and a considerable portion of the remainder, are devoted to a low-key account of the administrative charade imposed by authorities in several chains of command upon its author. On the KGB's rather clumsy effort at recruitment entrapment, see pp. 34–44.

19. *Medvedev Papers*, pp. 243–54; quotations on p. 249.

20. Ibid., pp. 354–64. See also pp. 301–50, where Medvedev describes in detail gross but furtive interference by postal authorities with his own correspondence with foreign colleagues, and related experiences, leading to his development of methods by which he successfully analyzed the censors' techniques. Chalidze, incidentally, in *To Defend These Rights*, presents evidence of interference with his correspondence with, for example, the president of the International League for the Rights of Man, in America, and the president of the International

Institute of Human Rights, in Belgium, in addition to evidence of prosecutions of Soviet citizens for addressing letters to foreign embassies or headquarters of foreign radio stations. See pp. 84–88.

21. *Medvedev Papers*, pp. 282, 297.

22. Ibid., p. 259.

23. Ibid., pp. 116–51.

24. Ibid., pp. 273–77; Svetlana Allilueva, *Tolko odin god (Only one Year)* (New York, 1970), pp. 201–11, 22. Allilueva writes of a friend, a talented ethnographer of Negro extraction, who was not allowed to visit Africa, of experts on Spanish literature not permitted to go to Spain, etc.

25. *Medvedev Papers*, pp. 178, 180.

26. *To Defend These Rights*, pp. 43–44.

27. Ibid., p. 48. On the next page, Chalidze refers to the "movement of armed forces into Czechoslovakia despite the guarantees of the 1955 Warsaw Pact renouncing the use or threat of force and renouncing interference in the internal affairs of signatory states," citing an official Soviet document in support of his statement.

28. Andrei A. Amalrik, *Involuntary Journey to Siberia* (New York, 1970), pp. 1–134, 195–205; Amalrik's remarks to Clarity quoted from Susan Jacoby, "Andrei Amalrik, Rebel," *New York Times Magazine*, July 29, 1973, p. 36.

29. Andrei A. Amalrik, *Will the Soviet Union Survive Until 1984?* 1971, pp. 95–106.

30. Ibid., p. 106.

31. Pavel Litvinov, "The Human Rights Movement in the USSR," *Index on Censorship* (Spring 1975), pp. 11–15, at p. 14.

32. *Sakharov Speaks*, pp. 228–29. Sakharov's statement was read on his behalf by his representative, Dr. Herman Feschbach.

33. The text of Sakharov's appeal was released by the International League for the Rights of Man on April 22, 1975. The wide range and high quality of Tverdokhlebov's thinking and implementing activity in the human rights field are apparent from even a cursory examination of his book *V zashchitu parv cheloveka (In Defense of the Rights of Man)* (New York, 1975). According to an "appeal" (obrashchenie) to *Novoe Russkoe Slovo*, dated April 25, 1975, Tverdokhlebov was, after the lifting of Chalidze's passport by the Soviet authorities and the departure of the physicist Boris Zuckerman and the mathema-

tician Alexander Esenin-Volpin from the USSR, "the last representative of the analytical tendency in the Soviet human rights movement," and his arrest indicated that the authorities had decided that "serious, nonpolitical study" of the juridical system was as dangerous as "even loud protests."

34. See *To Defend These Rights*, especially chapter 5, "Freedom of Movement."

35. See Ernest J. Simmons, "The Writers," in H. Gordon Skilling and Franklyn Griffiths, eds., *Interest Groups in Soviet Society* (Princeton, New Jersey, 1971), p. 279. Simmons quoted from English text of an open letter addressed by Chukovskaya to the Soviet leaders, published in the *New York Times*, November 19, 1966.

36. Leonard Schroeter, *The Last Exodus* (New York, 1974), pp. 366–67, reports Mikhail Epelman's effort (still unsuccessful at the time of publication of Schroeter's book) to invoke articles of the Declaration —including 13, 15 (the right to change nationality—in this case, of a spouse, and 10 (on compulsory jurisdiction of the International Court of Justice)—which, Schroeter notes, had been accepted without reservation by the USSR, and could therefore be considered, thought Epelman, legally binding, provided Israel, the only government authorized to bring the case to the World Court, had been willing to do so, which it was not. Chalidze, in *To Defend These Rights*, p. 97, construes Article 2 of the Declaration, asserting the availability of all rights referred to in it without regard to race, political opinion, sex, etc., as constituting recognition, "as a civil right," of the right to leave one's country.

37. *To Defend These Rights*, pp. 99–114; quotation at p. 106.

38. Schroeter, *Last Exodus, passim,* and especially pp. 34–36, 377–400. There is, an extensive literature on Soviet Jews in general and on the struggle of many of them, first to achieve rights and facilities of cultural identity and expression equivalent to those enjoyed by other non-Russian national minorities (limited as these are and have been since the advent of "Stalinism"), and then, as that effort met with no response by the authorities save obstruction, stony silence, and repression, to leave a country where they were neither accepted as Russians (even when subjectively fully assimilated into the dominant, Russian culture) nor permitted to live as Jews. Schroeter's study, a recent one, is a serious, careful work. See also, on problems especially relevant to our concerns here, Aleksander Voronel and Viktor Yakhot's two collections of articles, entitled, respectively, *I Am*

a Jew and *Jewishness Rediscovered,* both published by the Academic Committee on Soviet Jewry and the Anti-Defamation League of B'nai B'rith (New York, 1973 and 1974, respectively). Both consist of *samizdat* materials distributed in the USSR in or before 1972 and written by, among others, the physicists Voronel and Yakhot, both active participants in the Jewish movement; Larisa Bogoraz, who asks herself in her essay in the 1973 collection, "Do I Feel I Belong to the Jewish People?" and answers, in effect, that she is both a Jew and a Russian, and neither; and Andrei Tverdokhlebov, whose penetrating analysis in the 1973 volume of "anti-parasite" legislation seems unconnected with the problem of Jewishness. See also William Korey, *The Soviet Cage: Anti-Semitism in Russia* (New York, 1973). For analysis of aspects of early stage of Soviet Jewish protest, see Frederick C. Barghoorn, "Soviet Dissenters on Soviet Nationality Policy," in Wendell Bell and Walter E. Freeman, eds., *Ethnicity and Nation-Building* (Beverly Hills, 1974), pp. 117–34, especially pp. 126–31.

39. Schroeter, *Last Exodus,* p. 377.

40. Ibid., p. 386.

41. Schroeter cites the above-quoted statement by the HRC but gives no reference; Sakharov's statement is in *Sakharov Speaks,* p. 212. See also *Sakharov Speaks,* pp. 159–63.

42. Schroeter, *Last Exodus,* p. 378.

43. On Solzhenitsyn's decision not to leave Russia in 1970, see Per Egil Hegge, "Solzhenitsyn and the Nobel Prize," *Survey* (Spring 1972), pp. 100–111, at pp. 107–109. Excerpts from Shafarevich's statement— of which the full text was published in *Russkaya Mysl,* in Paris, on January 9, 1975—are in *Novoe Russkoe Slovo,* February 16, 1975, which also published the full text of Daniel's reply to Shafarevich. See also ibid., March 6, 1975, for the text of the "Declaration" by Rostropovich replying to Shafarevich. Quotations above are from cited issues of *Novoe Russkoe Slovo.* See also John Gruen, "Only in the West Can We Fulfill Our Art," *New York Times,* March 23, 1975.

44. Schroeter, *Last Exodus,* pp. 392–99.

45. Aleksander Voronel, "The Social Pre-Conditions of the National Awakening of the Jews in the USSR," in *I Am a Jew,* pp. 25–37, at pp. 28–29. Vernon Aspaturian's chapter, "The Non-Russian Nationalities," in Allen Kassof, ed., *Prospects for Soviet Society* (New York 1967), pp. 143–98, noted that already in the 1960's the regime had "restricted enrollment in higher educational institutions" for those

nationalities which had been traditionally "overrepresented," but he included in this category not only Jews, Georgians, and Armenians but also Russians; however, he stressed that Jews had suffered the greatest decline in "representation," See p. 176.

46. My estimate is based on data in Schroeter, *Last Exodus*, pp. 352, 375.

47. Roy Medvedev. "Blizhnevostochny konflict i evreiski vopros v SSSR" ("The Middle East Conflict and the Jewish Question in the USSR"), *Arkhiv Samizdata*, vol. 7, no. 496, 49 pp. in all, at pp. 28, 34–36; quotation at p. 36. The documents in A. S. are paginated separately rather than consecutively.

48. A summary and analysis of the Medvedev–Zand dispute is available in Korey, *The Soviet Cage*, pp. 287–90.

49. Schroeter, *Last Exodus*, p. 339.

50. Quotation from Christopher S. Wren, "Soviet Jews Worried Over Emigration," *New York Times*, December 20, 1974.

51. *Current* (newsletter of the Committee of Concerned Scientists), vol. 3, no. 1, March 1975, p. 9. The *New York Times* for February 7, 1976 carried a story by Christopher S. Wren entitled, "Seven Jews Who Returned to Soviet Say Life in Israel Is Harsh," reporting a press conference at which the returnees assaulted Israel as a "racist," exploitative, society. This seemed an effort, as Wren wrote, to "defuse" the emigration issue.

52. See, for example, Naomi Shepherd, "The Soviet Jews in Israel: Coping with Free Choices," *New York Times*, April 27, 1975. Shepherd reports, among other things, a 50-percent drop in arrivals in Israel in the first quarter of 1975, as compared with the corresponding period of 1974. See also Michael T. Kaufman, "Soviet Jews Are Discovering Difficulties in Adjusting to Life Here," ibid. March 8, 1975. Kaufman quotes Andrei Sedykh, editor of the emigrant Russian-language daily *Novoe Russkoe Slovo*, as saying that the Soviets had created "an army of unhappy people" in emigration. There is reason to believe that receipt of information by Soviet Jews still in the USSR about the difficulties of life abroad may have discouraged some from seeking to leave the country. Of course, Soviet propaganda, which usually conceals evidence of Jews' desire to leave— except in occasional cases in which a horrible example of "criminal" activity can be displayed—has made much of such favorable (from its point of view) events as vocal criticism, by a small number of former Soviet Jews abroad, of their unsatisfactory treatment, and the

efforts of a few hundred emigrants to return to the Soviet Union. See also *New York Times* unsigned dispatch from Tel Aviv dated July 6, 1975, entitled, "Fears Sharply Slash Immigration to Israel". This dispatch reported that less than half as many Jews had reached Israel in the first five months of 1975 as during the same period of 1974. One reason cited in the dispatch for the diminished rate of emigration—which, so far as I have been able to determine, continued in 1975 and 1976—was that Moscow issued fewer exit permits, although a few well known Jews with support, in this case abroad, received permission to depart. A defense of restrictive Soviet policy on emigration signed by Boris Shumilin, a high Soviet police official, was published in the *New York Times* February 3, 1976. Asserting that Soviet Jewish emigration to Israel decreased in 1975 by 50 percent compared with 1974 (only 11,700 left for Israel in 1975, he said), Shumilin attributed the drop to reports received from abroad by Soviet Jews of "lack of stability and security" and other unsatisfactory conditions in Israel. He praised Soviet "humanitarianism" and criticized "international Zionist circles" for allegedly seeking to make political capital of the issue of Jewish emigration from the USSR.

53. Schroeter, *Last Exodus*, p. 375.

54. Ibid., p. 376.

55. See ibid., pp. 13–28, for a nontechnical but informed discussion of the difficulties, in the Soviet context, of identifying the Jewish community and determining its number.

56. On the alternatives facing the Kremlin and the future prospects for Soviet Jewry, see, besides Schroeter, *Last Exodus*, pp. 397–400, Korey, *Soviet Cage*, pp. 326–28, and Leonard Schapiro, "The Soviet Jews," *New York Review of Books*, July 19, 1973, p. 4.

57. See statement made on July 25, 1974, by Professor Edward Allworth, Director, Program on Soviet Nationality Problems, Columbia University, in volume, *Détente*, before U.S., Congress, House of Representatives, Committee on Foreign Affairs, Subcommittee on Europe, 93d Cong., 2d sess., 1974, pp. 323–27. Allworth also included the Karelians, a nationality culturally akin to the Finns, in this category, along with, of course, the Jews. For extensive, relatively recent material on the increasingly active struggle of some Soviet Germans to enjoy what they have begun to perceive as their national rights, and in some cases to proceed to the German Federal Republic. See *Re Patria* (in Russian) published by *Posev* (Frankfurt, 1975). According to

official West German government figures, about 10,000 Soviet Germans emigrated from the USSR in 1973 and 1974, and the figure for 1975 appears to have been about 5,000. I am indebted for this data to Mr. Juozas Kazlas, an expert on the Soviet Germans. See also, on the Crimean Tatars, my above-cited chapter in Bell and Freeman, especially pp. 125–26; and, on that group and the Germans, the important study by Ann Sheehy, *The Crimean Tatars and the Volga Germans: Soviet Treatment of Two National Minorities* (prepared for Minority Rights Group, London, 1971). Indispensable background material on the Tatars and other deported peoples is in Robert Conquest, *The Nation Killers* (New York, 1970). It should be kept in mind that the Crimean Tatars—who, incidentally, are described in official Soviet sources not as Crimean Tatars but simply as Tatars— and the Germans, most of whom, like the Tatars, now reside in Central Asia (whither Stalin deported them, thousands of miles from their old homelands), have not been by any means fully "rehabilitated," if rehabilitation includes permission to return to lands where ancestors lived for centuries before deportation. It should be noted that five of the eight ethnic groups whose members were shipped off en masse to distant points during World War II, including the Chechens, Ingush, and Balkars, were quietly permitted to return to their original territories after Stalin's death, though certainly no full restitution was, or could be, made to them for losses of life and suffering involved in their deportation. The Germans, Meskhi, and Tatars were not granted even this boon.

58. See, for example, Aspaturian, "Non-Russian Nationalities," pp. 197–98, and Allworth, pp. 334–35. On the origins and earlier development of what Soviet sources call "Leninist nationality policy"—which, in fact, would more accurately be attributed to Stalin—see Frederick C. Barghoorn, *Soviet Russian Nationalism* (New York, 1956). See also the numerous relevant publications by John A. Armstrong, Robert Conquest, Hugh Seton Watson, Roman Szporluk, and other close students of Soviet nationality policy. There is wide agreement that Brezhnev's speech on December 22, 1972, in connection with the celebration of the fiftieth anniversary of the formation of the Soviet Union (there is dispute as to whether a historically appropriate date was chosen), signaled reaffirmation of the ideological and political correctness of a long-term assimilationist line. Some indication of form taken by this line is provided by Academician I. Mints's article in April 1975 on the celebration of the forthcoming thirtieth anniver-

sary of the Soviet victory over Nazi Germany. Mints referred to the "sentiment of national pride" experienced by the "Soviet people." See *"Pouchitelnye uroki istorii"* ("Instructive Lessons of History"), *Izvestiya*, April 3, 1975.

59. Valuable information and comment on the Ukrainian "renaissance" of the 1960's is in Bohdan R. Bociurkiw, "Soviet Nationalities Policy and Dissent in the Ukraine," *The World Today* (London), May 1974, pp. 214-26; quotation at p. 217. The quotation from Moroz is in *Boomerang: The Works of Valentyn Moroz*, ed. Yaroslav Bihun, with an introduction by Paul L. Gersper (Baltimore, 1974), p. 65.

60. Text in *Boomerang*, pp. 91-124. I have briefly summarized this essay in my "Soviet Dissenters," p. 124.

61. Bociurkiw, "Soviet Nationalities Policy," p. 219.

62. *Boomerang*, pp. 11-12, 50. Many other examples of appeals by Moroz and other Ukrainian dissenters, such as Vyacheslav Cholnovil, Svyatoslav Karavansky, and others, to Soviet constitutional principles—as distinguished from Kremlin practice—could be adduced. Some are mentioned in my above-cited article (note 59).

63. For details on the Soviet authorities' treatment of Moroz, see the pamphlet "Valentyn Moroz," published by Smoloskyp, Organization for Defense of Human Rights in Ukraine, Baltimore, Md. This is one of numerous informative pamphlets distributed by Smoloskyp.

64. *Boomerang*, pp. 72-89; quotation at p. 72.

65. Ibid., p. 85.

66. Ibid., p. 78.

67. Bociurkiw, "Soviet Nationalities Policy," pp. 219-25. See also item on Dzyuba in Smoloskyp pamphlet "Trials in Ukraine: 1973" (Baltimore, Md., 1974), pp. 3-5; and "Nationalities at Risk in CSCE," *Soviet Analyst*, July 17, 1975.

68. Bociurkiw, "Soviet Nationalities Policy," p. 221. See also "Nationalities at Risk in CSCE," which notes that despite efforts to counteract its influence, *Internationalism or Russification?* was "still widely read and discussed," and that "a further recantation" attributed to Dzyuba had been reported in official propaganda.

69. Barghoorn, "Soviet Dissenters," pp. 122-23, referring to I. Dzyuba, *Internationalism or Russification?* (London, 1968), pp. 102-13, 189, 194. See also Bociurkiw, "Soviet Nationalities Policy," pp. 221-22.

70. Bociurkiw, "Soviet Nationalities Policy," p. 223.

71. On Plyushch, see, for example, Bernard W. Hudson, "Dissent in a Straitjacket," *Times Literary Supplement*, April 18, 1975, p. 425, reviewing Tatyana Khodorovich, ed., *Istoriya bolezni Leonida Plyushcha (Account of the Illness of Leonid Plyushch)* (Amsterdam, 1975). The release and, in effect, the banishment of Plyushch probably resulted from the embarrassment to the Kremlin of widespread protest, on the part of Western mathematicians and other interested foreigners, regarding his treatment. Plyushch's arrival in Austria, "looking frail and trembling" but also "normal," according to a British psychiatrist, was reported in the January 11, 1976, *New York Times*.

72. Bociurkiw, "Soviet Nationalities Policy," p. 222.

73. See his book *Two Years in Soviet Ukraine* (Toronto, 1970); Barghoorn," "Soviet Dissenters," p. 123; Bociurkiw, "Soviet Nationalities Policy," p. 219. See also account of Plyushch's press conference in Paris, in *New York Times*, February 4, 1976, referred to on p. 83 and in footnote 167, chapter 2, p. 199.

74. See her earlier cited article "Ethnic Politics in the USSR," p. 21.

75. See Dimitry Pospielovsky, "The Kaunas Riots and National and Religious Tensions in the USSR," Radio Liberty Research, Munich, May 31, 1972 (CRD127/72).

76. Rakowska-Harmstone, "Ethnic Politics," p. 17.

77. *Soviet Analyst* (London), vol. 4, no. 9 (April 24, 1975), p. 8.

78. See, for example, Paul Wohl, "Long-Friendly Armenia Turning against Moscow," *Christian Science Monitor*, January 15, 1975.

79. *Sakharov Speaks*, pp. 132–33.

Chapter 4

1. Robert A. Dahl, "Introduction," p. 13, in Dahl, ed., *Regimes and Oppositions* (New Haven, 1973).

2. See, however, Frederick C. Barghoorn and Ellen P. Mickiewicz, "American Views of Soviet-American Exchanges of Persons," in Richard L. Merrit, *Communication in International Politics* (Urbana, Ill., 1972), pp. 146–67; also Mary Jane Moody, "Tourists in Russia and Russians Abroad," *Problems of Communism*, November–December 1964, pp. 3–14. Moody carefully documents the assymmetry of a situation in which, even on the purely quantitative dimen-

sion (leaving out of consideration the ideological, administrative, and judicial controls that help to account for qualitative differences in Soviet and Western foreign-travel patterns), it is overwhelmingly more difficult for Soviet citizens to travel, either to Communist or to non-Communist states, than it is for nationals of "bourgeois" states to visit—especially as tourists—the USSR and other "socialist" countries. It appears that no such study is available for the period since Moody's study was published, but the pattern she described has clearly not changed fundamentally.

3. Boris Meissner, in his penetrating analysis "Die 'friedliche koexistenz' in sowjetischer Sicht," *Europaische Rundschau,* no. 74/2 (Spring 1974), pp. 57–68, applies the expression "Janus head" to "peaceful coexistence." See p. 63.

4. Quoted from Constantin Olgin, "The Brezhnev 'Peace Offensive' and World Revolution," Radio Liberty Dispatch 251/74, (August 7, 1974), p. 3. Examination of Brezhnev's speech, referred to by Olgin and entitled "Za ukreplenie splochennosti kommunistov, za novy podem antiimperialisticheskoi borby" ("For Strengthening the Communists' Solidarity, For a New Upsurge of Anti-Imperialist Struggle"), in L. I. Brezhnev, *O vneshnei politike KPSS i Sovetskogo gosudarstve (On the Foreign Policy of the CPSU and the Soviet State)* (Moscow, 1973), pp. 144–93, indicates that Olgin correctly perceived the message conveyed by Brezhnev. On Khrushchev's "détente," see Vernon V. Aspaturian, *Process and Power in Soviet Foreign Policy* (Boston, 1971), pp. 775–84.

5. Valuable background on the semantics of "peaceful coexistence" is contained in Kohler et al., *Soviet Strategy for the Seventies* (Miami, 1973), chapters I, II, III. There is a very extensive literature on the Soviet "détente" policy that had its beginnings in the late 1960's but was most clearly manifested in the 1970's. Noteworthy are, for example, Josef Korbel, *Detente in Europe* (Princeton, 1972). Zbigniew K. Brzezinski, "The Deceptive Structure of Peace" *Foreign Policy,* no. 14 (Spring 1974), pp. 35–56, and several other articles by Brzezinski, perhaps especially his "The Competitive Relationship," in *Foreign Affairs* (October 1972); also Walter C. Clemens, Jr., "The Impact of Detente on Chinese and Soviet Communism," in the special issue on "détente" of *The Journal of International Affairs,* no. 2, 1974, and articles by Richard Pipes and others in the spring 1973 issue of *Survey,* and by Alvin Z. Rubinstein and others in the October 1974 issue of *Current History,* as well as David Finley's ex-

ceptionally good analysis in the opening part of his "Detente and Soviet–American Trade: An Approach to a Political Balance Sheet," in *Studies in Comparative Communism,* viii (Spring/Summer 1975), pp. 66ff. Marshall D. Shulman's article "Toward a Western Philosophy of Coexistence," in *Foreign Affairs* (October 1973), deserves special mention not only because, like Brzezinski's contribution to *Foreign Policy,* it realistically weighs the advantages and risks of "détente" from the point of view of United States interests, but especially because it offers thoughtful advice on how both the American government and the private sector in this country could rationally and creatively respond to a new, still-developing phase of international politics. The testimony and responses to questions of former Ambassador Foy D. Kohler on May 15, 1974 before the Subcommittee on Europe of the House of Foreign Affairs Committee contained in the volume entitled *Détente* published by that subcommittee and referred to earlier (see note 56, chapter 3), is of very special interest. Of course this is not the place to summarize the vast literature on "détente," a small sampling of which is referred to here. Perhaps it suffices for present purposes to note that there is considerable agreement among the authors referred to that Moscow and the West (led by West Germany and subsequently the United States) embarked on "détente" in response to the new situation resulting from events such as Western legitimation of the Moscow-dominated status quo in Eastern Europe, American weariness, and incipient isolationism after years of frustration in Southeast Asia, along with increasing Soviet concern about serious defects in the functioning of the USSR's economy, which, Moscow apparently hoped, could be remedied by massive infusions of advanced Western technology and managerial expertise, financed by the West on terms favorable to the Soviets: There was also hope in the West that in this situation, while intense competition for influence would continue, this competition could, more than before, be increasingly tempered by mutually beneficial bargaining in such fields as arms control, trade and scientific, medical, and cultural exchanges. There was a note of concern in many analyses, for example in those of Brzezinski, Kohler, and Rubinstein, lest hard Soviet bargaining and American ignorance of Soviet intentions produce benefits for Moscow far in excess of those that might be forthcoming for the United States. Thus, Brzezinski referred to the "asymmetry" of the Soviet–American relationship in his 1974 study. On the other hand, Shulman, Finley and Clemens, especially the latter, set a higher probability on an outcome in which the costs and benefits on both "sides" would be fairly evenly balanced. For a good summary of the literature on and the issues posed by "détente," which emphasized its dangers to the West if Western diplomacy could not bargain effectively with Moscow and make the East–West relationship a two-way street, see Gerald L. Steibel, *Detente: Promises and Pitfalls* (New York, 1975). Steibel's study was sponsored by the National Strategy Information Center.

6. Quotations in "Za ukreplenie," p. 190.

7. Quoted from an unpublished study by David E. Powell, "The Status of Soviet–American Relations," p. 8. This painstaking analysis, completed in January 1975, is my main source for comparing the 1970 and 1974 election speeches. My remarks on Brezhnev's 1974 election speech, however, are not necessarily fully compatible with Professor Powell's interpretation of that address.

8. Leonid I. Brezhnev, "Vse dlya blaga naroda, vo imya sovetskogo cheloveka" ("Everything for the Welfare of the People, in the Name of the Soviet Man"), *Pravda*, June 15, 1974, p. 2.

9. Powell, "The Status of Soviet–American Relations," pp. 8–18.

10. Ibid., p. 69, citing text of Mazurov's speech in *Sovetskaya Belorussia*, June 8, 1974.

11. Ibid., p. 69, citing *Foreign Broadcast Information Service* (Washington), July 3, 1974, p. R5.

12. Powell, "The Status of Soviet–American Relations," pp. 22–23, suggests this interpretation, noting Brezhnev's denunciation of alleged attempts by "imperialist circles" to obtain Soviet concessions in return for striking an East–West "bargain," and Podgorny's charge that some Western politicians sought to win from the "socialist countries changes in their domestic order according to the recipes of bourgeois democracy."

13. Ibid., pp. 24–29.

14. Kohler testimony at House Foreign Affairs Committee, p. 71.

15. Brian Crozier, "How Peaceful is Co-existence?" *Soviet Analyst*, vol. 4, no. 10 (May 8, 1975), pp. 1–2.

16. See *Conference on Security and Co-operation in Europe. Final Act. Helsinki 1975.* Department of State Publication 8826, General Foreign Policy Series 298 (Washington, D.C., August 1975), pp. 80,

114. On page 81, the document states that the signatories "will act in conformity with the purposes and principles of the Charter of the United Nations and the Universal Declaration of Human Rights and that "they confirm the right of the individual to know and act upon his rights and duties in this field."

17. The full text of Sakharov's statement of acceptance of the Nobel Peace Prize is the *New York Times,* December 11, 1975.

18. Semen K. Tsvigun, *Tainy front (The Secret Front)* (Moscow, 1973). A huge edition of 200,000 copies was published, indicating the importance attached to the book's message. It is interesting that this work was published during what now appears to have been the height of "détente."

19. Tsvigun refers specifically to "relaxation of tension" on p. 8.

20. See, for example, pp. 34, 52; on the latter page, Professor Zbigniev K. Brzezinski of Columbia University is assigned an important role in alleged subversive activities directed against the USSR.

21. Ibid., p. 93. Tsvigun accuses Shub of illegitimately attempting to obtain "specialist literature."

22. Ibid., pp. 17, 33.

23. Ibid., pp. 53–69.

24. Ibid., p. 396.

25. See Tsvigun, pp. 5–6, for an alleged case of a Soviet student who, starting from an excessive enthusiasm for watching foreign motion pictures, progressed downward, via acquaintance with foreigners who instilled "anti-Soviet" ideas in him, through expulsion from college, to spying for a foreign power, prosecution and conviction for espionage, and "severe punishment."

26. Quoted from Reddaway, *Uncensored Russia* (New York, 1972), p. 19, from an article by KGB General Malygin in *Molodoi Kommunist (Young Communist)*, no. 1 (1969), p. 59.

27. See Pavel Litvinov, *The Trial of the Four* (London, 1972), for text of the indictment against Ginzburg, Galanskov, et al., charging that the accused had "maintained friendly relations" with foreigners, who gave them "Djilas's book *The New Class* and other literature hostile to the Soviet system" as well as "anti-Soviet clippings from foreign papers" and, among other things, "money in Soviet rubles and foreign currency." Only Galanskov, however, was accused of having received money from a foreign source—and also of having violated currency regulations.

28. Max Hayward and Leopold Labedz, eds., *On Trial* (London, 1967) pp. 66, 114, 125, 128–29, 131.

29. See Chalidze, *To Secure These Rights*, p. 131 and pp. 209–46. It is apparent that the KGB was considering making a criminal case against Chalidze on the basis of his slight acquaintance with Sebreghts.

30. Quotation from a review by Bernard W. Hudson, "Dissent in a Straitjacket," of Tatyana Khodorovich, ed., *Istoriya bolezni Leonida Plyushcha (History of Leonid Plyushch's Illness)*, in *Times Literary Supplement*, April 18, 1975, p. 425. The statement about the sanctioning of the fifteen Action Group members is based on data culled from Reddaway, *Uncensored Russia*, especially pp. 150–70, and later press reports.

31. On Kovalev's arrest and Sakharov's protest, see *Chronicle of Human Rights*, no. 11–12 (September–December 1974), pp. 13–14; the same issue, p. 30, reported the founding of the Amnesty group, noting that it was the third "association of Soviet citizens independent of governmental or party control" that had affiliated with an international organization, the others being the Human Rights Committee, affiliated with the International League for the Rights of Man as well as with the International Institute of Human Rights, and "Group-73," formed in the fall of 1973 to assist political prisoners in the USSR, a function not attempted, at least on a group basis, by the Moscow Amnesty group, affiliated with the International Federation for Human Rights. Despite the fact that all three associations scrupulously respected Soviet law, such individual actions of some of their members as Turchin's open letter to Senator Jackson in support of the "Jackson Amendment," and indeed mere membership in what the Kremlin doubtless regarded as subversive groups (and, in fact, membership in any group not organized on the CPSU's initiative), presumably became part of the respective citizens' police dossiers, to be drawn upon, sooner or later, for use, if need arose, in a criminal prosecution. It is interesting, in this connection, that of the four persons who, as reported in the New York *Chronicle of Human Rights*, no. 4 (September–October 1973), founded "Group-73" in September 1973 and immediately sent greetings to an international conference of Amnesty International (Tverdokhlebov, Albrekht, Vladimir Arkhangelski, and Ilya Korneev), Tverdokhlebov and Albrekht had already suffered either police search or arrest, or both, by the spring of 1975.

32. Reddaway, *Uncensored Russia*, pp. 161–68.

33. *Chronicle of Current Events*, no. 17 (April 1971), pp. 37–41. Amalrik argued at the above trial that to try him for his views was in violation of both the Soviet Constitution and the Universal Declaration of Human Rights. A part of the videotape of the Cole interview was played during the trial.

34. Amalrik, *Involuntary Journey to Siberia*, 1–114, especially pp. 7–8, 47, 72, 107–108.

35. See, for example, Reddaway, *Uncensored Russia*, p. 80; John Dornberg, *The New Tsars* (New York, 1972), pp. 112–15; and especially the chapter on "Pavel," p. 24–37, in David Bonavia's perceptive *Fat Sasha and the Urban Guerilla* (New York, 1973).

36. Bill Murray, "Soviet Media Coverage of the Yakir-Krasin Trial: Variations on a Theme," Radio Liberty Dispatch (September 7, 1973), p. 3.

37. Peter Reddaway, "KGB Thuggery," *New York Review of Books*, March 6, 1975, p. 4. For text of the December 1974 letter to Sakharov, purportedly sent by a patently bogus "Russian Christian Party," see *Chronicle of Human Rights*, no. 11–12 (September–December 1974), p. 20. Sakharov's comment on the threats addressed to him, and his demand, in a letter to KGB head Yuri Andropov, for an end to pressure on him and his family and to persecution of his friends, is in Reddaway's above-cited article.

38. See, for example, the October 1974 and March 1975 issues of *Current*, the newsletter of the Committee of Concerned Scientists, and Christopher Wren, "Jews' Science Seminar Assailed in Soviet," *New York Times*, October 13, 1974.

39. According to an anonymous dispatch to the *New York Times*, May 6, 1972, reporting David Bonavia's expulsion for "systematic activity incompatible with the status of a foreign journalist," by "unofficial count, about twenty foreign correspondents" had been expelled "since the early 1960's."

40. Charlotte Saikowski, "Harassment in Soviet Union," *Christian Science Monitor*, June 6, 1971, p. 2. The Astrachan incident is referred to by Astrachan's wife, Susan Jacoby, in her book *The Friendship Barrier* (London, 1972). See her description in Chapter I, entitled "Ghettos and Guards," of the system of controls over foreigners resident in Moscow, especially p. 18.

41. *Chronicle of Human Rights*, no. 8 (March–April, 1974), pp. 21–22.

42. Ibid., no. 11-12 (September-December 1974), pp. 20-21.

43. On Kheifets's sentencing and Sakharov's protest against it, see ibid., p. 15. On Maramzin's arrest and Rene Cassin's protest, see ibid., pp. 25-26; for his release, see ibid., no. 13 (January-February 1975), p. 5, and "Soviet Writer Gets Suspended Sentence after He Apologizes," *New York Times*, February 22, 1975.

44. Peter B. Maggs, "Legal Controls on American Publication of Heterodox Soviet Writings," in Rudolf L. Tökés, ed., *Dissent in the USSR: Politics, Ideology, and People* (Baltimore, Md., 1975), pp. 310-28, *passim*, especially pp. 332-25 (quotation on p. 311). See also Chalidze, *To Defend These Rights*, pp. 291-94.

45. Quoted, from a monograph by Lunts entitled, in English translation, *The Theory and Practice of Forensic Psychiatric Examination*, by Vladimir Bukovski and the dissident Soviet psychiatrist Dr. Semen Gluzman, in their *samizdat* work (written in detention) "A Dissident's Guide to Psychiatry." See *Chronicle of Human Rights*, no. 13 (January-February 1975), p. 38. Apparently this extraordinarily perceptive work was smuggled out of the Perm camp, where Gluzman was confined at the time and, as far as I know, remains now.

46. Text of Amalrik's statement taken from *Chronicle of Current Events*, no. 17, quoted in *Moe poslednee slovo* (literally, *My Last Word*) (Frankfurt, German Federal Republic, 1974), pp. 108-109. This is a collection of final statements by persons found guilty in political trials during the years 1966-74, inclusive. Amalrik's final speech is briefly quoted by Bernard Gwertzman in "Amalrik Says Soviet Fears Ideas," *New York Times*, November 15, 1970.

47. For the Lasswell-Kaplan terminology referred to above, see Harold D. Lasswell and Abraham Kaplan, *Power and Society* (New Haven, 1950), especially pp. 55-102.

48. Sakharov's statement was published in the *New York Review of Books*, March 21, 1974, pp. 11-17, in an item entitled, "How I Came to Dissent". See p. 17 for quotation.

49. V. Petrov, "Internatsionalizm vneshnei politiki KPSS" ("The Internationalism of the Foreign Policy of the CPSU"), *Pravda*, December 21, 1973.

50. R. Kosolapov, "Leninizm—nauchnaya osnova politiki KPSS" ("Leninism—Scientific Foundation of the Policy of the CPSU"), *Pravda*, January 21, 1974.

51. For the text of the resolution as it was published, see *Izvestiya*, August 31, 1974.

52. "Uchitsya leninizmu—uchitsya pobezhdat" ("To Study Leninism Is To Learn How To Be Victorious"), *Pravda*, September 17, 1974.

53. See the long report by V. Kondrashov and M. Kotilevski in *Izvestiya*, October 10, 1974.

54. "Vospityvat ubezhdennykh patriotov" ("Bring up Convinced Patriots"), *Izvestiya*, January 29, 1975.

55. Text of Podgorny's speech is in *Izvestiya*, February 13, 1975.

56. Quotation in Christian Duevel, "The May Day Slogans of 1974," Radio Liberty Dispatch, April 24, 1974, p. 3. See also Duevel, "The October Slogans of 1974," Radio Liberty Dispatch, October 25, 1974, and slogan number 61 in *Izvestiya*, April 13, 1975.

57. Alec Nove, "Can We Buy Detente?", *New York Times Magazine*, October 13, 1974, at p. 34.

58. David Mutch, "West Germans Newly Concerned on Berlin," *Christian Science Monitor*, May 30, 1975.

59. For thoughtful, informed speculation on the succession question, see Grey Hodnett, "Succession Contingencies in the Soviet Union," *Problems of Communism*, March–April, 1975, at pp. 20–21.

60. Hedrick Smith, "Moscow Has Secured Detente Without a Risk of Open Society," *New York Times*, December 23, 1974.

61. Henry Kamm, "Ordinary East European Finds Some Drawbacks in Detente," *New York Times*, May 30, 1975, pp. 1, 16.

62. Smith, "Moscow Has Secured Detente," p. 16.

63. George W. Ball, "Capitulation at Helsinki," *Newsweek*, August 4, 1975, p. 13.

64. Irina Kirk, *Profiles in Russian Resistance* (New York, 1975), p. 117. This is only one of several statements to the same effect made by Volpin since his arrival in the West.

65. One of the most important background elements is what Moshe Lewin, in his thoughtful, well-documented study *Political Undercurrents in Soviet Economic Debates* (Princeton, N.J., 1974), terms Nikolai Bukharin's "gradualist approach to industrialization." See especially chapter 12, "The Inspiration of the 1920's," p. 328. Much has been written on the complex subject of continuities and links between Soviet dissent and the pre-Soviet revolutionary intelligentsia. Owing to such factors as the study—encouraged by the Soviet regime—of Russian classical literature and the influence of continuators of the prerevolutionary intelligentsia tradition such as

Boris Pasternak and, in a sense, scientists like Igor Tamm and his student Andrei Sakharov, "a class which is historically dead acquires, posthumously, ever new heirs and successors," as Richard Pipes noted in his chapter, "The Historical Evolution of the Russian Intelligentsia," in Richard Pipes, ed., *The Russian Intelligentsia* (New York, 1961), p. 54. More recently in his *Russia under the Old Regime,* chapter 10 (New York, 1974), Pipes has offered observations on the origin of the old Russian intelligentsia which are useful for understanding the problems of its Soviet successor. On Russian ambivalence, tsarist and Soviet, toward Western culture, which has been an important element in the susceptibility, but also the antipathy, of Russian and Soviet intellectuals toward the West, see George F. Kennan, *The Marquis de Custine and His Russia in 1839* (Princeton, N.J., 1971), pp. 118-33.

66. For a prediction, with special (but not exclusive) reference to the Ukraine, that as a result of repression, of which "surviving faith in the rule of law in the USSR" was a "certain victim," dissent will in the future "increasingly express itself through conspiratorial channels and its objectives and methods are bound to become more radical," see Bohdan Bociurkiw, "Soviet Nationalities Policy and Dissent in the Ukraine" *The World Today* (London, 1974), pp. 214-26, at pp. 225-26.

67. There is much evidence indicating that the CPSU leadership, in December 1971, instructed the KGB to silence the *Chronicle of Current Events* and generally to prevent further dissemination of opinions the Politburo regarded as subversive. See, for example, the letter addressed to the *Times* of London by Alexander Volpin and four other leading dissenters—who shortly thereafter emigrated—referring to a "command from on high" to that effect. Text of the letter is in *Arkhiv samizdata*, 1105, and Anatole Shub, "The Escalation of Soviet Dissent—and of Soviet Repression," *New York Times Magazine*, September 10, 1972, p. 92.

68. Albert Boiter, "Soviet Dissent and *Samizdat:* Summer 1973," Radio Liberty Dispatch, October 17, 1973, p. 1.

69. Albert Boiter, "*Samizdat* Review for Autumn 1974," Radio Liberty Dispatch, January 30, 1975, pp. 1-2.

70. Boiter, "Soviet Dissent and *Samizdat*" pp. 1-3; quotation at p. 1. Boiter noted, that the relatively small number of reported signatures to the published "letters" denouncing Sakharov and Solzhenitsyn

and the abrupt cessation of the campaign against them ten days after it began were indications that the regime's strategy had at least partly failed.

71. *Khrushchev Remembers: The Last Testament* (Boston, 1974), pp. 78–79.

72. On the last point, see, for example, the "Open Letter to Evgeni Evtushenko," by "A. Karanin," in Gunther Hillmann, *Selbstkritik des Kommunismus* (Munich, 1967), pp. 209–215. According to an editorial note to a series of Bukovski's works in *Grani* (Frankfurt), no. 65 (1967), pp. 9–10, "Karanin" may have been a pseudonym of Bukovski.

73. *Bodalsya telenok s dubom (The Calf Butted the Oak Tree)*, p. 50.

74. *Ibid.*, pp. 101–103.

75. Solzhenitsyn, *Bodalsya, passim;* L. G. Churchward, *Soviet Intelligentsia* (London and Boston, 1973), pp. 135–49; Zhores Medvedev, *Ten Years after Ivan Denisovich* (New York, 1973), especially pp. 57–63, 76, 120.

76. There is wide agreement among students of dissent and of the attitudes of the contemporary Soviet intelligentsia that the above interpretation of the relationship between repression and dissent in the late 1960's, and in the 1970's, is correct. See, for example, Reddaway, *Uncensored Russia*, pp. 18–19, and Churchward, *Soviet Intelligentsia*, p. 144. Indeed, its correctness presumably seems obvious to anyone who has carefully studied the reactions of dissenters to the Sinyavski–Daniel and Ginzburg–Galanskov trials, the invasion of Czechoslovakia, and relevant subsequent events.

77. Hodnett, "Soviet Succession Contingencies," p. 21.

78. For the translation of the last phrase, I have used the Russian text, earlier cited, p. 13. Remaining quotations are in *Sakharov Speaks*, pp. 118, 124–25.

79. *Sakharov Speaks*, p. 133.

80. Churchward, *Soviet Intelligentsia*, p. 164, so captions an excerpt from the Sakharov–Turchin–Roy Medvedev document.

81. Cf. the list of "tentative measures" in *Sakharov Speaks*, pp. 127–29, and in Churchward's somewhat different translation on pp. 165–67 of his *Soviet Intelligentsia*.

82. *Sakharov Speaks*, p. 173.

83. Relevant here is Erik Hoffman's observation, in "Political Opposition in the Soviet Union," in Barbara W. McLennan, ed., *Political Oppo-*

sition and Dissent (New York, 1972), pp. 329–79 at p. 373, that *samizdat* does not shed much light on such questions as the numbers of "active dissidents" and the breadth and intensity of support for "key oppositionist ideas."

84. See, for example, some pertinent remarks in Ellen P. Mickiewicz, "Introduction," to Ellen P. Mickiewicz, ed., *Handbook of Soviet Social Science Data* (New York, 1973), especially pp. 40–42.

85. See Frederick C. Barghoorn, "Factional, Sectoral, and Subversive Opposition," in Dahl, *Regimes and Oppositions*, pp. 67–70, 75–76; Churchward, *Soviet Intelligentsia*, pp. 139–49.

86. Churchward, *Soviet Intelligentsia*, p. 128.

87. Ibid., pp. 14, 54–55.

88. Ibid., p. 84.

89. Ibid., p. 142.

90. Ibid., p. 37.

91. See, for example, Mickiewicz's above-cited work, and also Robert J. Osborn, *Soviet Social Policies* (Homewood, Ill., 1970), and Merwyn Matthews, *Class and Society in Soviet Russia* (London, 1972).

92. Amalrik, *Will the Soviet Union Survive?*, p. 33. Amalrik's views are supported by George Feifer's observations, based on contacts with a considerable number of Soviet intellectuals. His friends, reported Feifer, included some of the most alienated people in the world, but they rendered no support to the Democratic Movement, partly out of fear, but also because they considered that Russian society had not yet reached a stage of development at which a political reform movement could gain sufficient support to justify the awesome risks involved in defying the tough, cunning, and ruthless Soviet rulers. See Feifer's "The Case of the Passive Minority," in Tökés, ed., *Dissent in the USSR*, pp. 418–37, especially pp. 422–24.

93. Vadim Belotserkovsky, "Soviet Dissenters: Solzhenitsyn, Sakharov, Medvedev," *Partisan Review* (Vol. XLII, No. 1), pp. 35–68, at pp. 44–45. See also "S. Zorin," and "N. Alekseev," who in *Vremya ne zhdet* (Leningrad, 1969), p. 44, assert that "the broad masses are beginning to think" and the authorities fear this process.

94. The quotation is from p. 370 in Erik Hoffman, "Political Opposition in the Soviet Union." Perhaps Hoffman presents a somewhat too positive picture. Cf. Richard Judy, in Skilling and Griffiths, *Interest Groups in Soviet Politics*, especially pp. 248–51. Judy perceived a "slow process of creeping economic rationality" at work, but ex-

pressed the opinion that while "analytical economics is fully compatible with rational humane socialism," a view he attributed also to young Soviet mathematical economists, the combination of "economic illiteracy" and "ideological paranoia" in the ranks of the leaders "guarantees the strength of more conservative forces for years to come." Quotations at pp. 249, 250.

95. See my above-cited chapter in Dahl, *Regimes and Oppositions*, pp. 27–88, especially pp. 53–70.

96. Moshe Lewin, *Political Undercurrents in Soviet Economic Debates* (Princeton, N.J., 1974), p. 214.

97. Ibid., p. 216.

98. Ibid., p. 230.

99. Ibid., p. 221.

100. Ibid., p. 246.

101. Ibid., p. 299.

102. Ibid., p. 241.

103. On Ossovski's views, see Boris Nicolaevsky, *Power and the Soviet Elite* (New York, 1965), pp. 132–33; see also Lewin, *Political Undercurrents*, pp. 354–55, and my chapter in Dahl, *Regimes and Oppositions*, p. 45.

104. On the latter topic, see, for example, Foy D. Kohler and Mose L. Harvey, "Soviet Science and Technology: Some Implications for U.S. Policy," *Orbis*, vol. 13, no. 3 (Fall 1969), pp. 685–708.

105. It may be relevant that the CPSU leaders moved in 1975 to reduce and perhaps eliminate the autonomy hitherto enjoyed, at least in the post-Stalin era, by the Academy of Sciences of the USSR. See, for example, Michael Parks, "Moscow Moves to Cut Autonomy of Prestigious Academy of Sciences," *Baltimore Sun*, May 27, 1975.

106. These remarks are to some extent on Deborah Shapley, "Detente: Travel, Curbs Hinder U.S.-U.S.S.R. Exchanges," *Science*, November 22, 1974, pp. 712–15.

107. Peter Reddaway, "The Resistance in Russia," *New York Review of Books*, vol. XXI, no. 20 (December 12, 1974), p. 36.

108. See my "The General Pattern of Soviet Dissent," in Peter J. Potichnyj, ed., *Papers and Proceedings of the McMaster Conference on Dissent in the Soviet Union*, pp. 1–35, at pp. 26–32.

109. See "Press Statement of Pavel Litvinov on March 22, 1974" Radio Liberty Dispatch, April 17, 1974, for full text, from which the above

portions were quoted. Litvinov appended to his statement a list of "individuals who today are paying with their physical freedom, livelihood and health"; he named Vladimir Bukovski, Viktor Khaustov, Leonid Plyushch, Vitali Rubin, Yuri Maltsev, and Vladimir Moroz, providing brief statements on each, and he appealed "on behalf [not only] of these people, but of countless others whose names may not be known to us," adding that "these human beings are the best that Russia has."

110. Peter Dornan, "Andrei Sakharov," p. 403.

111. Ibid., p. 405.

112. See, for example, his "Otkrytoe Pismo akademiku V. A. Engelgardtu" ("Open Letter to Academician V. A. Engelhardt"), cited here from *Almanakh Samizdata*, no. 1 (Amsterdam, 1974), pp. 9–10, in which Sakharov expressed indignation that Engelhardt—a distinguished Soviet biochemist—had, on an exchange visit to the United States, expressed the view that it was undesirable for American scientists to make public statements of the kind that Handler had addressed to Keldysh. In this communication Sakharov expressed gratitude to those abroad (and those inside the USSR) who had openly come to his defense.

113. Robert C. Cowen, "East–West Science—The Uneasy Detente," *Christian Science Monitor*, July 2, 1975.

Index